W9-CBO-779

GIBBS·SMITH
P
PUBLISHER
SALT LAKE CITY

An Architectural Guidebook to

PORTLAND

BART KING

WITH AN INTRODUCTION
BY MAYOR VERA KATZ

TO MY PARENTS, JANET AND MICHAEL KING, WITH GREAT LOVE.
AB IMO PECTORE.

First Edition
05 04 03 02 01   5 4 3 2 1

Text and photographs copyright © 2001 by Bart King

Published by
Gibbs Smith, Publisher
P.O. Box 667
Layton, Utah 84041

Orders: (1-800) 748-5439
www.gibbs-smith.com

Edited by Suzanne Taylor
Designed by Leesha Jones, Moon and the Stars Design
Printed in the U.S.A.

LIBRARY OF CONGRESS CATALOGING-IN-PUBLICATION DATA

An architectural guidebook to Portland / by Bark King ; with an introduction by Mayor Vera Katz.—1st ed.
        p. cm.
        ISBN 0-87905-991-5
1. Architecture—Oregon—Portland—Guidebooks.
2. Portland (Or.)—Buildings, structures, etc.—Guidebooks. I. Title.
NA735.P55 K56   2001
720′.9795′49—dc21′   00-012252

CONTENTS

Photo courtesy Zimmer Gunsul Frasca
© 2001 Timothy Hursley

ACKNOWLEDGEMENTS

No project of this nature is written in a vacuum; I would like to sincerely thank the following individuals for their assistance in the preparation of this book: The honorable Vera Katz, David Judd, Betsy Ames, Amy Schwartz, Daniel T. Crandall, Tim Hills, Charles White, Dedrea Decker, Dan Silva, Marian Crow, Randy Gragg, Rachelle L. Perry, Matthew Boucard, Pam Porter, Phil Rude, Angie Lawless, Mike Miller, Len Schiler, Lynn A. Spohn, Leslie Watanabe, Pete Kent, Jeff Hamilton, Kieran O'Brien, Paula Hamilton, Zimmer Gunsul Frasca Partnership, Beth Soresen, Reid Cooper, Karl Ockert, Danielle Birkin, Mark Kuestner, Marilyn Kirstead, Marc Hage, Nancy Fishman, Greg Baldwin, Matt Merenda, George McMath, Jon Tullis, Jeff Jaqua, Wendy Miller, Darryl Paulsen, Robert Liberty, Carol Shen, Steve Duin, Paula Stoeke, Jerry Arthur, and Brody vanderSommen.

I was also fortunate enough to receive the help of three learned gentlemen who graciously assisted me with suggestions, fact checking, and their impressive stores of knowledge. These men are Wallace Kay Huntington, Peter Meijer, and William Hawkins III. To them I offer my most heartfelt thanks.

I especially want to thank my editor, Suzanne Taylor. Without her, this project would never have happened.

Finally, my abiding gratitude and love to my wife, Lynn, both for her insightful suggestions and her unflagging support of this book.

MAYOR'S INTRODUCTION

There is no exact formula, no set of rules, for creating a great city. All that can be said is that a great city is created when the right elements come together to create a place filled with excitement, opportunity, and character—a city that enriches and inspires. The architects of this urban environment and of Portland's neighborhoods are its citizens, who bring these elements together. They are the architects of their future, one that is strategically planned and designed, and not left to chance.

Portland is a special place that honors the pedestrian, protects its green and open spaces, and understands that managing growth is best done when strategies are linked—connected to transit investment, employment, affordable housing, and design. This city—its leaders, its citizens, and the professional architectural community—realizes that congestion on its roads, the quality of its air, the vibrancy of its neighborhoods, and the health of its economy will be determined by what is built and where.

I remain impressed, just as when I was a newcomer to this city, by the hard work and passion of Portlanders to preserve buildings of historical character and function. The quality and number of national and local historic districts, and our commitment to preservation and the reuse of historic and older buildings spotlights our passion for meaningful architecture. This speaks clearly to our history and our frontier heritage. New and creative architecture plays within the lines and personality of this history, and with the light and air and special public places we treasure.

Today, our success is about integrating art and architecture, housing and community design. It is about the continual balance between historic and environmental preservation and development. It is about maintaining faith. If Portland's past is any reflection of its future, I have faith that its citizens are up to these tasks.

Welcome.

—Honorable Vera Katz
Mayor

INTRODUCTION

"Architecture, of all the arts, is the one which acts the most slowly, but the most surely, on the soul."–Ernest Dimnet, *What We Live By*

The nature of a city's architecture may not entirely dictate its nature, but it goes a long way toward defining it. The right balance of glass or wood or metal gives a structure tangible character; the height, shape, color, and essential physical nature of a building influences (or even determines) the experience that a person on the sidewalk has. This is not to overstate the case; as Ada Louise Huxtable wrote, nobody "believes that the architect can solve the ills of society." But the architect does create the environment of a city, and the architect's work shapes the interactions and experiences of those who come in contact with it.

At its best, architecture far transcends mere engineering in establishing a place for humans to work, relate, and exist. It is a form of sculpture which humans respond to from outside and from within as well. This human response can change with every step that is taken inside of a building, making the architect's work ever mutable and plastic. The quintessential job of the architect is to consider the interplay among open space, existing environment, client needs, and the human condition—and then create a form that works within that context. There are many solutions to any given project; what path should be taken? It is a genuinely complicated and daunting task, one that also involves coordinating construction contractors, geologists, electrical engineers, and a host of other professionals.

Yet for all that, when the work is finally done, in many ways the building is easy to evaluate.

The appreciation of architecture is both a simple and sophisticated response to the buildings around us. One can read architectural treatises and manifestos proclaiming the beauties or evils of "urban space," "democratically designed architecture," and other highblown concepts, but the fact is that the best way to judge a building is to simply look at it. Next, "use" it; walk into the building and see if its form and function are aesthetically pleasing and practical minded. While there are many historical styles and postmodern architectural mutations, there is something simple and essential beneath the metaphysical musings one often finds bandied about in architectural writing. Portland's most notable architect, Pietro Belluschi, wrote: "Architecture . . . goes beyond just saying that a form is Classical, International, or Modern, or Modernistic . . . you need the satisfaction of the eye."

But without the "satisfaction of the eye," most people are unlikely to go to the trouble of finding out more about a building. Portland has many buildings that satisfy the eye, and this book was written in response to my own curiosity about the variety of buildings I saw in and around Portland. This book is not intended to be encyclopedic; it is not a listing of all

Portland buildings, or even most buildings, but rather a collection of buildings that have distinguished or disgraced themselves in some interesting fashion.

Portland holds a distinctive place in the architectural pantheon of American cities. The original 150-year-old downtown area combines the strong architectural flavor of its past with the heady aroma of some distinguished modern buildings. Within a relatively small downtown district can be found nineteenth-century cast-iron-front buildings, skyscrapers, old brick warehouses, an 1890 train station with a 150-foot clock tower, five historic bridges over the Willamette River, and an assortment of museum, government, and retail buildings. Just behind the downtown district are two parks, one of which (at 4,683 acres) is the second-largest metropolitan park in the United States. Portland's magic lies in understanding that the sum of its parts creates a unified and pleasing environment; no one isolated architectural aspect of the city is necessarily world-class.

What downtown Portland may lack in terms of a single defining architectural symbol — like New York City's Empire State Building, San Francisco's Transamerica Pyramid, or Seattle's Space Needle—it more than makes up for in its civic planning, preservation of historic buildings, and overall attractiveness. It has a number of buildings that qualify as "small skyscrapers," that is, buildings that achieve distinctive levels of personality without being overwhelmingly gigantic. As writer James Mayer observed, "Although some cities dazzle from a distance like a five-carat diamond on a platinum blonde, Portland shines more like a half-carat promise ring. It bears closer scrutiny. And you actually can walk around in it."

The common thread among these features is the conscious planning that has gone into making Portland an aesthetically pleasing, safe, and accessible city. Particularly in the last forty years, there has been arguably no other U.S. city that has planned its urban and metropolitan environment with such care. And although not all buildings pay homage to the street experience of the city's pedestrians, enough of them do to truly make a difference.

Historically, the Pacific Northwest in the 1800s was an area claimed variously by Russia, Spain, Great Britain, and the United States, but by the 1840s, only the latter two were players, and the Anglo-American Oregon Treaty used the 49th parallel as a dividing line between American and British interests. The area Portland would become was a mere acre of land that was simply a rest stop for people traveling elsewhere. Stripped of its oak, cottonwood, and fir trees, it was appropriately named "The Clearing." Except for a small log hut and the broken mast of a ship, there were no buildings of any kind.

Oregon's first wagon train arrived in 1842, bringing roughly a hundred immigrants into the area. Most of these newcomers were farmers, but there were also opportunists and capitalists who recognized that the meeting point of two rivers as large as the Willamette and the Columbia created a potentially valuable expanse of real estate.

In 1843, Tennessee native William Overton claimed 640 acres on the west bank of the Willamette River. Overton asked one of the wagon-train pioneers, a lawyer named Asa Lovejoy, to pay the fee and fill out the necessary paperwork to file the claim on the land. For his efforts, Lovejoy received half of the claim. The filing fee was twenty-five cents, so Lovejoy got 320 acres for filling out some forms and paying a quarter. Shortly thereafter, Overton offered to sell the rest of the claim to a merchant named Francis Pettygrove. The asking price was fifty dollars.

After plumbing the river's depth, Pettygrove agreed to the deal. In 1845, Lovejoy and Pettygrove, unable to agree on a name for their town site, held a coin toss that would decide the town's name. Massachusetts native Lovejoy preferred "Boston," but Pettygrove won the flip and named the new town after the capital of his home state, Maine. Lovejoy, perhaps disenchanted with Portland after his failure to name it, sold his share in the city for approximately $390 to Benjamin Stark, a ship cargo master who would later go on to serve as an Oregon state senator.

Portland was built on a small, dense scale. The city's original 1846 plat established sixteen city blocks, each measuring a mere two hundred square feet, tiny as compared to those of other major American cities. This maximized the ratio of prized corner lots and provided better access to the Willamette River. The resultant compact grid in the city's center is still eminently friendly to pedestrian traffic ("the streets are too narrow for anything but camel traffic," complained Charles L. Chapman), and allow a great deal of sunshine to fall in the city streets, no small consideration in Portland's overcast climes.

Portland was essentially carved out of what was a primeval forest; it was nicknamed "Little Stumptown" for the ubiquitous stumps in the streets. Stumps outnumbered residents for many years, and it was common practice for taxes or fines to be waived in exchange for voluntary stump removal. With no shortage of timber, Portland's first buildings were constructed of wood. In the modern downtown area, nothing remains of Portland's original, largely residential architecture. The first masonry building in town was constructed in 1853, and cast-iron fronts on buildings became popular in the 1860s, as was the fashion at that time on the east coast. Construction of cast-iron structures was quicker and cheaper than all-brick buildings, while also allowing for more ornamental expression and bringing more light inside.

In 1872, a fire raged through the area of Morrison and Front Streets and was followed by what would be called the Great Fire of 1873. Together, the two infernos destroyed thirty city blocks. The Great Fire alone caused an estimated $1.3 million dollars in property damage at a time when the total worth of the town was only $8.8 million. Cast-iron structures burned readily in these blazes, and this, combined with changing architectural directions, resulted in cast iron being gradually phased out of new construction.

By the mid-1870s, nearly all of the new downtown buildings were stone or brick edifices. From 1890 to 1915, better elevators and the introduction of the steel frame made it possible to quadruple the four-story maximum height of downtown buildings, and skyscrapers could be built far higher than a person would wish to climb. The Lewis and Clark Exposition of 1905—which itself spawned many short-lived but exotic buildings—marked the beginning of a development spurt in the city, as financial institutions and commercial companies opened their own buildings downtown. This architectural growth corresponded with the extension of Portland's streetcar tracks. As transportation often predicates development, commercial structures began to spring up along the car lines, and, as the lines continued extending, Portland's residential areas also began to mushroom.

Beginning in 1893 and continuing into the early twentieth century, there was a nationwide swell of support for the "City Beautiful" movement (also known as the "American Renaissance"), a movement whose goal it was to improve cities through conscious civic planning. Many of America's finest public works stem from this era, including the New York Public Library and the redesign of the Great Mall in Washington, D.C. The city of Portland got a park evaluation in 1904 from famed landscape designers the Olmsted Brothers, and another in 1909 when the Civic Improvement League was formed to hire an expert who would create a plan to help make Portland an "ideal city." The league hired British architect Edward Bennett, who advised the planning of a transportation center with a post office and railway station, a cultural center with a theater and a museum, and a government center around City Hall. Although his complete plan was never executed, modern Portland does have three city areas that meet his descriptions.

The muted quality of light during Portland's overcast winters, springs, and falls became a primary consideration for architects working in the Willamette Valley, as illustrated by the following anecdote first related by lumberman Gordon Swope in the 1870s. A San Francisco woman staying in Portland with her relatives for a month experienced rain or drizzle through much of the first three weeks. Frustrated that her stay was coming to an end without any "good" weather, she asked the family's young daughter, "Does the sun ever shine in Portland?"

"How would I know?" the girl replied. "I'm only five."

While cast-iron and brick buildings tended to be dark in color, terra-cotta—which came into vogue between 1907 to 1920—put an off-white, reflective sheen on dozens of downtown government, commercial, and retail buildings. Terra-cotta could sheathe the entire exterior of a building or be used for decorative purposes. In general, buildings built during this period were an average of nine stories tall, came right up to the property line, and had cornices, which meant the buildings actually hung over the sidewalks. To avoid the chance of Portland sidewalks becoming darkened canyons, a 1918 building code revision limited building height on street-facing walls to 110 feet, with an increase of four vertical feet allowed for every one foot of setback from the street. Although these height restrictions would later be lifted, their idea was sound, as was the common practice of including a retail base on the bottoms of tall buildings. (Decades later, this practice became legally required in Portland.)

Everyone wants a room with a view, but modern buildings can have over one hundred feet between "windowed walls." This was not a problem in Portland's early office buildings; they reached significant heights, but often had no practical method of air ventilation other than opening a window. As to illumination, electricity was usually of low wattage and inconsistent supply. Therefore, "light courts," somewhat like courtyards for skyscrapers, were often cut into large buildings so that interior rooms could have access to natural light and ventilation. These interior courts had to begin at the top of the building, but they did not usually go to the bottom of it. Instead, they often ended in a skylight for a second-floor public space.

Unsurprisingly, because of the nation's economic downturn, little construction occurred in Portland during the 1930s. Post-World War II buildings took on a more modern cast, complete with metal and glass exteriors, beginning with Belluschi's pioneering Equitable Building in 1948.

While new companies were attracted to Portland, and the post-war boom resulted in new construction, ironically, the greatest impact on the Portland's architectural heritage would not have to do with what went up, but with what came down. Despite the pedestrian-friendly environment, it was America's love affair with the automobile that nearly undid Portland. A city "improvement" called for the Harbor Drive expressway to be constructed right through the heart of Portland's historic riverfront district. The six-lane expressway, completed in 1942, was designed to aid automobile travel and to provide work to returning war veterans. For this project alone, seventy-nine structures (mostly cast-iron) came down.

Few in the city appreciated the fact that the largest collection of cast-iron buildings outside of New York's SoHo District was being torn down. In the mid-1940s, Portland city

Introduction

planners invited celebrated New York civil engineer/civic fascist Robert Moses to create a plan for the city's future redevelopment. Moses is now infamous for laying waste to much of New York City in the first half of the twentieth century. His suggestions legitimized further destruction in Portland as Moses advocated tearing down Union Station and adding long bridge ramps that would dump automobiles right downtown. Out of the 200 cast-iron buildings in Portland, 180 were eventually destroyed. Of the massive bloodletting, a local paper noted that the few remaining historic buildings "stand out more defiantly than ever—not as simple-minded leftovers . . . but as avenging angels. Glass and the enlightened mass may have taken their toll, but [the buildings] that remain remind us of something perhaps missing. . . ."

While local architect Pietro Belluschi's work in the 1940s would inspire a trend of buildings to be built by Skidmore Owings and Merrill in the following two decades, widespread demolition (usually resulting in parking lots) continued throughout the 1950s. This eventually resulted in the 1968 adoption of a then-precocious Historic Landmark Commission, which officially interwove a preservationist policy into the city's planning process. This philosophy was strengthened by the National Historic Preservation Act two years prior. By virtue of Mayor Neil Goldschmidt's leadership, Portland adopted a Downtown Plan in 1972 that, among other things, created a focus on developing architecturally "emphatic points, unique physical designs for identifiable areas, and . . . [preserving] historic or architecturally significant buildings." The Downtown Plan also created the framework for future legacies such as Waterfront Park, Pioneer Courthouse Square, and light-rail.

In 1978, the city's Metropolitan Service District ("Metro") was created as an experiment in regional planning. This agency has authority over three counties and is best known for drawing the nation's first urban growth boundary in order to contain suburban sprawl and keep the city's core alive. All this planning paid off somewhat in the 1980s, as twenty-five major downtown construction projects were built. The 1988 Central City Plan focused on reclaiming the Willamette River as "a link, rather than a barrier" between the east and west sides of the city. The Convention Center, new Rose Garden, Oregon Museum of Science and Industry, and east-side river walkways/parks all stemmed from this project. The 1990s saw the 2040 Regional Framework Plan continue the city's tradition of providing sometimes noteworthy architecture within the framework of urban design and planning.

Currently, Portland can certainly be held up as an architectural success story; it is a city of modest proportions with an unusually high ratio of historical buildings coexisting with modern ones in an interesting tapestry. There is also a variety of distinct neighborhoods and colleges around the city that date from 1850 to 1950, which contain their own interesting architectural specimens. Here's to the hope that good design—and the watchful eye of design review commissions and committees—can keep new buildings in the city up to the standards of Portland's past.

✦   One of the attractions of the 1905 Lewis and Clark Fair was "The Trail," a re-creation of the route Lewis and Clark took across the continent. The fair's version had a life-sized cow made of butter and a village of Native Americans who ate dogs. Small wonder the fair drew almost 3 million visitors.

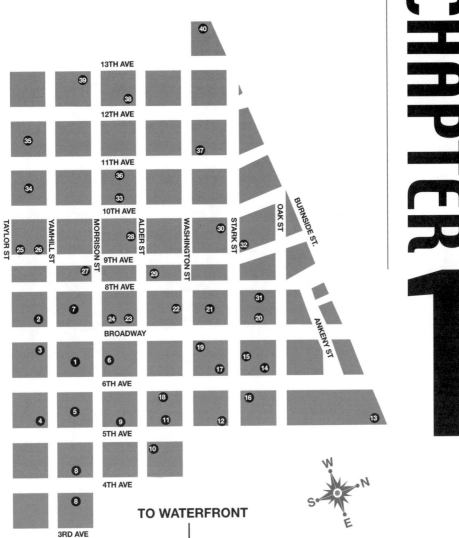

13TH AVE

12TH AVE

11TH AVE

10TH AVE

9TH AVE

8TH AVE

BROADWAY

6TH AVE

5TH AVE

4TH AVE

3RD AVE

TAYLOR ST

YAMHILL ST

MORRISON ST

ALDER ST

WASHINGTON ST

STARK ST

OAK ST

BURNSIDE ST.

ANKENY ST

TO WATERFRONT

W
N
S
E

DOWNTOWN—COURTHOUSE SQUARE AND ENVIRONS

1a *Pioneer Courthouse Square*

CHAPTER 1

DOWNTOWN–
COURTHOUSE SQUARE
AND ENVIRONS

"No other city has worked as hard as Portland at relating projects to each other. It's a Greek ideal–every project has a responsibility to the past and to the future."

—Greg Baldwin, Portland architect, 1990

1 PIONEER COURTHOUSE SQUARE 1984

Between Fifth and Sixth Avenue, Morrison and Yamhill Street
Architect: Willard Martin (Martin/Soderstrom/Matteson)
Additional design elements by Douglas Macy, Robert Reynolds, Lee Kelly,
Terence O'Donnell, Spencer Gill

It may seem strange to begin a guide on architecture with a space that is essentially empty, but the Pioneer Courthouse Square is not just a nexus of downtown activity; it reflects the architectural themes found around it in a myriad of ways, and it interacts with the public more successfully than any other spot in the city.

A primary challenge to any architect in downtown Portland is how to deal with each site's downward slope to the Willamette River. Some people report feeling mild vertigo on their first visit to Pioneer Courthouse Square, caused by their effort to find a point of orientation or horizontal line of composition to anchor their sightline. While these people are no doubt easily dizzied, it is interesting to note how Willard Martin dealt with the slope while incorporating it into a variety of shapes and lines that fit in creatively with the surrounding buildings. This resulting area combines elements of the Greek agora and the Roman forum in its open-air setting and creative seating arrangements, which are designed to facilitate both small group interactions and central viewing of the square.

3

1b   *Pioneer Courthouse Square*

While the square was not built until the 1980s, its history begins in the 1800s, with Bavaria-native Henry Hilgard (1835–1900; name later changed to Villard), who owned the company that built the first transcontinental railroad line into Portland. The first railway car arrived in 1883, with Villard and Ulysses S. Grant aboard. To occasion this event, Villard had hired the prestigious New York firm of McKim, Mead and White to design the Portland Hotel on this site. Construction began in 1882 but ended the next year when Villard's fortune crumbled. The site was then abandoned for five years with only the foundation completed. The site was nicknamed "Villard's Ruins" at the time; two victims of violent murder were found on the site before work on the hotel was continued and completed. (Material from the hotel's foundation is beneath the fountain on the west side of the square.)

Financiers completed the Portland Hotel, and it resided here from 1889 to 1951. The construction of this magnificent Queen Anne structure effectively moved downtown's social center westward, leaving Old Town and the Yamhill District to molder for a number of decades before their contemporary resurgence. (Further information about the Portland Hotel is located at the northeast corner of the square.) After the Portland Hotel was demolished in 1951, this block was a parking lot for thirty years.

In 1980, a worldwide design competition for a city square that would encourage day and evening patronage year-round was announced, with 162 official designs submitted. One of the announced design specifications was that the square should not kowtow to a particular school of architectural philosophy, but rather should be varied in its approach and mindful of the city's historicity.

Although Martin's design was chosen, the city mayor and many businesspeople disapproved of the square's open-air aspect (as opposed to an enclosed space). They feared that it would attract vagrants, so Mayor Frank Ivancie killed the project in 1981; but a groundswell of support for the square resurrected it, and after much political heat was expended, construction began.

The light-rail lines on the north and south sides of the square inspired the terra-cotta-covered columns that support canopies to shelter waiting passengers. The terra-cotta is a reference to the extensive terra-cotta sheathing of the surrounding buildings, and the capitals of the columns are intended to reflect the floor lines of the Jackson Tower to the south and the American Bank Building to the north. The "fallen" column in the northwest corner of the square has broken apart much as a column actually would, although this one, being made of concrete, bears no mason's marks. The capitals also afford one a close-up look at the roses, aphids, and ladybugs that decorate the other columns.

The use of redbrick is an obvious link to Portland's many downtown brick structures—including Nordstrom's brick fort to the west and the brick bus-mall to the east—yet the light colors of the surrounding buildings provide a welcome contrast to the deep red of the square.

Homage is paid to Portland's cast-iron architecture by the inclusion of the Portland Hotel's wrought-iron gate in its original location and by the cast-bronze posts and beams (called a *pergola*) on the northwest side, which also emulate the style of cast-iron columns in the Yamhill District.

One can call this approach to building "context-sensitive" or simply "good taste," but either way, it is a success. There have been complaints that this square is overly referential, or that it is a vulgar hodgepodge of styles. But given Pioneer Courthouse Square's historically and architecturally meaningful location, fun-spirited and clever execution, and the obvious pleasure the public takes in interacting with it, these charges are hogwash, and they flow off the square like water off a brick.

✦ This location was part of William Overton's original land claim. The parcel was sold to the city of Portland for $1,000 in 1856. The property has increased in value slightly since then.

✦ On October 13, 1985, a memorial service for the square's architect, Willard K. Martin, was held. Martin perished when an antique plane he had restored crashed in the Southwest as he and his son looked for cliff-side ruins to sketch.

1 c, d   *Pioneer Courthouse Square*

2 Fox Tower

2 FOX TOWER 2000

805 SW Broadway, between Taylor and Yamhill Streets
Architect: Thompson Vaivoda & Associates

One acid test for a skyscraper is whether its appearance is instantly recognizable on a city's skyline. In order to achieve this distinction, a large building often needs a distinctive top, like KOIN Tower, Jackson Tower, or even the 1000 Broadway Building. Yet this twenty-seven-story, stepped-back building has clean lines, is interesting to look at from a variety of angles, and avoids extraneous excesses, all without being a classic tower. It is indisputably more attractive on the curving east side, as the west boxes itself in with straight lines, yet its forms coalesce into a shiny and unique shape that somehow remains elusive.

Onlookers to its construction were witness to the huge hole the project began with, which became the 462-space underground parking garage, the city's deepest. An earlier version of the building had this garage in a podium base just above the legally required ground-floor retail space, but the design was wisely adjusted. The initial construction looked promisingly slender as the forty-by-forty-foot elevator core was built before the steel frame of the building, but the final mass has perhaps proved to be a trifle overwhelming. Although the city council fended off attempts to increase the building's height, the tower efficiently fences in Pioneer Courthouse Square's southwest corner and dwarfs Jackson Tower.

Fox Tower's distinctive multi-planar design and its stepped-back base were partially intended to prevent an unfriendly shadow from falling on the square, but some shade has been unavoidable. To test if the building falls within the city's standards, go to Pioneer Courthouse Square at noon on the spring equinox (March 21). If more than half the square is covered in the Fox's shadow, it is not following city regulations and should be immediately destroyed.

✦ Margaret Sanger (founder of the American birth-control movement) was arrested here in 1916 for disseminating "Family Limitation" literature.

✦ This spot was originally the site of the Heilig (later called the Fox) Theater, which was a brick Romanesque structure built in 1911 and designed by architect E. W. Houghton. Renovated in the mid-1950s, it hosted many road-show productions.

3 JACKSON TOWER 1912

Originally the Oregon Journal Building
Southeast corner of SW Broadway and Yamhill, southwest side of square
Architects: Merrit Reid and James William Reid (San Francisco)

The Reid brothers had already designed the Fairmont Hotel in San Francisco and the Hotel del Coronado in San Diego at the time of this commission. In Portland, the Yeon Building and the lamented Oregonian Building (razed in the late 1940s during the city's rush to judgment on "outdated structures") were among their accomplishments. Many of their buildings featured faces of glazed terra-cotta, and the Jackson Tower is no exception. Although towers were popular choices for newspaper buildings at the time of its construction, there are no other surviving buildings in Portland quite like the steel-framed Jackson Tower, and given its prominent downtown location, it now stands as one of a kind.

This building is tied to its surroundings by its creamy brick and white terra-cotta trim from the roof balustrade nearly all the way down to the base. It is crowned with a square clock tower. The arched base of the tower

3a, b *Jackson Tower*

received a fieldstone covering in 1953, while restoration in 1975 resulted in stucco being used in lieu of terra-cotta.

The tower was intended from the first to be illuminated at night, with bulbs screwed directly into the terra-cotta, making it a bit difficult to re-wire. Doric columns are obscured *behind* the clocks; perhaps this was not the best design choice. The clock faces are twelve-and-a-half feet across. The clocks originally ran on battery impulses from the basement of the building, but they were switched to steady electrical power in 1922. They chimed up until 1941, and today they have to be manually reset twice a year for daylight saving time.

✦   This building is named after Charles Samuel Jackson, publisher of the *Oregon Daily Journal.* During the time that the *Journal* occupied the tower, the clocks chimed every fifteen minutes.

✦   Because of its 1,800 light bulbs, the Jackson Tower was turned off during World War II to protect Portland from Axis powers and to save electricity. The savings on the power bill must have been impressive, as the lights were not turned on again until almost thirty years after the war's end.

3c   *Jackson Tower*

4 *Pacific Building*

4 PACIFIC BUILDING 1926

520 SW Yamhill Street, southeast corner of Pioneer Courthouse Square
Architects: A. E. Doyle; designed by Charles K. Greene

" . . . one of the two or three finest edifices ever to grace the Portland skyline."
—E. Kimbark MacColl, *The Growth of a City*

This is an attractive, blocky structure that somehow combines the Italian Renaissance with the Chicago School. The Italian details include a light-colored brick façade and overhanging red tile roof, while the Chicago touches are crisp, geometric windows, nearly flush with the walls. The Pacific Building

has Portland's familiar decorated cornices and off-white terra-cotta at the base of the structure. It has been noted that the Pacific Building refers in its height and color to two nearby buildings that were already finished at the time of its construction, the American Bank Building and the Jackson Tower.

This is one of three Italian Renaissance buildings created by A. E. Doyle's firm with Charles K. Greene as the primary designer. The precursor to the Pacific Building was the Bank of California, which has an identical cornice. Just to the south, the Public Service Building completes this architectural triple play, a great series of buildings that ended with Charles Greene literally dying of starvation. (See "The Public Service Building" for the rest of the story.)

✦   The building site was originally called the "Million Dollar Cowpasture" because the palatial Henry W. Corbett home (1875) and its outbuildings existed on the spot and a cow was sometimes tethered on the grounds there. When the last trees on the site were cut down, the *Oregonian* noted: "Nestling now in a forest of towering buildings, the old trees . . . are a breath from the past, but must leave now . . . so that another pile of brick and mortar and concrete and steel can have room."

✦   A. E. Doyle moved his architectural firm into this building upon its completion. The main lobby's lights, marble, and metalwork are still beautifully impressive.

✦   This was the first project of Italian-born Pietro Belluschi (1899–1994), an architect with superlative understanding of architecture as a social art and who went through significant and influential professional evolution. More than twenty years after the Pacific Building's completion, he would employ a not-dissimilar window scheme in his Equitable Building.

5 PIONEER COURTHOUSE/PIONEER POST OFFICE 1869–75

Originally the U.S. Courthouse, west wing addition 1903
555 SW Yamhill, due east of Pioneer Square
Architect: Alfred Bult Mullet/Addition: James Knox Taylor

Described as "out-worn and out-grown" by a local paper in 1927, Pioneer Courthouse is the oldest public federal building in the Pacific Northwest and the second-oldest federal building west of the Mississippi. The classic Italianate structure is still a testament to dignity and grace, despite the fact that since the early 1900s there have been repeated attempts to tear down this three-story, sandstone-walled building. To date, recalcitrant judges, preservationist groups, and red tape have prevented that from happening.

The original courthouse was rectangular, with wings added to the west side in 1903. Sixty-nine years later, the firm of Allen, McMath, and Hawkins finished an extensive restoration at a time when the preservation/restoration movement was still in its infancy. The spectacular results helped raise local awareness of the importance of keeping and maintaining historical buildings.

This site was put up for sale in 1933; luckily, there were no buyers at that time, due to the Great Depression. It was put up for sale again in the late 1950s, and stood virtually empty until 1968, when the efforts of Judge John F. Kilkenny and Congresswoman Edith Green ensured that the building would be restored and used; it was rededicated in 1973. As a reward, Edith Green got the left-handed compliment of having the appallingly ugly G. S. A. Federal Building (Skidmore, Owings, Merrill, 1975) at 1220 SW Third Avenue named after her.

As mentioned with Pioneer Courthouse Square, Portland city blocks slope down toward the Willamette River. The challenge to the architect of large buildings is to aesthetically deal with this slope, and Alfred Bult Mullet did so by leveling the entire site within the block and placing the building within a perimeter wall, with grounds descending to the sidewalk.

The building itself follows a very formal design, as is proper for a structure of its nature. It has Greek elements in its pediments, but the overall structure is usually referred to as Palladian. From outside, view the octagonal wooden cupola on top of the hip-and-gable roof. If the courthouse is

5a *Pioneer Courthouse—east side*

5b   *Pioneer Courthouse Cupola*

open, run the gauntlet of guards to go inside the cupola to get an interesting view of Pioneer Square. On the way, enjoy the oak and walnut woodwork and ash trim throughout the building, which has aged handsomely. Also view the second-floor courtroom, which comes complete with a fireplace. At the cupola, view the roof's chimneys that were part of the original construction; five of these fireplaces are still functional.

Just inside the main entrance on the west side entering the post office, note the flanking wooden carvings of *caryatids* on each side. Caryatids are female figures forced to carry great weights on their shoulders. They represent the women of Caryae, a Greek community in Asia Minor. These women were bound to slavery as punishment for treachery in the ancient Persian Wars. Their male counterparts are named *atlantes,* named after the god Atlas, who supported the earth. These particular caryatids originally graced the old Kamm Building.

In front of Pioneer Courthouse on the southwest corner are two iron structures on the sidewalk. These cover stairways that go down to public restrooms. Although they are presently locked to prevent illicit activities, it would be a fine thing to have them renovated and opened to the public again.

The building's architect was also a supervising architect of the Treasury Department and designed the Navy and State buildings in Washington, D.C. Although not an extravagantly rich man, he made a mint on one of his projects in San Francisco; namely, the San Francisco Mint, a building that closely resembles this courthouse.

Noted local architect Ellis Lawrence (1879–1946) organized the Portland chapter of the American Institute of Architects. This same group would later suspend Lawrence from the Portland chapter for the preservationist crime of drawing up an office building to replace Pioneer Courthouse during one of its threatened demolitions.

✦ Here are some serious suggestions for this site that never happened: Office building, city park, bomb shelter, workhouse for unemployed girls, greyhound racetrack, and, inescapably, a parking lot. Fred Meyer (original surname, Grubmeyer) favored a business use for the building and felt that a park would attract too many children and women, needlessly crowding the downtown area.

✦ *Location, location, location:* As with so many public buildings, Pioneer Courthouse raised a hue and cry among Portlanders upon its construction. The reason for the controversy? It had been built too far away from the heart of downtown. Local wags recommended setting up a Pony Express station to link the post office with the city's center.

✦ A. E. Doyle had a grandson, architect and preservationist George A. McMath, who also made a huge impact on the city's buildings. McMath assisted in the restoration of this building and dozens of others in Portland. His first architectural job was with a firm founded by Donald J. Stewart, a member of Doyle's original firm.

6 AMERICAN BANK 1913–14

Originally the Northwestern National Bank
621 SW Morrison Street, north side of the square
Architect: Doyle, Patterson, and Beach

This spot may look like a good place to put a bank, but it is apparently a somewhat snakebitten location; the building that preceded this one had a portion unexpectedly collapse and the rest had to be torn down. This successor is pure classical material. Granite-based Corinthian columns partially encircle the base of the building, and the terra-cotta decoration includes griffins and eagles. Local giants Henry L. Pittock and Frederick Leadbetter were the principal organizers of the Northwestern National Bank Company (and this building's construction), which went out of business in 1927. There was a memorable "run" on the bank in 1927, with crowds of people jostling to get inside the building before their funds could disappear. The two financial institutions that followed in this building also failed.

6 a, b   *American Bank*

The smooth brickwork on the front of this building was originally buff; it was painted white in 1983. The primary entrance features bronze hardware as well as a marquee that was redone in 1936 (according to Pietro Belluschi's designs) and again in 1984.

✦ Part of architect Doyle's classical leanings can perhaps be explained by the fact that he studied at the American School of Archeology.

7 NORDSTROM'S BUILDING 1978

701 SW Broadway, between Morrison and Yamhill Streets
Architect: Ernest C. Wilson

The Orpheum Theater was torn down to make way for this daunting full-block, brick-faced building as part of a downtown renewal plan. As such, the three-story building has been an asset in getting foot traffic into the area, although the squat structure with angled corner entries does not do much else to recommend itself to the aesthetically minded.

8 PIONEER PLACE 1990
PIONEER PLACE EXPANSION 2000

Due east of Pioneer Courthouse between Yamhill and Morrison Streets
Architect: ELS (Berkeley)

Although the opening of a shopping mall is hardly cause for rejoicing, the fact that a small and tasteful (and, at $134 million, expensive) one was put in the city's center helped maintain a vital downtown. Complain all you want, but it could be worse—a lot worse. Some cities have dropped huge malls or stadiums in their downtown areas, while the scale of these two shopping areas is in keeping with the relative scope of the surrounding zone. The public art helps keep it tolerable, and the glass rotunda of the western block ensures plenty of natural light for GAP shoppers at the base of the building. A similar atrium serves the same purpose in the expansion, shooting light down and creating the "English park" feel the designers planned. The expansion's garden was created by the installation of eighteen mammoth metal-stemmed and fiberglass-petaled sculptures. Salmon exteriors and terra-cotta trim pay homage to the locale. Inside, the west block uses more natural wood, while fake stone is on display to the east.

Pioneer Place was built by the Rouse Company (Maryland) after the purchase of three downtown blocks, a feat not replicated till 1999 when Gerdling/Edlen Development Company purchased the Blitz Weinhard Brewing Company site.

✦ On opening day in 1990, the escalators at Pioneer Place broke down because of the considerable heft and volume of Portland shoppers. Opening day for the expansion a decade later included the dropping of large clumps of confetti from the mall's roof onto the heads of shoppers below.

8 a, b   *Pioneer Place*

9 MEIER AND FRANK BUILDING 1909, 1915, 1932
621 SW Fifth Avenue, northeast corner of the square
Architect: Doyle and Patterson

The Meier and Frank Building was constructed in three installments and four parts. It was also local architect A. E. Doyle's first major commission, and a darned big one at that. This building eventually ended up being a fifteen-floor, steel-framed structure in what became the center of Portland.

Meier and Frank had a smaller building designed by architects Whidden and Lewis constructed on this site in 1898. In order to plan for what was initially only an annex to the building, A. E. Doyle traveled to Chicago with store president Sigmund Frank so that Frank could see what the latest architectural crazes were in department stores. Frank came back from the trip wanting two additional floors on the building, along with "modern" windows and white terra-cotta facing. Doyle originally wanted to use the same yellow brick face as the original Whidden and Lewis building had, but once he converted to using white glazed terra-cotta, it was utilized in the majority of his subsequent downtown designs. Terra-cotta completely covers the Meier and Frank Building, with the exception of the granite bases to the corner pilasters. Its usage is noteworthy in its sheer quantity if nothing else and does imbue the Meier and Frank with reflective light aplenty.

There are a variety of decorative elements to observe here, including ornamental panels, the great roof balustrade, pilasters, and the belt course. Smaller embellishments run the gamut from wave scrolls to egg and dart, and even a stylized Art Deco geometric design on the second floor.

The Meier and Frank Building is still a large and impressive structure. Interestingly, despite its size, it was built without an interior light court, a fairly standard feature on buildings that were its contemporaries. Years after

9 a, b *Meier and Frank Building*

its construction, A. E. Doyle self-deprecatingly called his creation a "big dry goods box punched full of holes for light."

Aaron Meier and Emil Frank both hailed from Germany. In 1870 they formed a business partnership that continues in name today. In 1967 Meier and Frank was purchased by the May Company, putting an end to the firm's motto: "Portland's Own Store."

✦   Four years before the design of this building, A. E. Doyle had visited Italy and Greece to study classic architecture. That same year he also worked for Henry Bacon, designer of the Lincoln Memorial.

✦   The unexpected death of Sigmund Frank in 1910 was partially responsible for the piecemeal nature of the store's construction.

✦   Overhauling the building with the most modern available equipment has included the installation of an automatic sprinkler system, nineteen elevators, and Portland's first escalators!

✦   A young "big-eared" employee of the store who worked in the necktie department in 1922 went on to become an international star. No, not Alfred E. Neuman, but Clark Gable.

10   YEON BUILDING 1911

Northeast corner of SW Fifth Avenue and Alder Street
Architect: Reid Brothers (San Francisco)

True to the Reid brothers' building tendencies (see the Jackson Tower), the Yeon Building is a palace almost completely sheathed with white terra-cotta. The building is spruced up with a nice colonnade at the top, as well as some terra-cotta decoration on the very top floor above the columns. Like the Jackson Tower, the Yeon Building originally had light sockets built right into the terra-cotta of the cornice for nighttime illumination. This cornice has since been taken down for safety reasons.

Canada-native John Baptiste Yeon (1865–1928) was a lumberjack who came to Portland in 1885 with $2.50. An obviously motivated and canny man, he was a millionaire in the lumber business by the time he was forty. It wasn't long after then that he became interested in real estate, and the Yeon Building, upon its construction, was the tallest office building in the state. His wealth assured, Yeon turned his focus to improving Oregon's roads. He was a key figure in the construction of the Columbia River Highway, and he was also paid a yearly stipend of one dollar in his capacity as the official Multnomah County Roadmaster.

11 FIFTH AVENUE SUITES HOTEL 1912

Originally Lipman, Wolfe & Co.
506 SW Washington Street, west side of Fifth Avenue between
Alder and Washington Streets
Architect: Doyle and Patterson

The Fifth Avenue Suites is a good companion structure to the Yeon Building across the street. It is a ten-story, half-block, white terra-cotta building with a wide variety of decorative flourishes. Wreaths, frets, medallions, and other embellishments work their way across the front of the building.

The original decorative cornice of this building caused quite a stir when one of its terra-cotta lion's heads fell one hundred feet to the sidewalk below. Nobody was injured by the clay Leo, but the scare resulted in the inspection of all downtown cornices and the subsequent modification and/or removal of several of them. Some of this building's lion's heads were replaced by fiberglass models.

Lipman, Wolfe & Co. was founded in Sacramento in 1850 by Solomon Lipman as a merchandise store. The Portland branch was opened in 1880, and this building served as a dry-goods store in its initial incarnation. Another store chain (Frederick & Nelson) picked it up as a department store until 1986.

Subsequently boarded up, a decade later the interior of this building was completely reworked by ZGF Partnership in its makeover to the Fifth Avenue Suites, an establishment designed to handle overflow guests from the Vintage Plaza Hotel. Over twenty million dollars later, the building had been salvaged from decades of downturn to a new version of the building it never was.

✦ Miniature Douglas fir trees can be delivered to rooms here at no charge.

12 BANK OF THE WEST 1916

Originally First National Bank, aka Oregon Pioneer Savings
and Loan Building
401 SW Fifth Avenue, southwest corner of Fifth Avenue
and Stark Street
Architects: Coolidge and Shattuck (Boston)

It has been observed that this building looks like a cross-pollination between a Greek temple and the Lincoln Memorial. Although the designers

12 a, b   *Bank of the West*

may have erred on the side of producing a somewhat unwieldy mass of a structure, it is an undeniably impressive bank. Features to notice include lots of concrete, which covers lots of steel, and Doric columns supporting a massive block of a portico. There are carved friezes on the cornice and enta-blature at the top of the building, with "swags" (a design imitating draped cloth) on the attic story. Also high up you will notice anthemions decorating the roof, which are flat honeysuckle decorations. After taking in the splendor, step inside for a shock—the dropped ceilings are lower than many living rooms.

✦   In a fine example of "networking," Abbot Mills was the First National Bank president during this building's construction. The architect, W. A. Coolidge, just happened to be a former Harvard school chum of his. It's not *what* you know . . .

✦   Above the entrance to the bank, two stone women flank the message *"Alis volat propiis,"* which is Latin for the Oregon state motto, literally, "By means of one's own wings one flies." So why do I need a bank?

13 U.S. BANCORP TOWER 1983

Aka Big Pink
111 SW Fifth Avenue, between Fifth and Sixth Avenues, south side
of Burnside Street
Architect: SOM/Pietro Belluschi, consultant

Standing unchallenged in its domain, the coppery U.S. Bancorp Tower is a towering Portland landmark not easily missed. Architect A. E. Doyle's wish for a bank tower in this vicinity was granted in the form of this, the only major building in Portland nicknamed after an album by The Band. This tower is also one of the few modern skyscrapers in the city to successfully avoid the pitfalls of both the boringly offensive concrete/steel/glass boxes and also the perceived postmodern follies of the Portland Building.

As the two opposing angles of Portland's city streets meet on Burnside, the architects allowed these angles to form the mass of the U.S. Bancorp Tower. Big Pink employs no right angles in its basic exterior form, so depending on one's line of vision to it, it can appear deeply stepped-back or nearly two-dimensional. It has a "stepped" granite base, which is reiterated in glass at the top, giving it a simple but effective ornamental look that works well with a building of its vast scale. (It has almost seventeen acres of space inside.)

13 a, b   *U.S. Bancorp Tower*

Size and shape aside, the Big Pink's real allure lies in its color. Seen in the setting sun from the northwest or in the dawn sun from the east, the appeal of this tower shines clearly through. Usually dusty rose or copper, the Bancorp Tower can do marvelous things with the light of morning and dusk; this process was memorably described by Gideon Bosker and Lena Lencek as "light silently spanking a parallelogram of glass and granite." The play of light on its surfaces was what most concerned Belluschi, who approached this building's design as much as a sculpture as a skyscraper. It can appear to be light pink, silver, deep copper, and nearly black, all in the same day.

Part of the magic of the tower's reflective abilities has to do with the window's light thresholds; depending on the amount of light on them, they either darken and absorb light, or they lighten and reflect it. The surrounding granite can thus be either darker or lighter than the nearby glass at different times of the day. As such, it is probably the most dynamic building in the city.

The resultant success enhanced Belluschi's already formidable reputation as one of the nation's leading architects, and it also did much to ameliorate some of SOM's transgressions on Portland's skyline. (One can still healthily despise the tower's adjacent mall/plaza.) Admittedly, a Portland building had been erected that took not one iota of consideration of the surrounding architectural context into account (the Portland Design Commission wrote that the tower had no connection to Portland's "setting or past"), but in this particular case, who cares?

✦   At 536 feet high, the U.S. Bancorp Tower is eight feet shorter than the Wells Fargo Tower, even though Big Pink has two more floors.

✦   The only available venue for the legions of Portland's stair racers has been the "Run on the Banks," a race to the top of the city's two tallest buildings, the Wells Fargo Tower and the U.S. Bancorp Tower, a total of eighty-six stories.

14   WELLS FARGO BUILDING 1907
AKA THE U.S. NATIONAL BANK BUILDING (FORMERLY KNOWN AS THE PORTER BUILDING)
SW Sixth Avenue and Oak Street, southwest corner
Architect: Benjamin Wistar Morris III

Adjoining the U.S. National Bank is the Wells Fargo Building, also now known as the U.S. National Bank Building. This twelve-story building was

14 *Wells Fargo Building*

considered a "skyscraper" in its day, and was the tallest building in Portland at the time of its construction. It also qualified as the city's first steel-framed skyscraper. This aside, the viewer is likely to notice its wide variety of textures and colors visible on its exterior surface.

At the bottom, above granite bases, is a covering of limestone that extends up in arches for two floors. After a terra-cotta buffer zone (with a white wave pattern on a blue background), the brick is decoratively laid out in diamond and cross patterns all the way to the upper floors, where colorful terra-cotta and green keystones resume, ensuring that this structure looks like no other office building. The balustrade at the top, as well as the wreaths and keystones below, are terra-cotta. At the top, below the copper roof cornice, are the words "WELLS" on one side of the building and "FARGO" on the other.

A Portland native, Benjamin Wistar Morris III went on to gain prominence in New York. When he first began there, he assisted with the plans for the New York Public Library. He was later affiliated with the Metropolitan Opera Company and helped develop the plans for what became Rockefeller Center.

✦ The site that the investors in this building had originally wanted was at Fifth Avenue and Alder Street, but the cost of the property was prohibitive, which explains the present "remote" location.

✦ *Big Rock Department:* The doorstep of the Wells Fargo Building's impressive entryway required the largest piece of granite ever shipped to Portland at that time.

15 a   *U.S.National Bank Building*

15 U.S. NATIONAL BANK BUILDING 1916, 1925
321 SW Sixth Avenue, south side of Sixth Avenue and Broadway
Architect: A. E. Doyle

This is a truly beautiful building, and the most impressive of its kind in Portland. Constructed in two stages (the Sixth Avenue portion in 1916 and the Broadway section in 1924), the U.S. National Bank is a terra-cotta temple acknowledging the power of the dollar, and an impressive place of worship it is. Constructed by Doyle as a Roman monument, the grandeur of the lobby was so impressive that early in the bank's history, Portland officials tried to impress visiting dignitaries with a visit to the building.

Although technically a reinforced concrete building, this looks more like five stories of Italian palace; the exterior Corinthian columns are fifty-four feet high, and at the time of the bank's construction were described as embodying "the soaring power of finance in a wealthy civilization." Makes one feel a bit queasy, doesn't it? If not, perhaps the dead birds trapped in the netting around the capitals will. The base of the bank is faced in granite, the rest in a grayish-pink terra-cotta that was designed especially for the structure. The cornice and balustrade at the top are purely classical, and there is a cornucopia of details, including fish scales, urns, rosettes, lions' heads, and yes, even cornucopias. Perhaps a better term would be "horns o' plenty," as they are being blown into by cherubim.

Inside, the Renaissance interior has to be seen to be appreciated; it's an amazing space, with thirty-foot-high ceilings, dignified light fixtures, and Italian (white), Belgian (black), and Hungarian (red) marble. The ceramic bas-reliefs on the ceiling were hand carved and hand painted, and have never had another coat applied to them. The interior plaster decoration is frankly amazing. It has been posited that this building's Roman style and lavish decoration may have been a response to the nearby First National Bank, which was also under construction at the time. If so, Portland benefited from the rivalry.

Note Avard T. Fairbanks's carved bronze doors on the east and west sides of the building. The theme of the east side is the development of transportation; the west side illuminates "international good will." Although deadly earnest, they are also indisputably impressive. (You should come by for a viewing when the bank is closed.)

✦   Fred Baker made all the light fixtures in here in 1917. The same Fred Baker rewired all the fixtures in 1975.

✦   The bank was expanded westward a few years after its construction. One of Doyle's proposals at that time was for a "U.S. National Bank Tower." This would have constituted a sixteen- to twenty-one-story office tower coming from the front top of the building. Budgeted at a proposed cost of $1,000,000, it was never built, but then you already knew that.

✦   The steel used in the bank's original safety deposit boxes was originally intended for French cannons in World War I. Keep an eye open for the Rose Festival crown while down in the vault; that's where it's stored.

15 b   *U.S. National Bank Building*

16a   *Bidwell and Co. Building entrance*

16   BIDWELL AND CO. BUILDING 1924

Originally the Bank of California, aka Durham & Bates Agencies, Inc.
330 SW Sixth Avenue, southwest corner of Sixth Avenue
  and Stark Street
Architects: A. E. Doyle; designer Charles K. Greene

This two-story Italian Renaissance building looks a bit like an upscale stone jail, although that's not actually stone you're looking at. Rather, it is terra-cotta dressed to resemble granite stone blocks. Its base is marble, and the roof was originally a red clay tile. It is a solid and attractive building, one that conveys the stability of its institution while letting in significant light through its west side with a series of sizable arched windows. It is also a nice down-to-earth counterpoint to the perhaps overly decorated U.S. National Bank across the street. An extensive year 2000 renovation by Greg Baldwin suits the building well.

Chief designer Charles K. Greene's next building for Doyle's agency would be the Pacific Building, followed by the Public Service Building, which has the same exterior lights.

✦   The Bank of California existed at this location for fifty years before moving to its location across from O'Bryant Square.

✦   Before this building's construction, the Portland Public Library was located here.

16b   *Bidwell and Co. Building*

17 THE COMMONWEALTH BUILDING 1948

Originally the Equitable Building
421 SW Sixth Avenue, between Washington and Stark Streets
Architect: Pietro Belluschi

"In this country we (architects) are inevitably kicked between fashion and dead tradition."
—Pietro Belluschi in a 1931 letter to Frank Lloyd Wright

Perhaps Portland's most seminal building, this was the first big commission that Belluschi's firm handled after World War II. The Equitable Building was the first completely sealed and air-conditioned building of its size in the U.S.; it was the nation's first truly modern structure in a variety of ways. The Equitable was also a trailblazer in its use of double-glazed windows, giving it a handsome and distinctive green look. Wrapped entirely in glass and aluminum, it is called a "curtain-wall" building, meaning that the exterior wall keeps out the weather but is non-load-bearing. Although there had previously been commercial skyscrapers with a regular, geometric look, nothing quite like this building had ever been seen.

17 *The Commonwealth Building*

During the early 1940s, Belluschi became aware that there was going to be a huge surplus of aluminum from the war effort, and he was interested in using the material for a project. A new formula of reinforced concrete was used for this building's design, allowing a thinner frame and more room for glass and sills of dark green aluminum, which made a nice contrast with the metal's silver sheen elsewhere. The incredible smooth appearance of the building is no deception; nothing protruding more than seven-eighths of an inch from the surface was permitted.

Perhaps the best news about the Equitable was that at its original height of twelve floors, it did not dwarf buildings in the surrounding area. (It was near the city's building code height limit at the time; it has had another floor added since.) Combined with the building's slender width, the sleek Equitable seems entirely balanced in composition, going neither too high or too wide, but appearing just right. As such, it is generally heralded as a landmark architectural work in the city, and has justifiably and often been acknowledged as one of the best U.S. buildings of the twentieth century.

The downside of native son Belluschi's pioneering work was that it served as a very powerful modernistic influence on downtown's future. By virtue of this early example, a Portland precedent had been set for the mush-rooming of other metal and glass boxes. This would ultimately result in an undistinguished skyline of reflective right angles in places, as Belluschi's basic style was widely imitated, but his restraint and tastefulness were not.

The original mural in the lobby of the building was designed by Belluschi and executed by house painters for fifty dollars. (The client had rejected a modern work of art estimated at $10,000.) The Equitable's lobby was re-designed in the 1970s, but Belluschi disliked it so much that he avoided visiting the building until Soderstrom Architects and Belluschi re-did the area in 1987. After that restoration, Belluschi signed his name to the lobby's re-created mural, a work that lends a rounded and organic theme inside a very geometric building.

As a measure of the Equitable's impact on its designer's career, Belluschi was awarded the high honor of being elected as a fellow of the American Institute of Architects (AIA) after its completion. In the boom years be-tween 1945 to 1950, Belluschi's office employed twenty-eight people and completed nearly two hundred jobs. Two years after this building's comple-tion, Belluschi went to Massachusetts to be dean of architecture at MIT. In 1972, he was awarded the highest honor an architect can aspire to, the AIA Gold Medal. (The award was not given without controversy, however, most of which concerned Belluschi's serving as an "architectural consultant" on projects, and was not given out again for a number of years afterwards.)

Across the street to the east, the First Farwest Building (remodel finished 1983, SOM) deserves notice for taking into account the Equitable Building. When architects talk about a "quality urban space," they are referring to the area between and around buildings; here, SOM shot for quality urban space and got it. The First Farwest Corporation purchased and significantly remodeled the 1940s existing building on this site, raising it from five to eleven stories and encasing it in aluminum curtain walls in lieu of the previous blue- ceramic-tile wall covering. (It had been known as the "Blue Building.") The result is a structure entirely compatible in terms of surface and size with its more famous neighbor. It may not be as distinctive, but it does present a unified face to the neighborhood.

✦ Pietro Belluschi was prepared to use aluminum in the structure of the building itself until the idea was rejected by local fire marshals because of that metal's low melting temperature. Belluschi initially had a high opinion of aluminum; he wrote without much prescience in the May 1943 *Architectural Forum* that "fire resistant aluminum alloys will do away with concrete fireproofing as now used in steel structures."

✦ One of Pietro Belluschi's lesser-known works during the war years was a temporary Japanese relocation center in Portland.

✦ Pietro Belluschi's name is misspelled on a plaque outside the lobby commemorating the building's innovative heat pumps.

18 WILCOX BUILDING 1911

*400 Sixth Avenue, southeast corner of Sixth Avenue and
    Washington Street
Architect: Whidden and Lewis*

This building is nearly identical to the Stevens Building (*1914*, aka Farwest Assurance Building, 812-820 Washington Street). Both buildings were designed by Whidden and Lewis in a modern style and built to the same height. Both are steel-framed office structures with white terra-cotta sheathing on the upper floors and ample windows. The original terra-cotta on both buildings' lower floors has been removed, but there is substantial terra-cotta decoration in the Wilcox's cornices, and floors three through ten of its body are covered in smooth, relatively light-colored brick.

Architects Whidden and Lewis thought enough of the Wilcox Building to move their business offices into it after construction was complete. Theodore Burney Wilcox (1856–1918) was born in the thriving metropolis of Agawam, Massachusetts. While working in a Massachusetts bank,

18   *Wilcox Building*

Wilcox impressed a visiting Portland banker enough for him to offer him a job in Portland. The move worked out well for Wilcox; he achieved a net worth in excess of $10 million. Wilcox financed the Stevens Building as well.

Whidden and Lewis also designed the very similar 620 Building (*1907, 1913,* 620 SW Fifth Avenue). It was originally built as a six-floor building, with the top half being added years later. Originally called the Failing Building (aka the Gasco Building), it is handsome without being inspiring; it features a modest cornice, and cream-colored terra-cotta covers and decorates the top two floors.

19   THE HOTEL VINTAGE PLAZA 1894

Originally known as the Imperial Hotel, aka "The Plaza"
422 SW Broadway, northeast corner of Broadway and
*   Washington Street*
Architect: Frederick Manson White

The original Imperial Hotel is now called the Hotel Vintage Plaza. Its architect, Frederick Manson White, moved to Portland from Derby, England, and the Imperial Hotel is a very representative sampling of his work. This massive, six-story redbrick building was designed in a style both utilitarian and classical, with obvious Roman influences.

Noted for its many arches, it is a blocky and imposing building comparatively bereft of the formal decoration that adorned buildings only ten years its senior. There is some embellishment with terra-cotta and pressed brick, and the frieze below the cornice at the top is one of its few exterior decorative details. Nevertheless, the brick and clean archways form a beautiful contrast with the rustic stonework of the lower floors, and make for an imposing and unique building.

The Imperial went through extensive restoration in the mid-1980s. A poorly conceived glass front was removed from the front of the structure to again reveal the beautiful rustic rock face below the brick masonry.

✦ One can still see the hotel's former name over the Washington Street entrance in an intriguingly zany lettering style.

✦ Designated historic buildings in Portland receive a substantial tax break. In 1999, the Hotel Vintage Plaza's approximate value with that tax break was $649,000. Without the break, it would have been assessed at about $8.3 million.

19 *Hotel Vintage Plaza*

20   BENSON HOTEL 1912, 1959

aka the Oregon Hotel/New Oregon Hotel
309 SW Broadway, southwest corner of Broadway and Oak Street
Architect: Doyle, Patterson and Beach

This distinguished French Baroque brick building is modeled after the famous Blackstone Hotel in Chicago; it has a good deal of beautiful terracotta to take in among the dormers and pediments. The unique-looking and colossal mansard double-sloped roof is covered with copper and terracotta tiles painted to resemble copper. This helps to distinguish the thirteen-story hotel from its taller neighbors; the green copper over the windows helps as well.

The Benson's lobby utilizes Circassian walnut woodwork from Russia, a cost-effective substitute for the marble the original plans called for. Italian marble did find its way into the floors of the hotel, with Austrian crystal chandeliers above them and a stone fireplace to the side. The lobby was remodeled by Pietro Belluschi in 1930, a job that forced him into the unpleasant position of having to stay in the most sumptuous hotels in Los Angeles, San Francisco, and New York for research. Go to the lobby's balcony for an up-close look at the ceiling's plaster designs of acanthus, rosettes, egg and dart, etcetera.

Photo courtesy of Coates Kokes, The Benson Hotel

20   *Benson Hotel*

Norway-native Simon Benson (1852–1942) worked in the Pacific Northwest as a lumberman and farmer, gradually increasing his wealth and acquiring timberland with a skillful business acumen to the point where he earned over $4 million by selling his holdings in 1910. Benson then purchased this site from fellow lumberjack/self-made millionaire John Yeon. The hotel operated at a loss until Benson took over the management. Simon Benson is today remembered each day by thirsty Portlanders for his bronze "Benson Bubblers," the street fountains which he donated to the city in order to provide free and available water to his employees, keeping them out of local saloons and increasing worker efficiency. (The distinctive design of the bronze fountains came from A. E. Doyle's offices.) Simon Benson moved to Beverly Hills in 1921 but later returned to Portland, a wise move still appreciated today.

✦ In 1974, a local lawyer was arrested outside the Benson Hotel for wearing a President Nixon mask, in direct violation of a local statute against publicly wearing disguises, Halloween notwithstanding.

✦ Prestige has a price: one can come close to dropping a cool grand on a really nice room at the Benson.

21 UNION BANK OF CALIFORNIA 1969

407 SW Broadway, between Broadway and Park, Stark,
and Washington Streets
Architect: Anshen and Allen (San Francisco)
Barnes, Hilgers and Maslen, consultants

This fifteen-story International-style building is noteworthy for the grayish-green "dollar bill"-color slate it uses in its service core, which looks good when wet or dry. This slate was supposedly quarried in the same spot in Wales as Stonehenge's slabs. It provides a good contrast with the building's white sides, as well as matching the glazed windows, which tie in with the not-too-distant Equitable's green glass.

However, in terms of taking surrounding landscapes into account, this is the Union Bank's only concession. Although its vertical design features may be relatively predictable given its date of construction, it still has very strong presence and an attractive look in the sunlight. Unfortunately, it accomplishes this by virtue of perching up on its pedestal to separate itself from its neighbors, and by taking up a full block.

21 *Union Bank of California*

22 *Morgan Building*

22 MORGAN BUILDING 1913

720 SW Washington Street, between Broadway and Park Street
Architect: Doyle, Patterson and Beach

This redbrick office building with an off-white terra-cotta trim would have made for a nice commercial bookend with the Arlington Club; it's a strong, dignified and attractive structure. The columns on the ground floor are covered with a ceramic designed to match the terra-cotta after a remodel. The well-done cornice is made of machine-pressed iron sheet metal and bracketed nicely, and the terrific Art Deco entrance was done by the Oregon Brass Works in 1938. Although there are some aquatic embellishments on this building, the original tenants of it were primarily doctors.

23 CHARLES F. BERG BUILDING 1902/1930

Originally the Dolph Building
611–615 Broadway, between Morrison and Alder Streets
Architect: Kim Weber for the Grand Rapids Design Service (Michigan)

If you really want to see some Art Deco, go to south Miami. In Portland, your choices are substantially more limited. This gorgeous building is the best example of an Art Deco façade in town. (It is also one of the *only* examples in town.)

The front of the Berg Building is a rich black and gold, with panels of cream and dark aquamarine panels high up. There are designs of sunbursts, spirals, rain clouds, and peacocks on the third floor, with a zigzag pattern at the very top. The Berg Building has a very dark façade, which is a delightfully unexpected choice given the high percentage of white terra-cotta one finds in downtown Portland. The terra-cotta façade was applied in 1930 during a remodeling of the old Dolph Building, whose structural frame is still intact. Gold runs throughout the building's front, 18-karat gold at that, a usage that was virtually unheard of in U.S. buildings at the time. Only two other buildings in the country were gilded with 18-karat gold when this lavish Art Deco front went up on the Berg Building. The point of this entire fascinating spectacle was to draw women inside to buy ladies' apparel, but shortly after the building's completion, the Great Depression began. The design elements that this building showcases were to become extinct in the no-nonsense structures that came in the following decades.

The Grand Rapids Design Service had a firm in Portland known for its cutting-edge designs. The building's namesake, Charles F. Berg (1871–1932), lived in San Francisco, managed a store at the age of nineteen, and opened a shop in Portland in 1907.

✦   Interior details of the Berg that are now gone included a Tiffany elevator with chromium fixtures and frosted-glass lighting fixtures of bronze and silver. The women's lounge was designed to replicate Catalina Island's Submarine Gardens with silver-and-coral finished furniture, a mauve velvet divan, and an artistic submarine window scene.

23 a, b   *Charles F. Berg Building*

24 THE BROADWAY BUILDING 1917

Originally H. Liebes & Co. Building, aka Continental Crossroads
625 SW Broadway, west side of Broadway between Morrison
*   and Alder Streets*
Architect: John V. Bennes

There's a great lineup of terra-cotta details along the top of this small building, including lions' heads and ornamental blocks at the edge of the roof that conceal the tiles. The brick at the bottom of the building was added in 1971. All other terra-cotta is original.

Architect John V. Bennes (1867–1943) studied architecture in Prague, which is unsurprising as his cousin was a president of Czechoslovakia. He was a long-time Oregon resident and executed many terrific buildings in the area; he was the architect for Oregon State University for thirty years. In 1943, he moved to Los Angeles, thinking it would improve his health. It didn't.

25 THE STUDIO BUILDING/GUILD THEATER 1927

901–919 SW Taylor Street
Architect: Luther Lee Dougan

The eight-story brick Studio Building is a favorite of classical music lovers town-wide, as it is the only building to pay homage to composers like Schubert by displaying their busts in niches with name panels along the perimeter of the building. The attractive structure also has a nicely weathered mansard roof, interesting pillars, and decorative cartouches and medallions.

The two-story Guild Theater was constructed at the same time but has been maintained less rigorously; it boasts an empty niche, sticky floors, and lots of character; still, it was a neat stunt for Dougan to have built both structures together.

25 *The Studio Building/Guild Theater*

26 PYTHIAN BUILDING 1907

Originally Masonic Hall
918 SW Yamhill Street
Architect: William F. McCaw

This building features some of the city's most dramatic brickwork. Tan-colored bricks explode out of window casings and line up interestingly on its quoining. The patterns look great at a distance as well as close-up.

✦ The Fraternal Order of Knights of Pythias was founded during the Civil War to advance "Peace through Understanding."

27 ZELL BROTHERS JEWELERS/ZELL OPTICAL 1917, 1949
800–816 SW Morrison Street
Architect: John V. Bennes/Remodeled: Dougan, Heims and Caine

This unique building was originally designed with a terra-cotta exterior; an amazingly rich limestone replaced it in a remodel thirty-two years later for the current owners, and the flush windows put in then reflect the International trend of the mid-twentieth century, as pioneered by the Equitable Building to the east. The modestly sized building's marquee sign with clock and corner columns are all most becoming; it's a hybrid of old Art Deco retail design and the stripped-down cubes of the future.

Two talented Portland architects worked on this building, decades apart. John V. Bennes was responsible for a vast number of Portland buildings, while Luther Lee Dougan made many excellent local buildings for twenty-one years before joining with the firm responsible for the brilliant remodel of this building.

27 *Zell Brothers*

28 THE GALLERIA 1910

Originally Olds, Wortman, and King
Between SW Ninth and Tenth Avenues, Morrison and Alder Streets
Architect: C.R. Aldrich

The name may carry a malodorous whiff of a southern California shopping mall, but this building predates the consumer terrorism of the modern age. Sheathed entirely with white terra-cotta and five stories high, the first department store west of the Mississippi (Olds, Wortman, and King) was originally housed here, and the building occupied a full block; it was reputedly the only store in the entire Pacific Northwest to do so.

In 1976, the building was one of the first in town to be restored for commercial use as a downtown shopping center. In this case, shops were added to the first three floors and offices took the upper two. Renamed the Galleria at that time, the building's central light well was enlarged into a nice seventy-five-foot atrium.

✦ A. E. Doyle was the local supervising architect on this building.

29 WOODLARK BUILDING 1912

815 SW Alder Street, northeast corner of Alder Street and
*   Ninth Avenue*
Architect: Doyle, Patterson and Beach

Smooth, light-colored brick covers this crisp nine-story building. Terra-cotta arches are above the ninth-floor windows, but other than that, the building's windows are symmetrical and uniform.

30 PITTOCK BLOCK 1914, 1923

921 SW Washington Street, between Tenth and Eleventh Avenues,
*   Washington and Stark Streets*
Architect: Doyle and Patterson

The site of the present Pittock Block is the site of the former Pittock Home, inasmuch as Henry Pittock's house was here until the 1914 completion of his mansion on the hill. Just prior to his move out, Pittock leased the entire block to a California investor with the agreement that a worthy structure named after him be constructed on the site.

29 *Woodlark Building*

30 *Pittock Block*

And it was so. The reinforced concrete Pittock "Block" (more impressive than a mere building) was constructed with a smooth, light-colored brick on the exterior, with a minimal amount of terra-cotta embellishment. Store-fronts within the building were designed with marble bases. The north half of the block originally stood at three stories tall.

✦   The basement of this building housed a power station and distribution plant for the Northwestern Electric Company. Electrical currents flowed from the Pittock Block to other downtown buildings, powering elevators all over Portland.

31 *Capitol Building*

31 CAPITOL BUILDING NORTH END 1914, SOUTH END 1926

*aka the Pacific Telephone and Telegraph Co. Building,
the Pacific Bell Telephone Co. Building
310 SW Park Avenue, southeast corner of Park Avenue
and Oak Street
Architect: Edwin V. Cobby; Addition: A. E. Doyle and Associates*

This beautiful Italian building would not look out of place functioning as a public building in Florence. Pacific Telephone ordered a building that would fit in with the already present Benson Hotel and Oregon Hotel, and the glazed terra-cotta and rough-faced redbrick seem to match well with the Benson. The cornice and balustrade at the top are not terra-cotta but painted cast iron. The quartz-faced Capitol 2 Building (1969, WEBGROUP, designers Charles W. Endicott, H. Robert Wilmsen) at the northeast corner of Stark Street and Park Avenue is technically an addition to the Capitol Building. The architects' idea was to create an extension that was mindful of the original structure without simply copying it.

32 THE FEDERAL RESERVE BANK OF SAN FRANCISCO 1949

915 SW Stark Street
Architect: Pietro Belluschi

This is a brilliant street-corner design in a futuristic vein. At this point in his career, Belluschi used a flush, smooth surface on all his buildings and the Federal Reserve Bank was no exception. The dark granite base is broken up by large windows, and the contrasting white marble floors above have very regular openings that are one with the wall. Repetition within opposites; it makes for a winning combination. The corner entranceway gives this building a distinctive flair among Portland's many fine bank buildings, and also gives this building a whiff of a streamlined Art Deco look with a haughty International air.

32 *The Federal Reserve Bank of San Francisco*

33 GOVERNOR HOTEL 1909

Originally the Seward Hotel
611 SW Tenth Avenue, southwest corner of Tenth Avenue
*   and Alder Street*
Architect: William C. Knighton

Take your time looking at this building's exterior, because it's a real eyeful; one can only imagine what Portlanders made of this decidedly unusual building upon its construction. Decorative, almost anthropomorphic features run rampant across the top of this building, particularly at the northeast corner of the hotel.

The terra-cotta decoration on this building is unusual for Portland in that it follows none of the city's usual classic designs. In fact, it appears to be utterly idiosyncratic to any of its prevailing styles. The front of the Governor Hotel follows an abstract Art Nouveau/Native American pattern with geometric, boxy medallions, diamonds, and squares. The decorative front of the hotel is covered in creamy light brick and there are some stylized chains holding up the copper awning over the front entrance. (The entrance and lobby were originally at the corner of the building.) This hotel was built with two light courts; if one had an "inside" room, the bathroom was down the hall. If you had a prestigious "outside" room, you got a connecting bathroom shared with another room.

The hotel went through an exhaustive restoration in 1987, and few of the interior features are original, not to the building's detriment. The four-section sepia mural in the woodsy lobby is a nice rendering of a hackneyed regional theme: Lewis and Clark. The Governor is currently "married" to the Princeton Building to the west.

William C. Knighton (1867–1938), the architect of the hotel, became the official state architect in 1912, and then designed the Oregon Supreme Court Building in Salem. An idiosyncratic architect, he was known for working a bell motif (to some, it resembles a shield) into his designs, and many are evident here to the observant spectator.

✦ Rooms at the Seward were originally rented for one to two dollars a night.

✦ Alumni of Grant High School do not receive special rates here, despite the fact that the same architect designed their alma mater.

Photo © Andre Bodo, courtesy of Fletcher Farr Ayotte

34a   *Multnomah County Central Library*

34 MULTNOMAH COUNTY CENTRAL LIBRARY 1912–13

aka Central Library
801 SW Tenth Avenue, between Taylor and Yamhill Streets
Architect: A. E. Doyle (Doyle and Patterson)

Seventeen miles of bookshelves and 130 computer terminals, high ceilings in the reading rooms, and ample light combine here to make this library simply one of the best in the country.

A. E. Doyle worked in conjunction with the chief librarian, Mary Frances Isom, to lay out this building's interior. Isom had studied library science in New York before coming to Portland; she also organized libraries in French hospitals during World War I. She and Doyle went on a tour of some of the nation's libraries to avoid pitfalls made in other cities while searching for inspirational designs. The result was a very efficient interior layout that has been fairly well preserved over the years and through remodels.

The exterior of Central Library has a brick Georgian façade with the first floor, basement, and trim done in Indiana limestone. A. E. Doyle chose the Georgian style as "the most typically American architecture we have." He apparently derived specific inspiration for the distinctive arched window design from the Boston Public Library (McKim, Mead and White, 1888–92). While the basic form remains fairly unassuming, it is a building redolent of tradition and public service. Part of the external allure of this building is the surrounding cast-stone wall and railing that encircles it.

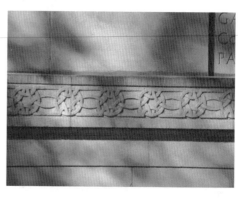

34b   *Multnomah County Central Library exterior detail*

Inviting benches with engraved names periodically appear in it, reducing the scale of what is nearly as wide a building as a Portland block can accommodate. If the library were a little closer to Belluschi's art museum, the two buildings would make a worthy architectural duo; the entrance to the Art Museum is very similar in design to that of the library.

Doyle felt that because of budgetary constraints, the library's exterior lacked the necessary decoration to make it a properly finished building, although in his address given at the library's opening he noted that this "is a library building, not an art gallery, nor a place for amusement . . . its architecture . . . (should reflect) surroundings of quietude and refined good taste." This philosophy worked in the building's favor as the library appears reasonably unfettered by extraneous decoration.

Much of the external detail of the library has stone inscriptions; three sides of the building are devoted to lists of influential individuals from the annals of western culture—in other words, mostly dead white guys. It is fun to run through the lists, wondering over Mary Frances Isom's selection process. For example, on the south side of the building, do we really need fifteen bookbinders listed, even on a library? And how could Muhammed be left off the list of religious leaders? Ah, well, it was a young and innocent age: Thomas Edison had not yet even distinguished himself enough to make the inventors list on the north side of the structure.

In 1991, structural weaknesses in the reading rooms on the second floor required the installation of steel scaffolding in the stacks for strength, and catalyzed discussion of an overhaul of the beautiful but antique building. The electrical system was particularly unsuited to deal with the needs of what has been transformed into a media center. The outside of the building was to be left alone, but the inside would be "technologized," brought up-to-date with earthquake codes.

Multnomah County chief librarian Ginnie Cooper oversaw an approximately $25-million renovation of the library by Fletcher Farr Ayotte (with McMath Dortignac and Hardy Holzman Pfeiffer Architects as design consultants). Taking place from late 1994 to 1997 (longer than the time it took to build the original structure), most of the interior was remodeled in a traditional yet creative homage to the library's heritage.

Ornamental plaster ceilings were restored and revealed, and two huge shear walls of reinforced concrete were put in to stabilize the entire building for seismic reinforcing. Throughout the interior, the building was completely renovated in the best sense of the word, with the original coffered ceilings in the lobby revealed again above the scagliola columns.

✦ The leaded glass dome in the third floor ceiling was originally above a cut-away hole in the third floor, allowing light to fall to down to the second floor.

✦ The library's Garden of Knowledge theme can be seen in its etched black-granite steps in the main lobby (by Larry Kirkland), as well as in the fourteen-foot bronze Tree of Knowledge in the Beverly B. Cleary Children's Library (Barbara Eiswerth and Dana Lynn Louis, artists). The tree cost $100,000 to make and install, and the entire cost of the project was paid for by an anonymous benefactor who likes metal foliage.

✦ Jamieson Parker (who later designed the Unitarian Church) was a seventeen-year-old junior draftsman responsible for the library's stone lettering. His misspelling of "Laurence Sterne" as "Lawrence" resulted in a fix-it job that can still be spotted.

✦ The original cost of the library was 21 cents per square foot, a fun sum to compare to the approximately $150-per-square-foot expense of the renovation.

34c *Library's Tree of Knowledge*

35 MEDICAL DENTAL BUILDING 1928

833 SW Eleventh Avenue, due west of the Central Library
Architect: Luther Lee Dougan

MEDICAL ARTS BUILDING 1926

aka Jeffrey Center
1020 SW Taylor Street, due south of the Central Library
Architect: Houghtaling and Dougan

The ten-story Medical Dental Building features a roofline populated with human forms and interspersed with caducei. (A caduceus is a scepter with intertwined serpents. The ancient god Hermes/Mercury carried one, as the Greeks associated serpents with healing and regenerative powers because of their ability to shed their skin and keep their eyes open for long periods of time. Aesculapius, the Roman god of medicine, is also associated with the snake.) Lower on the building are medallions profiling famous doctors over time. No doubt you'll recognize some of them; see if you can spot Dr. Doolittle. The essential shape and fenestration of this structure is fairly standard, but in its uses of textures, colors, and decoration, it really excels. It has a great little lobby, too, with some original bronzework, and a legitimate coffee shop on the ground floor that isn't part of a nationwide chain.

The eight-story Medical Arts Building has a huge arched portico supported by simple Tuscan columns. Terra-cotta ornamentation inside reveals a bust of Hippocrates, and a couple of porthole windows flank the arrangement. The outside of the building shows brickwork patterns arranged in a fascinating array on the façade; the quoining on the corners of the building leads up to panels with three-dimensional human figures gesturing just below the roof cornice.

✦ *Born to Build Department:* Most kids run away to join the circus. Luther Lee Dougan (architect of both of these buildings) ran away from home to eventually get an education and employment in architecture. Among his accomplishments: he lived for one hundred years, and he also designed the nearby Studio Building/Guild Theater.

35 c   *Medical Arts Building Entry Detail*

35 a *Medical Dental Building*

35 b *Medical Arts Building Entry*

36 PRINCETON BUILDING 1920–22

Originally the Elks Temple
614 SW Eleventh Avenue, southeast corner of Eleventh Avenue
*   and Alder Street*
Architects: Houghtaling and Dougan

This building really has a great deal of street presence. It is a good, conservative contrast to the far-out Governor Hotel; in fact, as of 1992, it is
essentially the Governor's west wing. The Princeton Building was originally built as the Portland Elks Lodge. The dignified Italian Renaissance
features of this building, which were inspired by Rome's Farnese Palace,
glow nicely in the sunlight, though given its gray color it is easy to miss
on an overcast day.

36a   *Princeton Building windows*

At the time of its construction, the Elks had money to throw around, and here they went about constructing the era's largest Elks Temple in the country. The exterior of the building is virtually all terra-cotta, with a metal cornice painted to match it. The surface includes a variety of window styles as well as bas-relief panels with female forms and rams' heads. They also spared no expense in constructing a tasteful yet hedonistic interior. The banquet and meeting rooms are lush, the library shows off its black-marble paneling nicely, and the original billiard room is festooned with cast-plaster parrots, snakes, and griffins. The columned ballroom is reasonably grand, a worthy site for a fête.

In one of local history's great ironies, the Great Depression loomed a scant decade after this profligate spending, and thousands of members who were unable to pay their dues dropped out of the Elks organization in the 1930s. The Elks had to give up the building in 1937. It sat vacant for two years, and then the Works Progress Administration (WPA) set one thousand seamstresses to work in the building's grand rooms, making clothes for the poor. During World War II, it served as a United States Armed Forces Induction Center. After World War II ended, at various times this building housed two athletic clubs, the perhaps no-less-athletic Pussycat Club, and the not-very-athletic ping-pong center named the Paddle Palace. The building was substantially renovated and redesigned as the Princeton Club in 1985.

✦   Before coming to Portland in 1903, architect Luther Lee Dougan worked for Frank Lloyd Wright as an office boy.

✦ Among the motivational inscriptions in Latin and English on this building, try to find the one that reads: "Elk Living in the Northern Sphere." (One assumes they meant Northern *Hemisphere,* unless there is a Planet of the Elks orbiting about.) *Magna est veritas et prevalebit.*

✦ Historian Virginia Guest Ferriday memorably described this building as "a derivation of the Farnese Palace with hints of naughtiness throughout its interior."

36 b   *Princeton Building*

37   PORTLAND TELEGRAM BUILDING 1922

aka Telegram Building, Franklin Institute of Sales
1101 SW Washington Street, northwest corner of SW Eleventh
*   Avenue and Washington Street*
Architect: Rasmussen Grace Co., Engineers

This building was constructed for the local newspaper of the same name. Founded by Henry L. Pittock (among others), it went through a variety of owners and eventually changed its name to the Portland News Telegram. In keeping with the tradition of giving newspaper buildings their own towers, this building, of redbrick with white terra-cotta trim, got one with a cupola right on the building's corner. Converted to lofts in the 1990s, this distinguished structure could use some exterior renovation; it would also be nice if someone set the clock.

37 *Portland Telegram Building*

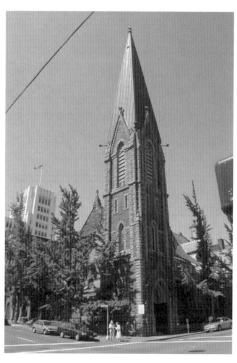

38 a, b   *First Presbyterian Church of Portland*

38 FIRST PRESBYTERIAN CHURCH OF PORTLAND 1886–90

1200 SW Alder Street, between Twelfth and Thirteenth Avenues
Architect: McCaw and Martin

" . . . the First Presbyterian Church seemed to me the outstanding [building] in the city."   —Visitor Ray L. Stout, on a 1900 trip to Portland

The First Presbyterian Church is certainly one of the most striking churches in Portland. It is a convincing stone Victorian Gothic, dramatic and authentic. The noteworthy façade of the building is locally quarried, coarse black basalt from Mount St. Helens with roughened sandstone trim. The church's corner spire leaps up 185 dramatic feet from the rest of the relatively low structure; its copper sheathing was added to it in 1929, replacing the original slate. (It was re-coppered in 1983.) Other features include projecting gables and sidelights between the buttresses, introducing more light into the church.

The carved interior woodwork defies description; it feels as if one is boarding some kind of Gothic seagoing vessel with its rich details and flowing lines. A 1999 renovation by SERA Architects and John Czarnecki & Associates resulted in the addition to the sanctuary of a magnificent pipe organ that was removed in the 1920s. Whether you're religious or secular, go see this church's interior.

39 TERMINAL SALES BUILDING 1926

1220 SW Morrison Street, south side between Twelfth and
Thirteenth Avenues
Architects: A. E. Doyle; designed by Frank Higgins

A quick check of this book's index will reveal that A. E. Doyle's credits in Portland put his architectural style's indelible mark on the city. His usual style is characterized as Classical Revival, and can be readily seen in buildings like the Multnomah Central Library. This makes the Terminal Sales Building unusual. It has a design considered modern for its era, making it one of Portland's few examples of a perpendicular Art Deco style. The eye follows the smooth, vertical concrete piers straight up for twelve stories, without any decoration or ornamentation on the way to spoil the ride.

Doyle's own firm was responsible for this building's execution, a notable exception to his usual embellished style. Times were changing in the

39 *Terminal Sales Building*

1920s, and businesspeople were interested in building upwards. The Terminal Sales Building is faintly reminiscent of huge skyscrapers back east, and although one can see in this building that the trend would lead to future monstrosities, it is still attractive and fresh today.

40 CRYSTAL BALLROOM 1914

Originally Ringler's Cotillion Hall
406 SW Fourteenth Avenue
Architect: Robert F. Tegen

This building was specifically designed to be a dance hall in 1914, and, remarkably, it still is. The exterior is a checkerboard brick front with arched bays across it, but it is the inside of the building that is amazing. The architect, Walter F. Tegan, was a German who had made similar revolving "ball-bearing" dance floors in other parts of the country. The tango was the latest dance in 1914, and although one could face jail time for dancing the forbidden tango in the early teens of the twentieth century, the building's third-floor dance hall was intended to capitalize on this infatuation.

Theoretically, the patented "elastic floor" could be adjusted to the differing needs of various dance steps by slightly giving way beneath the person's feet, giving even the severely rhythm-impaired a distinct advantage in keeping time.

The building was financed by an insurance agent named Paul van Fridagh and his sister, the daintily named Hortense van Fridagh. Despite this, it was named "Ringler's Cotillion Hall," after Montrose M. Ringler, a celebrated local dance instructor who was experiencing problems in his dance studio on Morrison Street, which shook overly much when streetcars passed by. It was Montrose Ringler's idea to solicit Tegan as an architect, and Ringler

40 *Crystal Ballroom*

maintained his dance studio in the building until 1921. If one was interested in learning the immortal dance steps of the "varsity drag" or "hesitation waltz," this was the place to do it.

Cotillion Hall continued as a dance hall until 1931. It then closed for four years until its purchase in 1935, when it reopened. Renamed the Crystal Ballroom in 1951, it was not a financial success and was subsequently closed again.

After a series of incarnations, the building stood vacant from 1968 until 1997, when it reopened upon its conversion to a McMenamins property. The company's happy tradition of decoratively painting every surface according to the dictates of a building's historical tradition held sway. Psychedelic folk art and the building's conscientious and creative remodeling make it a local favorite. To learn the entire history of the building, read the interesting book *The Many Lives of the Crystal Ballroom,* by Tim Hills.

✦ Montrose Ringler is credited with bringing the newfangled game named basketball to Portland.

✦ This building was originally designed with an elevator that would lift cars to extra parking in the structure's east half.

✦ Rudolph Valentino appeared here in 1923 to give dance demonstrations and make women's hearts throb. Decades later, another swarthy heartthrob would make an unofficial appearance: Frank Zappa.

CHAPTER 2

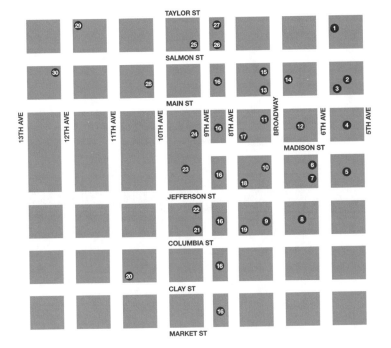

TAYLOR ST

SALMON ST

MAIN ST

13TH AVE
12TH AVE
11TH AVE
10TH AVE
9TH AVE
8TH AVE
BROADWAY
6TH AVE
5TH AVE

MADISON ST

JEFFERSON ST

COLUMBIA ST

CLAY ST

MARKET ST

N
W
E
S

DOWNTOWN—PARK BLOCKS

1 *The Public Service Building*

CHAPTER 2

DOWNTOWN– PARK BLOCKS

1 THE PUBLIC SERVICE BUILDING 1928

920 SW Sixth Avenue, between Salmon and Taylor Streets
Architects: Doyle, Patterson and Beach; Charles K. Greene, designer

Upon its completion, this sixteen-story Italianate building with an arched base and columned top qualified as Portland's tallest building, and it remained so for many years. The two wings of the building were originally two stories high, and were not raised to their present height of twelve stories until 1958. The base is granite, and the bottom two floors of the Public Service Building are gray terra-cotta, with the upper floor being covered in gray brick, a mildly surprising choice as Portland's gray weather might suggest picking a different hue for a building. Between the two sections is a charming line of stylized wave crests. The projecting cornice and dentils are terra-cotta.

The interior of the building is remarkable; the original bronze fixtures and beautiful marble walls have weathered some changes, but a $12-million renovation some seventy years after its original construction makes it quite a sight to see. Take note of the brass ornamentation of the elevator doors (courtesy of Belluschi), which are intended to represent the power companies that once dwelt herein. These original designs were copied throughout the building in its modern upgrade.

Charles K. Greene began the initial designs on this building, but left town before construction was complete. (Pietro Belluschi finished the project.) Greene had joined Doyle's office in 1909, and about a decade later, went abroad to study Greek and Roman classical architecture more closely, just as A. E. Doyle himself had done in 1906. Upon Greene's return, he was instrumental in the design of three Italianate buildings: the

Bank of California, the Pacific Building, and here, the Public Service Building. Greene was rewarded for his efforts by being banned from Portland by the Portland school board.

An openly gay man in the Portland of the early twentieth century, Greene faced initial prejudice, and, ultimately, rejection and forced exile. Greene threw parties attended by local high school students, and such a dim view was taken of this that he was eventually given two days to get out of town, exiled from the community that benefited from his masterful classical designs. He left before his last project, the Public Service Building, was completed. Despite his reports back to Stumptown that he was doing well in Los Angeles, he reportedly "died alone of starvation several years later."

A. E. Doyle himself died three weeks after the grand opening of the Public Service Building, in January 1928. He wrote a friend from his deathbed: ". . . sooner or later, we all put concrete foundations under our air castles."

✦   The Portland Gas and Coke Company and the Pacific Light and Power Company were two of the original occupants of the Public Service Building. A red-and-green-flashing ten-foot neon sign was placed on the roof that read "Pacific Power." It also had the words *heat, light,* and *gas* aimed in a different cardinal direction; from the front of the building, one saw a massive "Power." The sign was taken down in 1973, when the original red-tile roof was replaced by a metal one. Although downtown's main power plant is no longer in the basement of the building, it still houses the city's main power feeds.

✦   Speaking of power, the Public Service Building houses the force of nature known to mankind as "Niketown." Designed by BOORA Architects, this "entertainment architecture" makes for an interesting addition to the building.

2 SECURITY PACIFIC BUILDING/PLAZA 1980

Originally the Orbanco Headquarters Building
1001 Fifth Avenue, between Fifth and Sixth Avenues,
*   Main and Salmon Streets*
Architect: SOM

Portland through a looking glass.

This black, twenty-three-story skyscraper has been the target of any number of critical potshots over the years for its lack of imagination. It is simply shaped and covered in darkly tinted glass. Being as most structures

2 *Security Pacific Building/Plaza*

in Portland usually use lighter shades, one might glibly accuse this building of being insensitive to its surrounding context.

However, by reflecting back everything in its vicinity, this building creates an interesting kaleidoscope of images. The Public Service Building to the north looks great in reflection, and the Multnomah County Courthouse undergoes an interesting "underwater" effect on its west side from the reflected light coming off the Security Pacific Building.

3 HARRINGTON'S ENTRANCE 1912
Originally Congress Hotel Arches
1050 SW Sixth Avenue
Architect: Herman Brookman

On the southwest corner of the Security Pacific Plaza are open-air arches decorated with fruits, flowers, and rams. These terra-cotta arches were saved from the Congress Hotel, the building previously located on this site. The salvaged arches are fascinatingly Bacchanalian in their goat-like charm, though the addition of light bulbs all over seems a bit cheesy.

3 a, b   *Harrington's Entrance*

4 STANDARD INSURANCE BUILDING 1963

aka Standard Plaza
1100 SW Sixth Avenue, between Madison and Main Streets
Architect: SOM

To some, this building helped to herald in the new age of anonymous corporate structures that began sprouting in Portland (often courtesy of SOM)
in the 1960s. With the Standard, an attempt was made to integrate an open
plaza design with the building in order to make the skyscraper less forbidding. In contrast to the vertical, half-block, seventeen-story Standard
Building, the adjacent plaza sports curves, water features, a bridge, and a
ceremonial entrance to the building. The original plans eliminated the

sidewalks on Main and Madison, but objections from people unwilling to using the Plaza to get between Fifth and Sixth Avenues resulted in the sidewalks being left in place, although narrowed.

The Standard was ahead of its time in a couple of areas. The reinforced-concrete core allowed the builders to eschew columns from the center of the building to the outside walls. It also gave the Standard Plaza a fireproof interior stairwell, eradicating the need for exterior fire escapes and heralding in an age of modern buildings with unblemished skins. The Standard's second innovation was in putting its parking garage below street level.

German-born Leo Samuel (1847–1916) came to the U.S. only to be deserted by his uncle at the age of thirteen. He had one dollar, but he went on to found what was to become the Standard Insurance Company in 1906 on the theory that a West Coast insurance company could more efficiently serve local customers than those East Coast fellers.

✦   Randy Gragg, architecture reporter for the *Oregonian*, thought highly enough of the Standard Insurance Building's melding of art and structure and its efficient and civic-minded construction to rank it as a perfect "10," one of Portland's only buildings worthy of being called "great."

✦   One of Portland's most highly admired sculptures, Hilda Morris's bronze *Ring of Time,* is in the entryway on the west side of the Standard building.

✦   The Standard Insurance Building has a square, black, weather-forecasting beacon on top of it. Green lights on it indicate the weather is holding steady, white signifies a cooling trend, red is a warming pattern, and if you see it blinking, it's either going to rain or already is. It tends to blink often.

4 *Standard Insurance Building*

5 PACWEST CENTER 1984

aka Pacwest Tower, the "Icecube Building"
1211 SW Fifth Avenue, between Madison and Jefferson Streets
Architect: Hugh Stubbins and Associates (New York)

This gleaming, science-fictional skyscraper accomplishes the improbable: it forms a stylistic link with the Renaissance-style Portland City Hall, which is separated from the Pacwest Center by one avenue and almost a century of time. This was accomplished by giving the Fifth Avenue side of the Pacwest Center a low, U-shaped wing (topped with gable-shaped decorations), replicating the form of City Hall's wings across the street. Although primarily silver in appearance, the building's banded, darkly tinted glass gives it a Stygian anchor, lest it appear overly insubstantial. The Pacwest Center's stepped roofline allows it to avoid the accusation of evoking the skyline ennui that skyscrapers like the Wells Fargo Tower elicit.

Architect Hugh Stubbins may have created Portland's only building that seems to have paid respect to and updated the concepts of Pietro Belluschi's trailblazing Equitable Building. Like the Equitable, the Pacwest has a cool, even cold, aluminum look (the metal was imported from Japan) while also replicating a bit of the Equitable's smooth surface. By virtue of its size, the rounded corners help to accomplish this, giving it a hint of the streamlined style of an Art Deco variant, like that of a Greyhound bus, or a vintage chrome diner. This building would not look out of place on the cover of a pulp science-fiction magazine from the 1940s like *Astounding Stories.* ("See the City of the Future!")

5 a, b   *Pacwest Center*

6 *Ambassador Apartments*

6 AMBASSADOR APARTMENTS 1922

1209 SW Sixth Avenue, between Jefferson and Madison Streets
Architect: Carl Linde

One of the more fashionable addresses to keep downtown, this swanky locale should more properly be called the Ambassador Condominiums, although that title hardly has the same panache. The Jacobean building certainly offers the looker something to enjoy. Amazingly, its redbrick front *doesn't* feature terra-cotta, substituting Idaho sandstone in its stead. There is a nice roof balustrade, token balconies at the eighth floor, and escutcheoned, or projecting, windows.

✦   The smallest, cheapest, one-bedroom condo here was advertised for $148,000 in 1999.

7 UNIVERSITY CLUB 1913

1225 SW Sixth Avenue, between Jefferson and Madison Streets
Architect: Whitehouse and Fouilhoux

The brick-faced, reputable-looking University Club has an imposing façade, and it fits very well next to the similarly minded Ambassador Apartments. Nonmembers feel appropriately intimidated as they hurry past its double-gabled dormers, and members can glory in the knowledge that, for around a thousand dollars a year, they can walk into this Jacobean building as equals with the rest of Portland's high society that isn't hanging around the Arlington Club. The tall, narrow windows with thick mullions above the entrance and in the projecting bays elsewhere help to enhance this sensation; who knows what clandestine deals and super-secret handshakes are transpiring up there?

Founded in 1898, in the office of esteemed local architect William M. Whidden (City Hall, the Multnomah County Courthouse), the University Club was organized around the principles of academic brotherhood and the discussion of current events. Membership was available for a five-dollar initiation fee, followed by one dollar a month thereafter.

✦ Jacques Fouilhoux (1875–1945) was, believe it or not, French. He studied at the Sorbonne and moved to the United States in 1904. He initially worked for Albert Kahn in Detroit, and found that city so enthralling that he moved to Portland the next year. After leaving Portland, he was involved in the designs of the Rockefeller Center and the Chicago Tribune Building. He is the only Pacific Northwest architect to have won the French Legion of Honor.

✦ The club bar has over two hundred dice cups for wagering over who picks up the bill.

8 *The Oregonian Building*

8 THE OREGONIAN BUILDING 1946
1320 SW Broadway
Architect: Pietro Belluschi

As previously stated, it has been traditional for newspapers in major American cities to house themselves in distinctive buildings (often incorporating towers) as emblems of their status in the community. Although Oregon's most widely circulated newspaper, the *Oregonian,* once occupied a gorgeous clock-tower building, it needed a more up-to-date facility. Architect Pietro Belluschi studied newspaper plants across the country to prepare for this project and it shows; this looks like a newspaper plant. It's very efficient, and the interior layout has been widely praised for its design. Outside, the smooth surface, red granite and light limestone-sheathed building are not particularly appealing, although the green-tinted windows (and aluminum sashes) are the same type as are found in the Equitable Building. Described by the *Oregonian's* own columnist Steve Duin as a "mausoleum," it is perhaps a bit of a disappointment, but then it is more difficult to make an industrial office building segue aesthetically into a city than, say, a church.

✦ On the bottom floor, a concrete slab laid on a bed of sand was prepared for the 600-ton printing presses, with structural allowances made so that their vibration would not shake the rest of the building.

✦ The first issue of the *Oregonian* came out in 1850. Yearly subscription rates were five dollars.

9 LADD CARRIAGE HOUSE 1883

1331 SW Broadway
Architect: Joseph Sherwin

This is an example of a wooden building that has a touch of the Swiss chalet in it called "Stick style." It never really caught on in Portland, making this building a bit of a rarity with its wood decorations, lattice, garrets, and gables. In 1937, architect Van Ever Bailey remodeled this building for a construction company's offices, and he established his own office in the Carriage House as well. The first-floor carriage-house doors were remodeled; the current color scheme is a bit dolorous for Oregon weather. The real house that this outbuilding served was William S. Ladd's mansion, across the street where the *Oregonian* currently resides.

10 THE SOVEREIGN APARTMENTS 1923, 1967

Originally the Sovereign Hotel
710 SW Madison Street, between Broadway and Park Avenue
Architect: Carl L. Linde
Remodel: Wolfe-Zimmer Associates; Pietro Belluschi, consultant

This handsome, nine-story, reinforced-concrete building began life as what was euphemistically known as a "multiple-housing facility." Designed for

10   *The Sovereign Apartments*

the city dweller uninterested in housework, each micro-living area included a set of French doors looking out onto a micro-balcony, living room (complete with Murphy bed), kitchenette/dining nook, and bathroom.

Converted to apartments in 1938, the building retained its wrought-iron balconies and other original features. Gorgeous glazed terra-cotta covers the bottom two floors, and the terra-cotta quoining on the corners provides a nice contrast to the redbrick work on the bulk of the façade on the upper floors.

The original architect of this building, Carl Linde (1864–1945), also designed the Shemanski Fountain in the South Park Blocks. A German native, he moved to Oregon in 1906 and over the next fifteen years worked for a who's who of Portland architectural firms: Edgar Lazarus, Whidden and Lewis, A. E. Doyle, and Whitehouse and Fouilhoux. What's interesting is that he didn't have his architect's license in all that time. Of course, neither did anyone else; architecture was considered a gentlemanly occupation and it didn't become a legal, licensed profession in Oregon until 1919. Upon getting his license in 1921, Linde maintained his own practice for nineteen years.

✦   There was originally a quite large, lit roof sign atop this building facing northeast. Unsurprisingly, it read "Sovereign Hotel."

✦   *End of a Multiple-Housing Facility Era:* The Murphy beds were all removed from this building in 1973.

11 PORTLAND CENTER FOR THE PERFORMING ARTS 1987

aka New Theater Building
SW Broadway and Main Street, southwest corner
Architects: Barton Myers, BOORA Architects, ELS Design Group

There is a yin and a yang in all worldly affairs, and Portland architecture is no exception. Just as some buildings in the city utterly ignore the history and appearance of the area they are in—like many of the glass and concrete and/or steel boxes in town *(yin)*—so do some buildings strive mightily to not only fit in with their surroundings but even to provide aesthetic segues between them while simultaneously making their own unique statements *(yang)*.

That said, an important key to understanding the design of this postmodern structure is that it shares the block it's on with the First Congregational Church, which predates the arts center by nearly a century. At the time of its construction, there was much debate over which part of the Tao this building belonged to.

The exterior of the arts center has a glass-covered façade that makes it easy to see in and out of the building. The structure's shape, precise brick tones, and façade have been criticized for not fitting in well between the church to its south and the old-style theater to its north. Local architect George McMath said of it: "It looks like a bunch of pieces stuck together." Yet while the external form of the center may not be referential or unified enough for some, it is considerate of its surroundings on a practical level.

11a *Portland Center for the Performing Arts Entrance*

11b   *Portland Center for the Performing Arts skylight*

The First Congregational Church granted a ninety-nine-year lease on this property (which used to be its parking lot) for the development of the Center for the Performing Arts. A condition of the lease was that sunlight had to still fall on the stained glass on the church's north wall. To see how the architects allowed this to occur, check the gap between the two buildings on the west side of the block. You will see that the back of the Performing Arts Center has been cut away to allow this to occur. Also, the "fly," or staging area, above and behind the Newmark Theater, has been cut away to allow a view of the church's tower from the east side of the city.

The west roofline of the Performing Arts Center emulates the lines of the church's triangular roofline. The cornice lines of the Congregational Church were followed by the Arts Center's designers, as well as a different, lighter form of the church's distinctive checkerboard stone pattern on its walls, which also refers to the decorative brick of the Arlene Schnitzer Concert Hall and even the walls of the Heathman Hotel.

Walking into the Portland Center for the Performing Arts can be disconcerting. Entry into the building is designed to make visitors feel like they are onstage, so what they see is a floor design patterned toward them as a focal point, along with a lobby complete with a multilevel rotunda likewise focused upon the entrance. The fact that there may be a number of people in the balconies looking down only heightens the sense that the theatergoer has become an unwitting performer.

Above the cherry wood lobby is the central atrium, which rises to a glass-domed, "spectralight" ceiling. The colored glass decorations are not colored, but rather chemically treated so as to appear bluish at some angles, turquoise at others. The results can be spectacular on one of Portland's frequent sunny days.

Three theaters exist in this building. The Newmark Theatre is the larger theater in which to see events. It has two balconies and a main floor arranged in an Edwardian horseshoe design, along with an impressively massive stage and a retractable orchestra pit. The Dolores Winningstad Theatre (maximum capacity 280) is a more intimate setting and is where the city's Shakespearean troupe, the Tygre's Heart Production Company, puts on its shows. The red wood here (and elsewhere in the building) appears to turn black when the lights are turned down, focusing attention on the performance.

✦ In the late-nineteenth and early-twentieth centuries, some Portland theaters specialized in "box house" productions. These were so named because the balconies were curtained and divided, allowing the occupants to enjoy the show without compromising their identities. Why the need for privacy? Box-house shows specialized in a raunchy form of vaudeville, and the female performers not onstage served as "waitresses" for the balcony patrons. The egregious effects of Portland's then-widespread fleshpots, both in the theater and in houses of ill repute, may have contributed to a 1912 city vice report that conservatively stated that one-quarter of all trips to Portland doctors were for reasons of, shall we say, socially transmitted diseases.

12 GUS J. SOLOMON U.S. COURTHOUSE 1931

aka the Federal Courthouse
620 SW Main Street, between Sixth Avenue and Broadway
Architects: Whitehouse and Church (James Smith, Roi Morin,
*   Earl Newberry)*
1984 restoration: ZGF Partnership/Allen, McMath and
*   Hawkins, consultants*

This building was the last major building constructed downtown during the 1930s and was originally built around an inner courtyard. Like all courthouses, it is intended to strike people with awe, and upon entering the beautiful bronze Art Deco doors that decorate the Main Street side of this building, awe (or at least respect) would seem to be the appropriate sentiment. In 1932, the *Oregonian* reported that some of the pink, brown, and red marble of the interior lobby would be inlaid with gold, but that the metal would be safe, as "the rich material is so tightly held by the stone it cannot be extracted."

The lobby is sumptuously appointed in the same Art Deco style as the entrance, but it also mixes classical motifs with its deco elements. Cherry and mahogany wood and cast-bronze friezes, grilles, geometric shapes, and floral designs abound in this rich area; even the mailboxes are done in style, marked with cast-metal letters in black glass. In comparison, the sandstone exterior of the neo-classical building is somewhat modern and mildly frumpy in a Renaissance Revival fashion. The Doric columns in this concrete and steel building have shrunk right into mere flattened pilasters, making them a completely decorative element.

✦   With the shift of federal courtrooms to the Mark O. Hatfield Courthouse, new tenants have moved in, and the courthouse has lured filmmakers with its historic courtrooms. Two on the sixth floor and one on the seventh feature plaster roofs and impressive woodwork, and can currently be rented for about $500 a day.

✦   Architect Morris Whitehouse was a Portland native who studied at MIT and at the American Academy in Rome.

12 *Gus J. Solomon U.S. Courthouse*

13 Arlene Schnitzer Concert Hall

13 ARLENE SCHNITZER CONCERT HALL 1928

*Originally the Portland Publix, aka Paramount Theater,
the Portland Theater
SW Broadway and Main Street, northwest corner
Architects: Rapp and Rapp (Chicago)
Restoration: BOORA Architects*

This building was originally known as the Portland Publix theater when it hosted vaudeville shows, then the Paramount Theater in 1930 (because its owners had a contract with that film company to run their films locally), and then the Portland Theater again. Whatever era one chooses, the multicolored brick theater still clearly shows its original Italian Renaissance leanings. The arched windows on the outside of the stone-trimmed theater were not "bricked in," as they appear to be. The theater was originally designed that way so as not to have a blandly industrial brick front around the building. The walled-over windows do perhaps give the building an element of mystery, making one curious as to its interior.

The formal elegance of the concert hall's inner treasures must be seen to be appreciated. Marble, mirrors, vaulted ceilings, chandeliers, and decoration are everywhere; as one young patron exclaimed, "It looks like the *Titanic!*" Although the oceanliner predated "the Schnitz" by a dozen years, the regal detailing of each rings a similar chord in the viewer. As you walk in the grand main lobby on the east side of building, note the marble walls. They will feel warm to the touch because they're not marble at all, but painted Italian plaster. For the cool feel of real marble, feel the large marble ledge on the level just above the lobby's entrance.

The cream-marble statue of a nude woman coyly smirking *(Surprise)* facing the lobby entrance in front of the snack bar is the only one of the theater's remaining full-size statues. Intended to be a young woman "surprised" while bathing, she originally rose from a small fishpond in that very spot. (The circular floor pattern at her feet shows the fishpond's location.) She suffered a gunshot wound to the hand during a box-office robbery in the theater's infancy and has the battle scars to prove it.

Although vaudeville programs happened here early in the building's history, it was used primarily to show movies, which it did until 1971. An auction in 1975 stripped it of many of its features and statuary. (The colossal pipe organ went to a pizza parlor in Denver.) The new performing arts space opened in 1984, named after Harold and Arlene Schnitzer, who kicked in a cool million for rehabilitation of the structure. The restoration was just that; it was intended to bring the building back to its original opulence. It entailed work on new rigging systems, stairs, and elevators, as well as decorative restoration. The removal of the old neon "Paramount" sign from the east side of the theater resulted in its falling to the sidewalk in an impressive crash.

✦   In the balcony, you can still see the large apertures on the back wall where the projection booths were. You can also get a good case of vertigo, as the pitch of the balcony is quite steep.

✦   One street design plan was to permanently close Main Street between the Center for the Performing Arts and the Schnitz. This plan was modified to allow a retractable gate to close off the street during performances, but otherwise remain open.

14   1000 BROADWAY BUILDING 1991

aka the "Ban Roll-On Building"
1000 SW Broadway, east of the Heathman Hotel
Architect: Broome, Oringdulph, O'Toole, Rudolph, and Associates
(BOORA)

The egg-headed Broadway Building cost a reported $90 million to erect. It is rendered in pleasant enough colors, has a unique shape, and does feature its own imitation of a geodesic dome on top, yet it fails to impress some.

Architectural critic Randy Gragg described it as looking like "a robot, a bald offensive guard, or a perfume box." Part of the building's offensiveness stems from the misrepresentation of its plans. The extreme relative height of the tower was allowed by the city because promises were made that the site's original Broadway theater marquee would be restored, and that there would be a roof garden and restaurant. Don't bother looking for these features on the present tower; they weren't included after all.

Though not a particularly large skyscraper (a relatively modest twenty-three stories), the Broadway Building can look mighty impressive from downhill, on its east side. The building solves its parking needs in an interesting way with seven stories of car space between the offices above and the lobby below. Although it takes a while to notice, it does pay homage to its surroundings; look east at Park and Main and one can see an interesting replication in lines between the Arlene Schnitzer Concert Hall and the Broadway. Coincidentally, Seattle got itself a variation of this "robot/guard/box" building-type in the same year: the Second & Seneca Building.

✦ Tom Moyer distinguished himself as a boxer with 168 victories and 11 losses (total of amateur/professional matches). As such, he is the only Portland developer to erect skyscrapers who is in the Oregon Sports Hall of Fame.

14 *1000 Broadway Building*

15 THE HEATHMAN HOTEL 1927

Originally the New Heathman Hotel
712 SW Salmon Street, southwest corner of Salmon Street
* and Broadway*
Architect: DeYoung and Roald, Renovation: Carter Case

The "Great White Way" was the nickname given to the stretch of Broadway that housed the Portland Theater and other entertainment venues, and it was on the Great White Way that the Heathman Hotel was built in the Roaring Twenties. One of the last classic hotels in Portland, the Jacobean-style Heathman building seems to have been designed as a sober counter-point to the florid Renaissance stylings of the Arlene Schnitzer Concert Hall next door. The Heathman is a decidedly serious building, with just a little decoration in the way of quoining on the corners and windows and patterned brickwork.

In a way, this hotel was Portland's first KOIN Tower. In the 1930s, KOIN Radio moved into the hotel from across the street, resulting in some remodeling of the mezzanine level. By 1940, the work had resulted in perhaps the finest radio studio in the country. KOIN would stay here until the advent of their television station in 1953. A 1982–84 renovation coincided with work being done on the Portland Theater; the subsequent restoration of the block entirely energized the area.

✦   From the Heathman Hotel you can gain access to the Schnitz through the "secret passage" via the cigar room on the mezzanine level, a passageway uncovered during the 1980s remodeling. (You still need a ticket, though.)

16 SOUTH PARK BLOCKS 1852

SW Park Avenue between Salmon and Market Streets

Originally intended to be twenty-five blocks long, the Park Blocks were supposed to run all the way through the city to the Willamette River. In 1852, they were deeded to the city for park usage, but twenty years later, missteps in the estates of Daniel Lownsdale and Benjamin Stark allowed their donated blocks to go into private hands and be developed. If the park had run its intended course, these would have gone through and connected up with the North Park Blocks. In 2000, Neil Goldschmidt and Tom Moyer successfully organized an effort to buy back some of this space to make this nineteenth-century plan a reality in the twenty-first century. Stay tuned.

The tile-roofed Shemanski Fountain (1926) is at the north end of the South Park Blocks. The combination statuary/temple was commissioned by Joseph Shemanski, a Jewish immigrant. At the time, the fountain was criticized on "aesthetic" grounds by the Portland Arts Commission; its placement in front of the Arlington Club is ironic, as Jews were not allowed membership until the late 1960s. Statues of Abraham Lincoln and Teddy Roosevelt (which were dedicated by then vice president Calvin Coolidge in 1922) are seen as one goes south through the park. (Dr. Henry David Coe, presenter of these statues, was a lifelong friend of Roosevelt's.) The sculpture of Lincoln (1928, George Fite Waters) was initially criticized for its melancholy look, the Civil War apparently not being justification enough for a solemn expression.

✦ In 1853, numerous lots bordering on the South Park Blocks were deeded to fraternal organizations and churches, explaining the high ratio of churches now in this stretch of the city.

✦ This was once a dirt track known as The Boulevard where horse racing occurred.

17 FIRST CONGREGATIONAL CHURCH 1889–95
1126 SW Park Avenue
Architect: Henry J. Hefty (Switzerland)

Originally this Italian Gothic structure had three towers, but two shorter and rounder towers at the southeast and northwest corners were removed in the 1940s, modernizing the building. Now the church has only one tower,

17 a *First Congregational Church*

17 b *First Congregational Church tower*

and it is not wholly original. The real tower was heavily damaged in the Columbus Day Storm of October 12, 1962. Although some say it makes the building look a bit lopsided all by itself, the new 185-foot tower is well worth looking at; it has a mini-cathedral of its own on top. Much of the exacting detail at the top was obtained through sheet metal. (The repetition of small shapes of this nature, for example, diamonds, is called "diaperwork." Should the tower gather enough soot, its diaperwork will be dirty.)

At the time of its construction, skeptics nicknamed this church "the Holy Checkerboard" for its distinctive pattern of dark basaltic rock with lighter limestone. This church's interior can hold more than 1,000 people in a unique, downwardly sloped seating arrangement that features the unique combination of stucco and polished redwood. The west-side pillars of the church were replaced in 1996; you can see that the original stone gives way to new material.

✦ The financial panic of 1893 caused many church members to cancel their pledges to the church's construction fund, elongating its construction time.

18 OREGON HISTORY CENTER 1965–66, 1989

1230 SW Park Avenue, between Madison and Jefferson Streets
Architect: Wolf and Zimmer Associates/Pietro Belluschi, consultant
Addition: ZGF Partnership

This is home to a shop, museum, and research library. First-time visitors have fun finding the *real* front entrance to this squat, concrete-walled building; it has a somewhat confusing junction with the adjacent Sovereign Hotel, particularly on the park side of the building where it is fenced off.

Initially constructed in 1966, the city obtained the entire block surrounding it (including the Sovereign Hotel) twenty years later. This led to a bit of a dilemma, as the office building and apartments already existing on the property needed to be brought into the plan for the independently designed History Center. The solution was to paste a marble rectangle onto the Sovereign Hotel's west side; calling it an *aedicule* doesn't make it any less incongruous. Although it matches up with the original museum's 1960s lines, the net effect doubled the amount of dated-looking architecture on the site.

New entrances to the museum were opened, a plaza was added, and perhaps to distract the eye from the strange combination of the distinguished apartment building meeting the pillbox History Center's additions, two *trompe l'oeil* ("trick of the eye") murals were painted on the Sovereign's south and west sides. Walter Gordon (former dean of the University of Oregon School of Architecture) derided the "visually overwhelming" murals as being "intended to knock our socks off with Disneyland wonder." In any event, they depict prominent symbols from Oregon's history; while observing the west side, keep in mind that only the darkened center windows are real.

18 *Oregon History Center*

19 FIRST CHRISTIAN CHURCH 1922

*1315 SW Broadway, main entrance at northeast corner of Park
Avenue and Columbia Street
Architect: C. W. Bulgar and Son (Dallas)*

This is the only pioneering church in Portland still at its original location, although the present building is the church's fourth on this site. In 1919, while making plans for their congregation's new temple, the church board stated its architectural desire for something "very plain and substantial following straight lines. . . ." The result is a building with a roofline that is something of a mishmash; although it cries out for red tiles, for a time it had composition shingles. The becolumned portico's brick steps sprawl out distinctively on the block's corner, and the exterior walls on each side of it start at their bases with red brick, giving way to decoratively laid out combed-face gray brick and terra-cotta decorations farther up.

✦   This site was originally deeded by Daniel Lownsdale in 1853 (the same year he deeded his South Park Blocks to the city) as a spot for a "Female Seminary of Learning."

✦   Although the First Christian Church began its Portland congregation with five members in 1879, it miraculously managed to purchase this property merely one year later.

19 *First Christian Church*

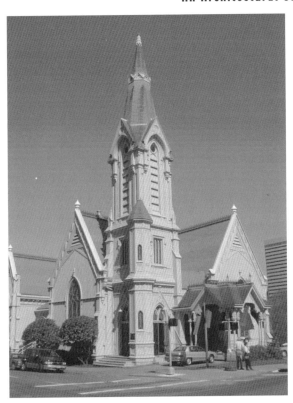

20 *Calvary Presbyterian Church*

20 CALVARY PRESBYTERIAN CHURCH 1882
aka "The Old Church"
1422 SW 11th Avenue
Architect: Warren Heywood Williams

This is one of the most revered churches in the Pacific Northwest. Naturally, the belfry is the first thing one notices, followed by the window arches, buttresses, and beautiful window work itself. Although the style of the church's exterior is Gothic, its materials are not. Traditional Gothic cathedrals are made of stone, while this church has been primarily done in wood (leading some to call it a "Carpenter Gothic" church), to no detriment of its appearance. The chimneys and steeples have clover dovecote motifs, while the interior of the church has an assortment of styles hidden within its plaster window moldings, vaulted, ribbed ceilings, and cast-iron columns. Stand back and appreciate its wealth of wooden detailings.

✦   Warren Heywood Williams designed this church and oversaw its construction as a generous gesture to the congregation. He moved to Portland from San Francisco in 1872, after Portland's ruinous downtown fires.

✦   The original stained glass of the church was made by Irvington's Povey Brothers.

✦   In the late 1960s, the church was up for sale. At that time, certain unbalanced parties advised moving the church to a new location on Sauvie Island.

21   SIXTH CHURCH OF CHRIST SCIENTIST 1932

1331 SW Park Avenue, northwest corner of Morrison Street
Architect: Morris H. Whitehouse and Associates

This is an imposing Art Deco-style building, with a ziggurat-like shape successfully designed to inspire awe. The massive face of the building gives little hint of what is inside. (What *is* inside is a central dome with a wheel-and-hub seating arrangement arranged around a sloping floor.) The intricate brickwork on the outside was the result of a directive to the architects to make the construction of the church utilize as much labor time as possible. Check the year of the church's construction if this "make-work" philosophy doesn't make sense to you; this is one of the few non-apartment buildings in Portland constructed during the Great Depression. (Coincidentally, the nearby Portland Art Museum is another of this rare breed.)

This building works very well with its surrounding context. Three handsome apartment buildings were built just to the south of the church between 1930 and 1931, including the excellent Jeanne Manor Apartments

21   *Sixth Church of*
Christ Scientist

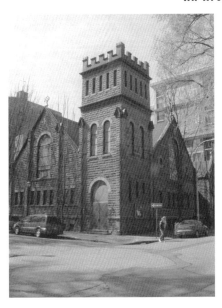

22 *Saint James Lutheran Church*

(Bennes and Herzog), which contains Art Deco elements in its piers, windows, and entrance. The popularity of apartment buildings in this part of town is partly explained by nearby Portland State University's refusal to allow dormitories on its campus.

✦ Morris Whitehouse's firm worked on the Temple Beth Israel five years previous to this church. Whitehouse himself came to be known as a designer of clubhouses for the rich.

22 SAINT JAMES LUTHERAN CHURCH 1908

1315 SW Park Avenue (at the southwest corner of Jefferson Street)
Architect: Unknown

One can almost imagine Christian soldiers emerging from this sturdy church. It has a battlement with crennelations, and the whole structure is made of rough limestone. The original wooden church was built here in 1890, to be replaced eighteen years later by this Gothic creation. The large tower deteriorated over the years and was removed in 1951. Over twenty years later, it was reconstructed on evidence found from old photos.

This church may have the distinction of having the worst addition ever built in the city. Look over the aluminum-and-glass structure to the south of the church to give your brow some new furrows; its blatant disregard for the original structure is unfathomable.

23   *Portland Art Museum*

23 PORTLAND ART MUSEUM 1932 AYER WING, 1939 HIRSCH WING
1219 SW Park Avenue
Architect: Pietro Belluschi

The Art Museum is noteworthy as the first building for which Pietro Belluschi received widespread acclaim. While it reflected the advancing march of Modernist architecture, its simple but effective use of natural materials and accessibility made it a truly innovative museum design. This building's trim work features real Italian travertine (a porous limestone), which provides a worthy contrast with the graceful brickwork, and helps focus attention on the serene formality of the museum's structure, which is a perfect complement to the rustic quiet of the South Park Blocks.

The Portland Art Museum was originally founded in 1892, with no pieces, no building, and $1,000 in the coffer. The first curator, Henrietta Failing, felt that the new museum building should be architecturally simple enough not to distract from the art itself. But before work began on the Ayer Wing, Belluschi had to overcome the head of the board of trustees who wanted the building in a Georgian style. Compounding the problem was the presence of senior architect Jamieson Parker (designer of the First Unitarian Church) on the board, a conservative man who most people had thought would get the commission for the museum.

Dismayed at what he viewed as such a backward-thinking proposition, Belluschi went to the highest source possible to back him up on his intentions for a much sparer design: Frank Lloyd Wright. Wright encouraged him, writing, "I think your exterior would mark an advance in culture for Portland." And Wright was right.

In a 1931 memo, Belluschi explained his view: ". . . that standard mask called 'style,' whether that be Georgian, Italian or English is just a bad formula and only our lack of imagination has tolerated its application on buildings where a new set of ideas had to be given a new form. . . . Let us not try to maim and twist the body [of the museum] to fit the suit but let us build a new suit consistent with the body."

The museum's initial Georgian design was eliminated in subsequent drafts. The initial plans also included designs for the expansion of the museum over the block it was situated on, although years (and even decades) would separate the construction of these different wings. But through similarity in design, the three wings suffer not at all for the intervening years between their construction. It is a building that ties itself to the past with its materials yet remains modern by virtue of its restrained ornamentation and functionality. While one could reasonably argue that the actual dimensions of the museum do not match up well with the adjacent Masonic Temple's mass, Belluschi did go to considerable trouble to research the surface patterns of Frederick Fritsch's brick buildings for inspiration.

The Ayer Wing is the most visible portion of the museum, facing the Park Blocks with a bayed façade. It projects symmetrically north and south from its centrally located entrance. Entering, one can enjoy natural illumination from "light monitors" in the entry and second-floor spaces. These do not cast the harsh localized glow that skylights can throw, instead diffusing and spreading the outside light in an inconspicuous fashion.

The Hirsch Wing followed seven years later, and it shows a further paring of any classical references. Inside, the skylighted sculpture court proved to be an effective addition to the museum's space. The central sculpture court was renovated in the late 1990s, amid much brouhaha over whether the addition of a door and the alteration of the ceiling compromised the spare and vaulting space Belluschi designed. Also at issue was whether the changes should be clearly recognizable as later construction or "embedded" into the original aesthetic Belluschi intended. Thankfully, the latter philosophy prevailed.

More recent additions include the Hoffman Wing, added in 1970 (Wolff, Zimmer, Gunsul and Frasca/Belluschi, consultant), and the newish Evans H. Roberts sculpture garden, between the Masonic Temple and Belluschi's museum proper, which was finished in 2000. Laid out by Topher Delaney (San Francisco), the garden needed to serve as a connection between the two wings of the museum, while still being security-conscious of the artwork to be displayed there. A glass wall and cable fences accomplish this fairly well. Also completed in 2000 were two new art centers (Ann Beha & Associates, Boston), helping to nearly double the gallery's available square footage at the end of the twentieth century. Original Portland Art Association founder Henry Corbett advocated long ago that the museum should showcase art using exclusively Oregonian subjects as source material; it took some time, but the new art centers, devoted to Native American and Northwest art, would please him.

✦   Over half of Pietro Belluschi's Oregon commissions were noncommercial; that is, museums, churches, and the like.

✦   An early coup for the museum came in 1913, when Marcel Duchamp's famed work *Nude Descending a Staircase* was exhibited shortly after its U.S. debut in New York.

✦   It was no coincidence that Belluschi got this commission; a member of the Portland Art Association since 1907, he became its president in 1926. Because of scant commissions with the onset of the Great Depression, Belluschi returned to Italy before the opening of his museum and didn't return for a year.

24   MASONIC TEMPLE 1924

aka the Art Museum's North Wing, containing the administration building and ballrooms
SW Park Avenue
Architect: Frederick Fritsch (Sutton, Whitney, Anandahl and Fritsch)

A 1924 design competition for this building resulted in a local architectural firm getting the biggest commission at that time of any in the state. Richard Ritz has noted that the large stone front of the building was considered plain for its day, which could be construed as a precocious modern touch.

It is easy to believe that the design of this colossus may have been based on one of the seven wonders of the ancient world, the Mausoleum of Halicarnassus. (Halicarnassus was a city in Asia Minor in the province of Caria. See more information in "Pioneer Courthouse.") Despite its relatively recent construction, the temple looks like an imposing refugee from some bygone era, or actually, eras, in that Roman, Persian, and Tuscan influences can be found in it. (The stone trim ornament was done to Frederick Fritsch's original design.) Its almost whimsical combination of historical

24 *Masonic Temple*

origins may qualify it as an example of "marbled-archeological architecture." Inside, the original layout was no less eclectic, as room themes of "Moorish-Oriental," Norman, and Louis XVI were designed.

✦   The budget of this monument was no less earthshaking: $1.25 million, a significant fortune in the 1920s. However, the local Masons could handle the costs after being organized in 1850 by Portland aristocrats like Stark, Couch, and the estimable Socrates Hotchkiss Tryon.

✦   The Masonic Temple currently contains the ballrooms and administration offices of the Portland Art Museum and is somewhat connected to Belluschi's Art Museum by a sculpture court; future additions may join the buildings more concretely, and the Art Museum no doubt is anxious to expand gallery space into the 191,000-square-foot temple.

✦   Architect Frederick Fritsch started early and ended too soon. He joined the Whidden and Lewis firm directly out of high school, but suffered from a painful illness that forced him to retire at age 38. He comitted suicide five years later.

25 TRANSCENDENCE 1995

*901 SW Salmon Street, northwest corner of SW Park Avenue
   and Salmon Street
Artist: Keith Jellum*

This bronze salmon flying/bursting through the brick corner of a seafood restaurant creates a good mix of art, architecture, and local flavor. Portland State University instructor and sculptor Keith Jellum is also responsible for the water-god sculpture of Mimir on NW Twenty-seventh Avenue between Upshur and Thurman Streets.

25 *Transcendence*

26 *Arlington Club*

26 ARLINGTON CLUB 1910

811 SW Salmon Street, at the north end of the South Park Blocks
Architect: Whidden and Lewis

"The big deals in town . . . are conducted over the lunch tables at the
Arlington Club. . . ."—Federal Judge Gus J. Solomon

This is a reasonably impressive Georgian building, complete with climbing ivy. It manages to impress and ward off the casual bystander while giving the member a surge of pride at belonging to such a reputable-looking structure. The sparkling white pillars leap out from the front of this redbrick, neoclassical building. Some of the terra-cotta that is visible in the balustrade, cornice, and belt course is painted off-white.

This is Portland's *elite* club. Once dubbed the "last bastion of gentile male chauvinism" by E. Kimbark MacColl, the club now admits Jews, blacks, and women—and they were admitted in that order, women finally in 1990.

So what goes on in here? When the Arlington Club originally met in 1867, their goals included having a "meeting place for discussing their own and Portland's destiny." Scary, huh?

A note on the architects: Boston native William M. Whidden (1857–1929) originally came to Portland from New York as an employee of the incredibly influential New York architectural firm of McKim, Mead and White. His job was to supervise construction of the Portland Hotel. Although he did return to the east coast, Whidden eventually hooked up with Massachusetts native and MIT graduate Ion Lewis in 1889. They formed a partnership and built an incredible number of residential, institutional, and commercial buildings in Portland. A. E. Doyle worked as an apprentice in their office for twelve years.

Ion Lewis was the architectural director for the Lewis and Clark Centennial Exposition in 1905. For some reason, he chose an architectural theme of Spanish building styles, and while plenty of red-tile roofs have been built since then in Portland, the historical connection with Lewis and Clark was oddly nonexistent.

✦ This is actually the second Arlington Club building designed by Whidden and Lewis. The first was at the northwest corner of Park Avenue and Alder Street.

27 PARAMOUNT HOTEL 2000

808 SW Taylor Street, at Taylor Street and Park Avenue
Architect: Curt Jensen & Associates

At its opening, this fourteen-story hotel was noted for its Styrofoam moldings and cheap construction materials, as well as a lack of attention paid to genuinely interesting design elements. Given its prominent location, this seems a bit of a boondoggle, but it does create an interesting silhouette against the sky.

28 CHAUCER COURT 1922–24

Originally the Odd Fellows Building
1019 SW Tenth Avenue, southwest corner of Tenth Avenue and
   Salmon Street
Architect: Ernest Kroner

The unusual overhanging canopies running across the top of the parapet of this building are called *baldachins.* These exotic features are usually found over altars, thrones or doorways in very important places. These baldachins were originally lit, and if you can imagine the downward cast of their light in the evening, it was no doubt quite an atmospheric structure for an Odd Fellow to enter. Terra-cotta ornamentation is also evident; below the two-story bay window is Portland's only terra-cotta marquee.

   This brick building is also unusual in that its construction was influenced by the spiritual beliefs of the Odd Fellows, a fraternal group

28 *Chaucer Court*

established in the seventh century that claims biblical roots for its organization. With that in mind, this structure looks a little like the offspring of a Gothic cathedral and an apartment building. The two-story cathedral-style windows on the top floor help suggest this. The building's original purpose was twofold as well, in that it was to serve as lodge building and home to retail offices. Sold by the Odd Fellows and remodeled in 1980 as part of a HUD project, the exterior of the building remains pretty much as it was.

German-born Ernest Kroner (1866–1955) was the right man to design a building with the esoteric metaphysical requirements his clients needed; his specialties were churches and schools.

✦ Portland's original Odd Fellows Hall at First Avenue and Alder Street had a tower that contained a 1,040-pound bell used for a fire alarm from 1861 to 1874. Its replacement was hung at First Avenue and Morrison Street and weighed two tons, with a fifty-pound clapper. It supposedly could be heard from Oregon City to Sauvie Island.

29 FIRST BAPTIST CHURCH 1892–94

909 SW Eleventh Avenue, south side of Taylor Street
Architect: Warren H. Hayes (Minneapolis)

The *first* First Baptist Church was built on Alder Street between Fourth and Fifth Avenues in 1870. In a quest to expand church size, a building committee was formed to cast about for a suitable site and architect to make the second First Baptist Church. The superintendent of the new church's construction recommended Warren H. Hayes for the job. Hayes had built over a hundred churches already at that point and was something of a specialist in the field.

This strong building, with its rustic texture and many arches of wedge-shaped stone, is unique in the Portland area for its true Richardsonian Romanesque style, in that it was based on Richardson's own Trinity Church in Boston. The First Baptist has more in common with the Dekum Building and the University of Portland's West Hall than with other local churches. The walls are solid stone, not just rock-faced. The source of the building material was sandstone quarried in Washington, with the exception of the darker rock at the base (which gives the building a nice contrast), and the polished granite columns at the entry.

✦ Sure, it's convenient, but nothing sucks the magic out of a beautiful bell tower faster than mounted public address speakers pointing to the four corners of the city.

29 *First Baptist Church*

30 FIRST UNITARIAN CHURCH OF PORTLAND 1924

*1011 SW Twelfth Avenue, southwest corner of Twelfth Avenue
and Salmon Street*
Architect: Jamieson Parker

This is an attractive redbrick church trimmed in stone with a polygonal copper-sheathed spire. The steeple, with its bull's-eye window and pilasters, was renovated in 2000. The Georgian Colonial-style church is now connected to the adjacent brick and terra-cotta Church of the Nazarene (Raymond W. Hatch, 1926) to the south. Housing one of the largest Unitarian congregations in the U.S., it is a building rich in civic and spiritual tradition; unfortunately, the church's interior does not reflect this in its original form, as a fire in the 1960s necessitated a remodel.

✦ Jamieson Parker was responsible for the Historic American Building Survey (a program designed to record Oregon's most important architectural specimens) in the mid-1930s. Surprisingly, none of the buildings initially surveyed were in Portland. He also designed Saint Mark's Anglican Church, 1025 NW Twenty-first.

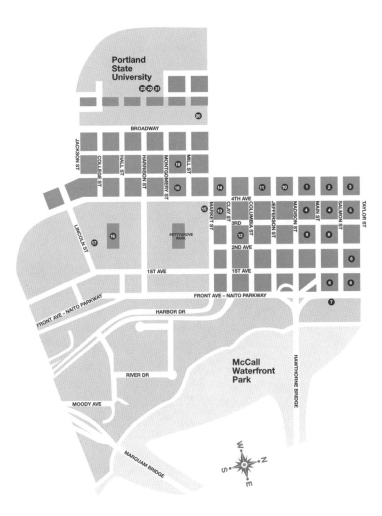

Portland State University

JACKSON ST
COLLEGE ST
HALL ST
HARRISON ST
MONTGOMERY ST
MILL ST
BROADWAY
LINCOLN ST

PETTYGROVE PARK

1ST AVE
FRONT AVE – NAITO PARKWAY
HARBOR DR
RIVER DR
MOODY AVE
MARQUAM BRIDGE

4TH AVE
CLAY ST
MARKET ST
3RD
2ND AVE
1ST AVE
FRONT AVE – NAITO PARKWAY

COLUMBIA ST
JEFFERSON ST
MADISON ST
MAIN ST
SALMON ST
TAYLOR ST

McCall Waterfront Park
HAWTHORNE BRIDGE

23 22 21
20
19 18
14
11 10 1 2 3
15 13 4 4 5
12 9 8
6
16 17
6 6
7

CHAPTER 3

DOWNTOWN—GOVERNMENT SQUARE, SOUTH AUDITORIUM DISTRICT, PORTLAND STATE UNIVERSITY

1 a *The Portland Building*

CHAPTER 3

DOWNTOWN—
GOVERNMENT SQUARE, SOUTH AUDITORIUM DISTRICT, PORTLAND STATE UNIVERSITY

1 THE PORTLAND BUILDING 1982

aka The Portland Public Service Building
1120 SW Fifth Avenue, between Madison and Main Streets
Architect: Michael Graves (Princeton, New Jersey)

"Architecture is the art of how to waste space."–Philip Johnson

One important key to understanding the Portland Building is that its architect, Michael Graves, was vastly more interested in how the building would look than how it would work. At this juncture, it is fair to say that Graves is as much a designer as an architect; *Time* magazine ran a year-2000 cover story on design with a full-page photo of a Michael Graves-designed toilet brush. Upon being awarded the national medal of the arts, President Clinton said that Graves "gets as much pleasure planning a large building as he does designing a spatula."

Since its construction, the Portland Building has not worked particularly well, and its surface design has been something of a hit-or-miss proposition. Considered to be the first large-scale postmodern structure in the U.S., the Portland Building has been criticized locally for its lack of pedestrian access on Fourth Avenue, for its unconventional design, and for just plain being ugly (in the eyes of some). The structure also set off a nationwide debate over the proper role of the then-new postmodern architecture. Nevertheless, the building qualifies as *the* worldwide symbol of the start of postmodernism. As such, it can be argued that it is the city's most architecturally significant building. It also qualifies as the city's most controversial structure.

Architect Michael Graves tried to refer to the styles and looks of other Portland building types in order to produce a contemporary amalgamation of what had gone before. The results of this context-sensitive approach is unquestionably a clever building, and one that shows thinking outside of the box—namely, the glass and metal box that modern skyscrapers had employed up to this point. As such, it gets points just for trying. The building was a one-of-a-kind at a time when large structures seemed to be noted for their banality. Though its basic form is fairly lumbering, and the rows of small individual-sized windows verge on the monotonous, the Portland Building offers the viewer much to look at, particularly from a distance. Terra-cotta strips line the building's sides, and the bluish-green base compares favorably to the trees in the Plaza Blocks. The building itself is essentially a box with a colorful tripartite column design and some colorful Art Deco about it.

Nevertheless, some of the isolated decorative elements, particularly the metal ribbons on the north and south sides, were entirely misbegotten. These "festoons" were originally supposed to be drapes, but the curves employed would have been too difficult to affix to the building. The ribbon was a compromise, and it was a bad one. It's one thing to incorporate whimsical elements into a building, but these were a wretched aesthetic touch. The view improves on the west side, where there are different ways to interpret Graves's aim with the building's distinctive look. Is the design supposed to represent a person? While the two "columns" with projecting capitals supporting a keystone at the top were a favorite design element of Graves's, it can also be interpreted as an anthropomorphic design. Or is it just plain old kitsch?

The genesis of the building began when a citizens committee was drawn up to solicit proposals. The head of this committee, William Roberts, persuaded his colleagues to hire noted architect Philip Johnson (New York State Theater/Lincoln Center, 1964, Trump International Hotel and Tower, 1997) as their advisor. Johnson, who had just won the AIA's Gold Medal, handpicked three entrants and then recommended Graves.

This was particularly galling to Pietro Belluschi, who had engaged in a series of public debates with Johnson in previous years about the proper role of the architect. These debates could be simplistically summed up as follows:

Belluschi: The architect should listen to the client while formulating original ideas that elegantly match the surroundings.

Johnson: The architect should be given free rein so that his authentic artistic expression can run free. Ever read Ayn Rand?

Belluschi actively lobbied the city council against the approval of the Portland Building on the grounds that Graves's conception (built in the style of "the enlarged jukebox or the oversized beribboned Christmas package") should be built in Las Vegas, not Portland. Mayor Frank Ivancie (of Pioneer Courthouse Square fame) favored Graves's plans, however, giving them the impetus for approval. (It should be noted that Belluschi, perhaps mellowing in his anti-Philip Johnson sentiments, later somewhat recanted his strong opinions about the building.)

Regardless, there have been serious problems with the building. Although it was the cheapest design submitted (built at a cost of $24.5 million), it has cost many more millions in subsequent earthquake proofing and leak fixing. Tiles on the lower portion have been repeatedly repaired; occupants have found the ceilings too low, ventilation noisy and inefficient, and windows too small. As of the year 2000, three floors have been cleared for reworking, and it is estimated that it will take $13 million to fix the building correctly. Admittedly, the original construction budget was very tight, so the fault should not be laid entirely at Graves's feet.

As if this weren't enough, there has been substantial debate over the placement of the nine-ton statue *Portlandia* over the Portland Building's entrance. The second-largest copper sculpture in the U.S., *Portlandia* is supposed to symbolize commerce, but she seemingly has nothing to offer for barter but her large trident. Despite attempts by Mayor Vera Katz to relocate *Portlandia* to a more visible location on the waterfront, the statue remains on the Portland Building, partially because of the vociferous complaints of the sculptor, who managed the triple play of selling the statue to the city, dictating its placement, and retaining rights to its image. This despite the facts that the statue was a year overdue, thousands of dollars over budget, and the idea for it came from an old Portland City seal. Now *that's* commerce.

✦ Architectural critic and historian Carter Wiseman called the Portland Building "a rather condescending exercise performed by a sophisticated academic on a culturally overeager community." Ouch.

✦ The Portland Building was awarded an AIA Honor Award after its completion. Architect Michael Graves followed up on his triumph with the Portland Building by introducing a line of his own crockery at Target. More recently, Graves won the AIA's gold medal (its highest honor) in 2001.

1 b *Portland Building*

2   Multnomah County
Courthouse

2 MULTNOMAH COUNTY COURTHOUSE 1911, 1914

1021 SW Fifth Avenue, entire block between Fourth and Fifth Avenues,
and Salmon and Main Streets
Architect: Whidden and Lewis

An American Renaissance-style building faced with Indiana limestone blocks, the county courthouse's most significant features are huge Ionic limestone columns from the third to the sixth floors on the east and west sides, which help give the building a magnificent governmental look.

This is actually the second Multnomah County Courthouse. The first one was built in 1886 and had a cupola with a promenade that allowed a view of the rustic landscape around it. The plans for the present building were ready in 1909, but the courthouse was not finished until 1914, when it became the largest courthouse on the west coast and Portland's largest single structure. After the courthouse was done, architects Whidden and Lewis were seemingly overpaid by $6,000, a large sum in those days. The two refused to give the architectural plans to an investigative league for further review, and that was apparently the end of the matter.

If you were outside the courthouse during the February 2001 earthquake, you would have noticed workers pouring quickly out of the building. They were wise. A structural engineering report predicted that the courthouse could not withstand much shaking without significant danger.

But don't let that stop you from gazing at the square-cut windows at eye level and blank walls around much of the building level as you walk to the carved, scroll-bracketed entrances on the east. Inside: Marble, marble, marble. Bronze lanterns greet one in the foyer, and the stairway has beautiful Italian newel posts.

Going up and investigating the other floors, extensive interior remodeling has taken place throughout the building. The courtrooms contain a large amount of scagliola (plasterwork imitating stone), which is a Whidden and Lewis trademark. Originally constructed around a central courtyard, the building's inner area has been filled in with a pillbox structure that houses offices and a jury room.

✦ *Multnomah* was a local Native American term for the Willamette River. Recorded by Lewis and Clark in 1805, it was originally written "Mulknomah," which sounds like a lesion on a slab of cheese.

✦ Hangings were executed in a courtyard to the east of the old court building. Last words by the convicted were allowed (just like in the movies!), and in one case, the soon-to-be-executed individual gave an eighty-minute speech before the trap door swung wide.

✦ Scant years after the courthouse's opening, confiscated alcohol was often poured down a drain in the central courtyard. Court workers put in a secret drain to divert the liquor into their own container. They were caught.

3 STANDARD INSURANCE CENTER 1971

Originally the Georgia Pacific Building
900 SW Fifth Avenue, between Salmon and Taylor Streets
Architect: SOM

The thirty-two-story Standard Insurance Center is minimalist in appearance, and while it gives the city a good historic example of the utilitarian approach taken to building skyscrapers in that era, it is not a particularly gratifying building to look at. At the time of its construction it was the highest reinforced concrete building in the country. Big whoop. More interesting is the fact that a timber company (Georgia Pacific) would pour so much concrete into a building that symbolized their corporate image, which is usually associated with wood.

The designers did try to personalize the block space with a plaza in front of the building, but as it's essentially just an expanse of granite, it may have had the opposite effect of what was intended.

The regular boxed, deep-set window spaces seem to be the epitome of predictable design, but architecture aside, the problem with the Standard Insurance Building is that it's too big. An entire city block occupied by a building like this is too homogenous an entity for the pedestrian to enjoy. But corporate egos are as susceptible to trying to outdo each other as junior-high schoolers, as every company wants to have the tallest building legally allowed on their lot. In order to bypass zoning permits and maximum height limits (which might vary from one location to another), developers in Portland have been known to put together multi-block parcels. They then simply transfer "air-rights" from one property to an adjacent one. That's what happened with this building.

✦ Out front is what has been dubbed the worst public work of art in Portland—*The Quest,* by Count Alexander von Svoboda, which shows intertwined nudes frolicking, swimming, gyrating, or just trying to escape from their highly visible locale. Locally, the piece is known as "Family Night at the YMCA" and "Three Groins in the Fountain" (although there are really *five* groins).

3 *Standard Insurance Center*

4 CHAPMAN SQUARE, LOWNSDALE SQUARE 1852

aka Plaza Blocks
Between Fourth and Third Avenues, Madison and Salmon Streets

These two historical blocks create the government square (or rectangle) for Portland. The squares flank an octagonal fountain with an immense bronze statue of a bull elk that traffic flows around. (Supposedly, a bull elk had once been seen grazing nearby early in the area's history; elks also typically symbolized majesty to Victorian society.) The local chapter of the Elks organization reviled the 1900 beast as a long-necked "monstrosity of art" that was anatomically incorrect. There has also been some debate over whether its hindquarters should face oncoming traffic.

Lownsdale Square commemorates the Spanish-American War. The list of Portland notables who served in this gentlemen's war reads like a "Who's Who" of Portland society. They were not in much danger; there were only 385 U.S. battle deaths in the war, compared to Spain's approximately 7,000. The exotic words inscribed on concrete projections around the statue honoring the Second Oregon volunteer infantry are famous battles from the Spanish-American War.

Kentucky native Daniel Lownsdale was a tanner by trade who came to Oregon at the age of forty-three. He staked a square-mile claim just west of the original William Overton claim and established a tannery. In 1848, he purchased Francis Pettygrove's half-interest in the Portland township for $5,000 worth of leather. Pettygrove went off to join in California's Gold Rush while, six months later, Lownsdale sold half of his new interest (or one-quarter total interest) of Portland to a cross-eyed man named Stephen Coffin for $6,000. Stephen Coffin (1807–82) was the principal partner with Chapman and Lownsdale in ownership of the original Portland town site. Mr. Coffin was elected in 1851 to the post of Portland's coroner.

William Chapman was a lawyer from Oregon City who subsequently purchased one-sixth of Portland's total town site from Lownsdale and Coffin in 1849. Chapman was arrested in 1851 for offering to slit a judge's throat in his own courtroom. In the 1850s, Lownsdale, Coffin, and Chapman predictably had a falling-out over land titles and were quite vituperative toward each other.

✦ The elk statue has also been called a "fossilized stag" and a "gargoyle quadruped." It was donated by two-time mayor and one-time Minister to Turkey (1892–93) David Thompson.

✦ Young roughnecks loitering hereabouts resulted in the passing of a 1924 ordinance segregating use of the parks to children, women, and male escorts of the women on one side and men on the other. (By checking the location of the squares' respective restrooms, you can guess which was which.) As of 1971, members of any gender can enjoy the elms, gingko trees, and sequoia. If you listen quietly, you can sometimes hear the prisoners exercising in the Justice Center to the east.

5 STANDARD INSURANCE PARKING GARAGE RETROFIT 1997
aka the "Boogie Woogie" Building, containing the Oregon Sports Hall of Fame
Between Third and Fourth Avenues, Salmon and Taylor Streets
Design and retrofit: GBD Architects

Primarily a parking structure, this building is interesting for the fact that the colorful beams and ties on the outside were added after its construction, in order to stabilize some structural cracking that had occurred. What had been merely a parking lot metamorphosed into something much more vibrant: the powerful Boogie Woogie Building. This is a rare case of external beams and a seismic retrofit actually improving the looks of a building.
✦   The Portland Chapter of the American Institute of Architects gave this parking garage a Merit Award in 1997.

6 WORLD TRADE CENTER (ONE, TWO, AND THREE) 1975
Originally Portland General Electric's Willamette Center
Architect: Zimmer Gunsul Frasca Partnership

This three-building, three-block complex was built in 1975 and went by the unwieldy title of "Portland General Electric's Willamette Center." Subsequently and ambitiously renamed the World Trade Center in 1988, it was then remodeled and expanded. The three buildings consist of an eighteen-story office tower with a private heliport (373,590 square feet). The next largest structure is the seven-story service building dedicated to the utility's engineering and power operations department. The third building is a three-story activities building, sometimes referred to as the "public block." (The hexagonal One Main Place may look like a part of this complex, but it was built five years afterwards by SOM.)

The genesis of the layout ideas for these buildings is interesting. The architects researched the approach that Georges Eugene Haussmann used

6 *World Trade Center*

for Paris in the mid-1800s, specifically his plans for the *Place de la Concorde* (Square of Peace) in the Champs Elysees, which emphasized open plazas and wide boulevards. Haussmann was more than a century ahead of his time in his design of stores at street level that would spur foot traffic.

ZGF employed these ideas at the Willamette Center and somehow also managed to be pioneers in this respect in the mid-1970s, a sad statement on U.S. urban planning in the twentieth century. The buildings are sheathed in a smooth gray granite-and-glass exterior: one wonders what Haussmann would make of the skywalks between buildings, but they sure do look good.

✦ During the French Revolution, the Place de la Concorde was the site for the decapitation of hundreds of people (including King Louis XVI and Marie Antoinette) by guillotine. Portland followed destructive suit in a less bloody fashion, as mere historic cast-iron buildings were razed to make room for these ambitiously titled structures. Salmon and Waterfront Park does mark the spot where the first man hung in Portland, Dunford Balch, was strung up in 1859 for the murder of his son-in-law, Mortimer Stump.

✦ The original plans for this complex called for an outdoor ice-skating rink to create "a small urban theater." The idea was nixed by a killjoy utility commissioner.

✦ The water quality of the Willamette River has been a criminal embarrassment for a while. In 1937, in a test of the river's water, ten healthy "fighting" trout were lowered into the waters off the riverbank here. Nine minutes later, all were dead. Sixty-three years later, the river would qualify as one of the Environmental Protection Agency's dreaded Superfund clean-up sites.

7 MCCALL'S WATERFRONT RESTAURANT 1949

Originally Portland Visitors' Information Center
1020 SW Naito Parkway
Architect: John Yeon/Wick, Hilgers, and Scott, associate architects

Considered an architectural monument in many circles, this building is a prime example of the widely disseminated International style, a style that would eventually lead to increasingly sterile and severe buildings world-wide. Ironically, the Chamber of Commerce initially requested that Yeon create a log building to symbolize the city. He didn't listen, choosing instead to create a building noteworthy for its pioneering use of plywood.

Yeon used a Japanese-inspired concept of screens for the views into and out of the original building. A strong sense of geometric spaces predominated the design of the structure, and it was groundbreaking, clean, and prominently located. Not everyone was in love with the building; the Portland Men's Gardening Club chose to rip out the flora they had previously agreed to plant around the building as a protest against its design. The minimalist building was well thought of in architectural circles upon its completion, yet it has fared less well than its contemporary, the Equitable Building. Nearly razed in 1967, it housed the Bureau of Architectural Planning before its subsequent incarnations as the Portland Facilities Management Building and McCall's Restaurant. It has been rendered a different structure by the changes wrought upon and around it; Yeon himself purportedly yearned for its destruction as he witnessed the architectural context coming up in the area.

8 MARK O. HATFIELD UNITED STATES COURTHOUSE 1997

aka the Federal Courthouse
1000 SW Third Avenue, between Salmon and Main Streets
Architects: Kohn Pederson Fox (New York)/BOORA Architects

"Architecture, like dress, is an exercise in good manners, and good manners involve the habit of skillful insincerity—the habit of saying 'good morning' to those whose mornings you would rather blight, and of passing the butter to those you would rather starve."   —Roger Scruton, *London Times,* August 14, 1984

Measuring sixteen stories high on its east side, the Federal Courthouse is the most ambitious building constructed in Portland during the 1990s and certainly the most expensive public building in Portland. Although it was completed under budget, total building costs were in the majestic $129-million range—the fifth-highest cost for its size of over forty federal court-houses built in the 1990s. Majesty was what the architects had in mind when they gave the courthouse a wholly intimidating pedestrian experience away from the building's front. It is a building that attempts to have good manners in its main entry to the west, but one that essentially remains aloof to the city.

The top of the courthouse has an overhanging roof that has led to its nickname of the "Schick Razor Building"; it is one of the elements the courthouse employs on its exterior form that creates a distinctive whole. The courthouse manages to look different from every side, yet not appear to be mishmash; it is a masterful testimony to the power of Senate finance committees and the long arm of the law.

The courthouse is oolite on the outside and cherry on the interior; while this may make it sound like an architectural confection, *oolite* (sometimes called "egg stone") is a limestone with small, rounded concretions that look something like fish eggs. It can come rough or smooth; this building shows both textures on its sides and columns. Cherry wood was used in the courtrooms for a uniform red beauty.

Although the courthouse began with fifteen courtrooms constructed, the offices on the fifth, sixth, and seventh floors of the building were designed with high ceilings in the event they ever need to be converted to

8 *Mark O. Hatfield United States Courthouse*

courtrooms as well. High ceilings are *de rigeur* for courtrooms because of atmosphere. In the course of meting justice, a certain reverent ambience is necessary, and one doesn't find that with ten-foot ceilings.

Federal buildings don't have to follow the same local strictures that other public buildings do in terms of their art budget, but at $1,065,000, the Hatfield Courthouse did not stint. The water art on the first floor uses the technique of rippling the wall itself to make its fascinating pattern. The ninth-floor terrace has some very whimsical bronze sculptures by Tom Otterness that use the timeless themes of education, justice, and aquatic rodents. The view from the top floor is a work of art unto itself, and one of the best in the city.

✦   Distinguished state senator Mark O. Hatfield nearly served as Richard Nixon's vice-presidential running mate in 1968; the *Miami Herald* went so far as to print it in headlines as a done deal. Spiro Agnew, probably the worst vice-president in history, was chosen instead.

9 JUSTICE CENTER 1983

1111 SW Second Avenue, between Main and Madison Streets
Architect: ZGF Partnership/Pietro Belluschi, design consultant
Inner detention areas by Walker, McGough, Foltz, Lyerla (Spokane, Washington)

City, county, and state branches of government are all present in this handsome, eighteen-story, concrete-faced example of "postmodern justice facility architecture." Like the Portland Building, the Justice Center is a pioneering postmodern structure; perhaps unlike it, the Justice Center conveys its homage to Portland's past with impressive dignity and civic virtue.

Immediately noticeable in front of the Justice Center's arcade on the west side are two beautiful cream-colored columns made from an Italian limestone called travertine. It is porous and somewhat "holey," which gives it a distinctive look designed to symbolize the two aspects of justice in the building itself: the courts and the enforcement of the law. While the columns are terrific, whether they match up in color and form with the building behind them is open to debate. In sculptor Walter Dusenberry's words, they are there to "perfume the slammer." One person's perfume is another's malodorous scent. Decide for yourself.

The west front colonnade is a great tie-in with City Hall's design, and provides the Justice Center with a base for its overall column-like design, but the glass is the Justice Center's most notable feature. Above the main

Photo courtesy Zimmer Gunsul Frasca
© 2001 Timothy Hursley

9 a   *Justice Center*

9 b   *Justice Center lobby detail*

threshold on Third Avenue is an enchanting work of stained glass by Ed Carpenter. One can view it close-up inside on the second floor, where the natural light coming through the beveled and colored glass makes a beautiful illumination on the gleaming steel details of the three-story, barrel-vaulted interior lobby of the Justice Center. Incidentally, the glass roof of the lobby is meant to convey the openness of the judicial process within the building.

That's a nice trick for a building that doubles as a jail; it's open and shut. The blue, concave reflective glass center above and behind it only transmits light to the interior of the building through 16 percent of its panels onto community space for the jail. There is also a concave glass feature on the handsome east side of the building, though it looks out onto a parking lot instead of the historic park on the other side.

The windows of the Justice Center on the fourth through eighth floors are unusual. Wired apertures above the concave, reflective glass center front the area where the prisoners exercise. The slit windows to either side of the glass center are jail cells, which reputedly offer a magnificent view of the Park Blocks and the Portland Building to the west. These have been specially designed to make it virtually impossible to see into the space from outside. It is possible to get a limited view from the inside *out,* however, so doubtless, many inmates have gazed across the Plaza Blocks and debated whether the Portland Building is a good postmodern match for the Justice Center. (They certainly have a better view than the Portland Building's employees with their boxy windows.) In any event, the design challenge of incorporating a secure area for accused miscreants within a public building on such a significant site was admirably met.

The tenth floor is an indoor *and* outdoor exercise area for the inmates; the five stories above that are police offices.

Inside, on the ground floor of the building as one passes through to the Second Avenue side, are examples of prisoner artwork, some of which is often quite good. Continuing, one descends one of two curved stairways, which come to a halt at some very fine Art Deco newel posts. These can be lit up and seem to always feel warm to the touch. And warmth may be the feeling that the triangulated tower of the Justice Center imparts: a glowing feeling of beauty and practicality combined together.

✦   In the mood to be deputized? Go to the top floor and visit the Portland Police Museum.

✦   Through a vagary of governmental financing, funding for the Justice Center came from the Federal Highway Administration's bridge program.

✦   For a taste of Portland's original justice, missionary and pioneer Dr. Elijah White laid out the following "White Code" for the Willamette Valley in the 1840s: (*1.) Whoever shall take a life shall be hung. (2.) Whoever willfully shall burn a building shall be hung. (3.) Whoever shall steal an article of more than a beaver pelt shall receive fifty lashes and pay back twofold.*

10 *Portland
City Hall*

10   PORTLAND CITY HALL 1895

*1220 SW Fourth Avenue, between Jefferson and Madison Streets
Architect: Whidden and Lewis/Renovation by SERA Architects*

"The urns of fate from which destiny flows."

That is not a description of a milk bucket by a self-important dairy rancher. Rather, it is a newspaper description of the roof corner ornamentation of Portland's City Hall, a delightful gray and pink four-story building executed in a style known as Renaissance Revival. Architect Peter Meijer has noted that no other public buildings in Portland can boast of the palette of materials that City Hall and Multnomah County Courthouse contain, as a result of Whidden and Lewis's East Coast aesthetics and knowledge of European materials. As for the decorative four-foot urns on the roof, they are lightweight replicas of the original solid limestone ones, which were deemed too dangerous to passersby and replaced during the 1990s remodel of the building.

City Hall actually sits upon a site that was prepared for a differently designed seat of city government in 1892. At that time, ground was broken for a city-hall building designed by Henry Hefty; its plans called for a two-hundred-foot bell tower, or *campanile*. When Whidden and Lewis got the commission, they planned on having a domed cupola on the building. Although this was considered a bad idea in the 1890s, since Wells Fargo Tower now looms to the south, these proposed tops would have given City Hall a physical presence that would serve it in good stead now.

When City Hall was constructed, it had one of the state's first steel frames. On the exterior, it has a granite face with nice column cornice decorations and balustrades at the top of the building. A rotunda for coach drop-offs in front is supported by paired Scottish Aberdeen granite columns. The entrance on Fourth Avenue shows the original scagliola-faced columns on the interior, lurking behind newer ones; these exterior column shafts have an interesting design. (A courtyard was once located on the side of this building.)

After slipping into a sad state, a brilliant two-year remodel of the building began in 1996. At $228 a square foot, the final cost was almost double what had originally been approved for the project. Most of the funds were spent on the steel frame structure, elevators, and fireproofing and safety measures. (Ironically, after the successful and expensive renovation, the city was fined $1,170 by OSHA for having an overly low balcony railing on the second floor.)

Only $3 million went to refurbishing City Hall's historic features, which include marble floors and wrought-iron frames on the elevator shafts. The restoration of the original four story atrium courts was particularly noteworthy. The glazed white tile is mostly original, having been covered up in the 1930s during a renovation.

Across the street from City Hall to the east is Terry Schrunk Plaza. Formerly the site of flophouses, a recruiting center for the armed forces, and a parking lot, this plaza centers on a small brick amphitheater. The sixteen-ton, twenty-two-foot high rock is from China's Lake Tai. Some controversy ensued upon this gift from the Chinese government to Portland as to its placement. As various branches of government went through a series of evasive maneuvers on taking responsibility for the abstractly-shaped limestone (a process called "passing the stone"), the mayor made the command decision: it would sit within sight of City Hall, as the gift had been intended to. "The bigger the rock, the more significant the cultural exchange."

✦ Upon this building's completion in 1895, a grand total of thirty-four employees worked here. In order to use all of the building, the Oregon Historical Society had exhibits on the top floor.

✦ City Hall's rotunda on SW Fourth Avenue shows the marks where a 120-foot construction crane crashed down just after the renovation had begun.

11 WELLS FARGO TOWER 1972

Formerly First National Bank Tower, First Interstate Bank Tower
1300 SW Fifth Avenue, between Columbia and Jefferson Streets
Architect: Charles Luckman and Associates

The question an architect should ask him or herself before beginning an urban project is not *whether* they are going to pay attention to the existing surroundings while working on their designs. Rather, the question should be *how* they will acknowledge their surroundings. The cardinal rules of design should read: "Always design from the bottom up, and while you're at the bottom, look around a little bit, won't you?"

11 *Wells Fargo Tower*

This building is a prime example of what happens when an architect does not take these considerations into account. It is part of a group of structures that began to emerge in the 1960s which made a complete break with anything worthwhile that existed in the city's past. Size mattered to the client and architect involved with this project, and their aim was to make as big of a building possible on Portland's homey little blocks. Here, the result was this monolithic monstrosity that blocked off the horizon and left little room for pedestrian interaction.

Part of the problem stemmed from the fact that at the time of these buildings' construction, big corporations housed their headquarters exclusively in downtown high-rises, as opposed to the now-common practice of going to the suburbs to build a low, sprawling company "campus," as Nike has done in Beaverton. These outlying areas usually have better parking and lower rental rates, though none of the cachet of a downtown tower.

The "corporate chic" epitomized by the Wells Fargo Tower is utterly charmless. Not only is the building aesthetically sterile, but also its podium-based garage isolates the building from its surroundings. The passerby can choose to gaze up in awe, or keep eyes averted from the inhospitable spectacle; there certainly is nothing to look *into*. At best, this building (and others of its ilk, like the twenty-one-story Hilton Hotel [1963, SOM, 921 SW Sixth Avenue]) can be termed "International"; at worst, they are simply out of context with the surrounding area, an unimaginative blight of Brobdingnagian proportions.

At 539 feet tall, the Wells Fargo Tower is simply overwhelming and it creates an aesthetic effect as subtle as a jackboot in the face. Sure, it has a flared bottom. Who cares? The marble on the base is one-sixteenth inch thick, pasted onto metal lathing. The thinness of this veneer is symbolic of the shallowness of the building's artistic ambitions. It has been consistently vilified over the years as an out-of-scale and out-of-place eyesore, which slightly lessens the pleasure of hurling brickbats at it now.

Described by writer Ivan Doig as "huge and sleek and featureless," this tower helped provide the political impetus to change city zoning laws in order to prevent a mushrooming of future behemoths.

The real crime of these buildings, particularly the Wells Fargo Tower, is that they were allowed so close to City Hall. In contrast to its neighbor, the seat of city government looks like a mushroom, utterly overwhelmed by corporate power.

✦   The Council on Tall Buildings and Urban Habitat currently ranks the tallest building in the world as the 1,483-foot Petronas Towers in Kuala Lumpur, Malaysia. It's big, but soon to be overtaken. The Wells Fargo Tower, at 544 feet, is the 414th highest building in the world. Hoo-ha. (For national comparison, the Empire State Building is 1,250 feet high.)

12 KOIN TOWER 1984

aka KOIN Center, "The Mechanical Pencil"
222 SW Columbia, between Second and Third Avenues
Architect: Zimmer Gunsul Frasca Partnership

This thirty-five-story orange brick tower with the blue crown is as close as Portland has come to its own Chrysler Building; it gives the city a postmodern, Art Deco spire to be proud of. The KOIN Tower's setback lines give it an appearance that is instantly recognizable on the skyline, and as with the Fox Tower, this is one of the most important things a downtown skyscraper can accomplish. Although it is a true postmodern building that combines historical influences with its Spanish, Gothic, and Art Deco traits, it isn't a kitschy structure like the Portland Building, and has perhaps worn better on the eyes over the years because of this.

The base of this tower is brick and limestone; looking upward, its most advantageous exterior features are the multi-faced corners that cast shadows and are particularly beautiful where the tower "steps in" toward the top. The KOIN Center (while obviously less blocky) has a common stylistic link with buildings like the Sixth Church of Christ Scientist on Park Avenue. In another architectural similarity to buildings on the South Park blocks, it has been noted that the windows at the bottom of the tower resemble those of the Portland Art Museum.

Given its small base, it is impressive how high the tower goes without being a monstrosity. After a three-story base, there are two main stepped-back sections to the tower, with a galvanized steel top, and from a distance, it looks a bit like a misplaced peg from a children's erector set. The tower has not gone without its critics; commuters coming out of the tunnel on Highway 26 lost a view of Mount Hood, and its design elements have been called "nostalgic." But the KOIN hardly suffers in comparison to its neighbors. East of the KOIN Tower is the Marriott, which squats on the waterfront like a mutated seashell. Try walking around the backside of it sometime to appreciate how bad its street interaction is and to better value the KOIN Tower.

✦ The condos in Fountain Plaza, high atop the KOIN Tower, have some of the best views in town . . . and a high-visibility entrance at the tower's base.

12 *KOIN Tower*

THE SOUTH AUDITORIUM DISTRICT

aka Portland Center, New Town

This area has an interesting lineage (see "Corbett" for more information.) Once home to Portland's most colorful ethnic neighborhoods, it deteriorated enough after World War II to be selected as the urban spot to get a shot-in-the-arm by getting razed. Over two thousand people were evacuated, with fifty-four blocks being subsequently leveled. The I-405 interchange and the South Auditorium District were the result.

The Portland Development Commission (formed in 1958) got the South Auditorium Renewal Project physically initiated in the early 1960s, giving Portland a leading role in the nation in urban renewal. It was funded by private, city, and federal funds, and the firm of Skidmore, Owings and Merrill were put in charge of the plans and design elements. The idea was to make this district a model for urban renewal by inoculating it with new buildings. Its specific method to accomplish this was to preserve Portland's small block sizes and then combine retail, residential, and recreational spaces together in the area in a way that would promote commerce and draw people to it.

Twenty-four blocks were converted into three huge ones, with pedestrian walkways replacing the lanes where traffic had formerly run. While the result was aesthetically about what one would expect from a SOM project from that time period, the improvement to the area was non-negotiable. It is a mildly generic and sterile environment, but also one that is quiet, efficient and well-laid-out, and it has certainly been successful in increasing the city's take in revenues from the previously anemic tax base. It is also noteworthy as being perhaps the nation's only successful urban-renewal project from this era.

✦   When the initial federal grant funds for the urban-renewal project came through, the plan was to build a coliseum in the South Auditorium District.

13   IRA C. KELLER FOUNTAIN 1970

aka Forecourt Fountain
SW Third Avenue, between Clay and Market Streets
Designer: Angela Danadjieva Tzvetin of Lawrence Halprin
*   and Associates*

This is perhaps the most popular fountain in Portland. Like the Lovejoy Fountain, it is designed to imitate water in its natural environment. Although it is essentially just a grouping of various concrete shapes, the fountain has waterfalls, placid eddies, slowly running spots, and foaming surf, all presented in an area that promotes interactions of an equal range of possibilities. One can find a quiet nook and ruminate, take a misty stroll, or sit on a big block and get pounded. It's a darned creative mix of angles and pumps, and the people-watching is enjoyable as well.

✦   Ira Keller was the head of the Portland Development Commission, the agency responsible for the South Auditorium District project; he was named Portland's First Citizen in 1972.

13   *Ira C. Keller Fountain*

14 *Portland Plaza*
Condominiums

14 PORTLAND PLAZA CONDOMINIUMS 1973

aka the Norelco Building
Between Clay and Market Streets, Fourth and Fifth Avenues
Architect: DMJM

Very nicely situated for viewing from the east side, this reflective, three-towered condo structure acquits itself quite well, particularly considering its less-distinguished contemporaries in town dating back to the sixties and early seventies.

This building had a cameo as a futuristic structure in the PBS film of Portland author Ursula K. LeGuin's book, *The Lathe of Heaven.*

15 200 MARKET BUILDING 1973

aka the Black Box
200 SW Market
Architect: Rudat, Boutwell and Partners

Although seemingly just the city's dark glass-curtain-walled precursor to Security Pacific Plaza, the two buildings are different enough to warrant mention. First, at eighteen stories, the Black Box is significantly shorter and blockier than its cousin downtown. And although it has less interesting surroundings to reflect than the Security Pacific Building, the Black Box may be a more successful building by virtue of the denseness of its black opacity, as well as for the creative terraforming that places it in context on its space. Seen from a distance, one must admire the terraced landscaping and multilevel podium that went into this building's planning.

16 LOVEJOY FOUNTAIN/PLAZA

In Lovejoy Park, between First and Fourth Avenues, Harrison
and Lincoln Streets
Designer: Lawrence Halprin and Associates (San Francisco)

More interesting than the surrounding buildings, this fountain (along with Pettygrove Park) help to make this section of town work. The idea was to imitate the natural cascades of the Sierra Mountains, and although the firm selected was not from these parts, the result comes admirably close to its goals in an impressive piece of landscape architecture. To be sure, there is an awful lot of concrete imitating nature (were *real* boulders too hard to come by?), but all the angles and planes combine to create a splendid splash.

17 VILLAGE AT LOVEJOY FOUNTAIN APARTMENT COMPLEX 1999

245 SW Lincoln Street
Architect: Fletcher Farr Ayotte

If you want to hold the urban growth boundary, you need high-density urban design. The completion of this five-story, L-shaped building made the block it sits on the densest in the city. As such, it fits in perfectly with the city's urban growth boundary goals. The fact that it's a wood framed building that is rounding out the final development of the South Auditorium project (noted for its extensive use of concrete) is interesting. Of course, there's no wood on the outside of the building; that honor goes to stucco.

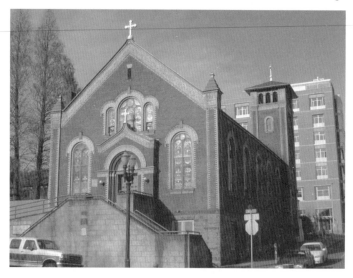

18   *Saint Michael the Archangel*

18   SAINT MICHAEL THE ARCHANGEL 1901
SW Mill Street and Fourth Avenue
Architect: Joseph Jacobberger

When Saint Michael's was designated a historic landmark, it helped it avoid the wrecking ball that took down the surrounding neighborhood. This handsome church has a square bell tower with a pyramidal roof; its stained glass was by the Povey brothers. In some ways, this church is the only touchstone to the past of the area's former Little Italy, a redbrick reminder of a bygone era surrounded by concrete and glass. It was originally constructed of building materials donated to the church.

PORTLAND STATE UNIVERSITY EST. 1955
Bordered by SW Tenth Avenue to the west, Sixth Avenue to the east, Market Street to the north, College and Jackson Streets to the south.

As there is not always a clear delineation between the PSU campus and Portland proper, PSU seems to be enmeshed within the city itself. PSU was the original site of Lincoln High School; the old Lincoln High School building was purchased in 1952, and the college was created three years later as a city college.

This campus was the site of an urban-renewal project in the mid-1960s, a development intended to revitalize the decaying southwest and southeast parts of downtown Portland with new architecture and civic planning. At the turn of the century, the campus plans to expand eastward, beginning with the $33-million Urban Center. Should the campus continue this expansion, it could link up with the South Auditorium District, successfully linking two urban-renewal projects currently separated by parking lots and forgettable buildings.

✦ Currently, 15,000 students use this facility, which is spread out over forty-nine acres in the city.

19 PORTLAND STATE UNIVERSITY URBAN CENTER 2000

Between SW Fifth and Sixth Avenues, Montgomery and Mill Streets
Building architect: Thomas Hacker and Associates/Plaza: Walker
& Macy

This block is certainly the most important PSU development that exists away from the inward focus of the Park Blocks. Among its significant accomplishments, it provides a worthy setting for the new locale of the College of Urban and Public Affairs. Students in this program can gaze out their plentiful classroom windows at a new university district in the area, past the informal containment boundary that Broadway has posed in the past, and into an urban square that replicates Pioneer Square's success at combining public transportation with open space and art.

The Urban Center itself defies description by presenting an almost bewildering array of looks to the different cardinal directions, all presented within the context of a brick structure that opens up nicely to the outside by revealing the interior through steel and glass. The plaza's design is subtly simple and pleasing, co-existing amiably with the abstract public art, which is swirled into both the plaza and building.

19 *PSU Urban Center*

20 LINCOLN HALL 1911
Architect: Morris Whitehouse

The brick color of the old Lincoln High Building (called Lincoln Hall, or "Old Main") established the color template for future construction. Unfortunately, its dignified and well-constructed style was not also emulated. This building has great Corinthian columns on the front; I assumed that there had been large windows between the columns that were bricked-over due to remodeling, but a 1914 postcard of the building belies that.

✦ Though exiled from the building, Lincoln High School (established 1869) is probably the second-oldest public high school west of the Mississippi. The AAA building to the east of Lincoln Hall was the former site of Lincoln High School's "playground."

21 ALUMNI ASSOCIATION OFFICES CIRCA 1900
aka Simon Benson House
Between the Blackstone Apartments/Ione Plaza on
*   Montgomery Street*
Architect: Unknown

This once-sadly-neglected, two-and-a-half-story Queen Anne-style home was formerly located at 1504 SW Eleventh Avenue. Described as looking like "a boarded-up meth lab" by a local columnist, it became a bit of a *cause célèbre* when robbers stole several leaded glass windows from the home. The ensuing attention paid to the recovery of these also brought higher visibility to the rescue and restoration project for the house, which carries a weighty historical significance.

The first phase of the building's new lease on life began with a four-block move in a windstorm to Portland State University in 2000, highlighted by the replacement of the original rocks from the previous site around its foundation. Simon Benson, a man known to have frowned on public drunkenness, may have been irked by the champagne-and-cheese crowd on hand to cheer the home's move. On the other hand, his heart may have been warmed to see such effort being given to a house that lingers as a reminder of the once-majestic residential character of this area.

22   *Blackstone Apartments*

✦   Simon Benson (*nee* Bergersen) was a local philanthropist who lived in this home for twelve years. Among his other accomplishments, he donated Multnomah Falls to the city of Portland in 1915, and invested in the Multnomah Falls Lodge and Columbia Gorge Hotel. The hotel that bears his name in town is probably the ritziest digs around.

22   BLACKSTONE APARTMENTS 1930
1831 SW Park Avenue
Architect: Elmer E. Feig

An Egyptian motif denotes this distinguished four-story apartment building of variegated brick with cast-stone decorations. Note the pharaohs at the entry; it shares features with Feig's Morland Apartments near Lloyd Center.

23 PORTLAND STATE UNIVERSITY LIBRARY 1967, ADDITION 1987

aka the Branford Price Millar University Library
Architect: Skidmore, Owings, Merrill

This five-story building is noteworthy for curving around the large copper beech tree in front of it. The original building was merely a blocky concrete, glass, and brick affair with an admittedly good view. The design of the remodeled structure is conservationist in nature, having been designed thus to preserve the tree, which has its own booster club, the Copper Beech Society. The library was built in two parts; the 1987 addition is the part that curves. Inside, one can differentiate the old from the new by looking at (or tripping over) the floor demarcations. The library sports an appropriate "bookend" look and copper roofing on its front overhang.

The firm of Skidmore, Owings and Merrill (aka SOM) began in the late 1930s as America's purveyors of modernism (also sometimes called the International style or corporate modernism); they were uninterested in ornament, but they were committed to the glass-and-steel, curtain-walled skyscrapers of the new age. In the 1960s, SOM was instrumental in working on urban-renewal projects in the South Auditorium District and Portland State University that revitalized decaying areas of Portland with new architecture.

Across from the library is Neuberger Hall (1967, Wolff, Zimmer, Gunsul, Frasca), an ugly glass and aluminum box, but to its south is the old Shattuck School (now called Shattuck Hall), a beautiful Georgian brick structure by architect Floyd A. Naramore, architect of the Portland School District. If one walks down Shattuck Hall's north side, one can get a glimpse of Piggott's Castle on the hills to the southwest. (See "Piggott's Castle.")

23 *PSU Library*

CHAPTER 4

ANKENY ST

ASH ST

PINE ST

OAK ST

STARK ST

WASHINGTON ST

ALDER ST

MORRISON ST

YAMHILL ST

TAYLOR ST

SALMON ST

4TH AVE

3RD AVE

2ND AVE

1ST AVE

FRONT AVE – NAITO PARKWAY

WILLAMETTE RIVER

MORRISON BRIDGE

N
W   E
S

YAMHILL HISTORIC DISTRICT

1 *Skidmore Fountain*

CHAPTER 4

YAMHILL HISTORIC DISTRICT

"We have taken away from the man in the street all the stereotyped little ornaments, cornices, cartouches . . . but we have not yet been capable of giving him back the equivalent in emotional value."

—Pietro Belluschi, Reed College address, December 1950

The Yamhill District stretches roughly from Salmon Street on the south, Fifth Avenue on the west, and Burnside Street on the north. (I have slightly altered the boundaries in this section.) The city's 1846 plat was eight blocks in length and two blocks deep. The blocks were oriented to the river, not to the points of the compass, which explains the "street skew" mismatch that would later develop between the northwest and southwest sections of Portland where they meet at Burnside Street. During the early 1860s, Portland's commercial heart was Front Street (now Naito Parkway) with its wharves and river traffic. This, in turn, led to a building boom on Front, First, and later, Second Avenues.

The first buildings in the area were wooden New England–style buildings, and they proved eminently flammable. Cast-iron, Victorian Italianate storefronts came to predominate in this area after the Great Fire of 1873. Portland's 200-hundred-foot blocks divided nicely into eight 50-by-100-foot lots. These could be further cut to lots only 25 feet wide. While some Yamhill and Old Town buildings were quite large, some were ambitiously called "block" buildings even when they were only a half-block, quarter-block, or even less in size. In parts of Old Town and the Yamhill District, one can see that these buildings show signs of early urban planning, as belt courses and cornice lines are continued from building to building, despite variances in design and construction date.

While the architects of these older buildings devoted great care to their façades, they usually left the sides bare. Assuming that a building's neighbors were at least as tall as it was, that was well and good; however, in many instances, a two-story building was next to a four-story building, which was

127

next to a three-story building, and now the decorated fronts with the bare walls (combined with the empty holes created by parking lots) creates a certain staccato unevenness to the eye of the pedestrian.

The Yamhill District remained the city's center until the construction of the Portland Hotel (1889) heralded the rise of a new city core to the west. This move inland was hastened by Portland's increasing population, and a new railroad, which cut into passenger travel on the Willamette River. The Yamhill District's flooding problems, particularly the Great Flood of 1894, also proved a powerful deterrent to businessmen, who sought the higher ground of the west.

These factors led to the Yamhill District's increasing seediness beginning in the 1890s, with many cast-iron buildings becoming warehouses or going untended. A renaissance of sorts came with the 1914 opening of the Yamhill Public Market, a highly successful farmers' market that lasted until 1933. But riverfront businessmen killed the goose that laid the golden egg by moving the Public Market to an indoor site on the riverfront in a building called the Sea Wall Market. This gigantic warehouse proved a disaster. Produce retailers balked at selling their wares inside the building, and the project failed. (The *Oregon Journal* took over the Sea Wall Market from 1948 to 1961, and when they moved out, it stood vacant until its demolition.)

As noted in the introduction, the 1940s began a city improvement plan that wiped away many of the area's original buildings, and most of what was left was demolished in the 1950s to make way for parking lots. The attitude toward tearing down old structures was gradually replaced by a preservationist spirit, and by 1975, the Yamhill District was designated a historic district and found a place on the National Register of Historic Places.

✦ The Great Fire of 1873 reduced the fortunes of Meier and Frank to the point that they were forced to dip into the savings account of Sigmund Frank's wife, Fannie Meier, which held fifty-eight dollars.

1 SKIDMORE FOUNTAIN 1888

First Avenue and Ankeny Street
Sculptor: Olin Warner

This extremely attractive cast-iron fountain is named for Stephen Skidmore, who designated in his will that his estate build a fountain to provide water for Portland's "horses, men and dogs." Today, it is considered somewhat bad form for men to drink from it, although four granite cups attached by chains were once connected to the fountain for just that purpose. (Portland's Benson Bubblers were still decades away.) A bronze basin is held up by handmaidens and a column of granite, and horse troughs below are fed by lion's-head spouts. There was a proposal to top the fountain with the likeness of the fire chief at the time, but the mayor nixed it.

Illinois native Stephen Skidmore (1838–83) came with his family to Portland via the Oregon Trail when he was eleven, and he grew up to become a druggist and city councilman. Skidmore visited the 1878 World's Fair in Paris, where he was most impressed with the fountains exhibit at Versailles. Dying from consumption at the age of forty-four, he left $5,000 of his $175,000 estate for a fountain.

Olin Warner was chosen for the project; he was a noted sculptor of the day whose work included five gigantic heads depicting the human races for the Philadelphia train station. The fountain was constructed during the same weeks that the original Portland home of Skidmore was torn down just a few yards away. Skidmore's mother had been caught in that house during a flood of the area in the early 1860s and died of a severe cold she developed as a result.

As the heart of the city quickly moved first to the Yamhill District and then uptown, the area around the Skidmore Fountain became so downtrodden that in 1896 there was a concerted effort to relocate the fountain westward to a more vital district or to the Park Blocks. Nonetheless, despite the turmoil and tragedy that swirled around it, the fountain's maidens still serenely hold their plate aloft, adding a substantial dash of beauty and history to a grateful city.

✦   Stephen Skidmore also left $100,000 of his holdings to his business partner and friend, Charles Sitton, who also died young. In 1891, he was found in his buggy with a handkerchief drenched in ether clenched to his face, the apparent victim of self-medication for migraines. He was forty-one. Not to be macabre, but Olin Warner also suffered an unusual fate. While bicycling in Central Park in 1896, he suffered a stroke and fell beneath a horse's hooves. The combination was fatal.

✦   Henry Weinhard offered to run a hose from his brewery to the Skidmore Fountain in order to have it be a beer fountain on its opening day. City leaders, fearing for the welfare of horses (no mention of the dogs), declined the gracious offer.

✦   *The day the maidens burned:* In 1957, city employees attempting to clean the bronze nymphs used acid, causing them dire harm and necessitating a full restoration.

2 NEW MARKET THEATER 1872
50 SW Second Avenue, just southwest of Skidmore Fountain

NEW MARKET BLOCK, SOUTH WING 1871
SW First Avenue, south of the New Market Theater
Architects: William W. Piper and E. M. Burton.
Renovated 1983: SERA, Allen, McMath and Hawkins

Architect E. M. Burton came to Portland from the Midwest in 1854, nine years before William Piper, who arrived in answer to an advertisement for proposals to build the Multnomah County Courthouse. (The two joined forces on the courthouse project, winning two hundred dollars for their submission. It was demolished in 1910.) The work the pair accomplished independently and together resulted in scores of cast-iron buildings being built in the north end of town, including these two.

The site of this building and the Skidmore Fountain was originally Portland's Pioneer Cemetery; the last bodies were removed in 1854, clearing the way for Captain Alexander P. Ankeny's financing of this building.

The outside of the long, narrow, Victorian Renaissance–style New Market Theater is impressive. It has remarkable detailing, with huge, arched carriage-entrance portals on the First Street side, large Corinthian columns, and beautifully arched windows. The cast-iron work of the first floor segues

2 *New Market Theater*

into brickwork for the top two, and then it's on to a fairly massive cornice. Spotlights illuminate the elaborate details on the façade in the evening, making a spectacle worthy of a fine theater.

It is called the New Market Theater because the first floor of the building was dedicated to a two-hundred-foot arcade that boasted twenty-eight *marble* produce stalls. This resulted in a building that housed a unique combination of produce market and theater. In the memorable words of Terence O'Donnell and Thomas Vaughan, it had "cabbages on the first floor, tenors on the second."

The theater's cultural achievements occurred upstairs. The original 1,200-seat theater in this building was on the second and third floors. (It has long since been torn out.) "What cultural achievements?" you might ask. Well, the New Market qualified as the most high-class theater north of San Francisco. Performers included Baird's Colossal Minstrels, Fannie Davenport, and Janauscek. (Yes, *the* Janauscek.) Shooting exhibitions took place here, and General Ulysses S. Grant enjoyed the recital of a poem at the Theater, sometime before becoming one of the worst presidents our country has ever had.

Complications during construction of this building led to the dissolution of the partnership between Piper and Burton. Piper's final work would be the Deady Hall (named for "whiskey judge" Matthew Deady) at the University of Oregon. Unable to collect his fees for this work, Piper sold his practice, retired, un-retired, worked eight more frustrating years, and finally, in 1886, boarded a train to visit his sister in Ohio. At Medicine Bow, Wyoming, William Piper screamed, "Help me, help me! Will no one save me?" Throwing open the door to the railcar, he then threw himself from the train. Whether the University of Oregon or the reduced demand for cast-iron architecture was to blame, nobody did help him.

His building, at least, *did* receive assistance. Although the north wing's cast-iron columns were torn down in the 1950s, a substantial renovation of the theater took place in 1983. Among other things, architects found that the complex ornamentation on the top of the building was badly damaged. William J. Hawkins drew the plans, and a sculptor re-created the finials and other detailing in fiberglass. A greenhouse was eventually added to the north side of the building, and mezzanine office floors took the place of the original theater space. While the interior remodel of this building does not warm my heart, the intent was good.

Next door to the New Market Theater on the First Avenue side is the New Market Block. This building preceded the theater by a year, taking the place of an orchard. The agricultural theme of the locale is revealed in the detailed grape clusters visible on the main columns at the corners and in the center of the building. Scrolls, leaves, and brackets also jut out to merge into the belt cornice. The "A" in the threshold plate probably refers to Captain Ankeny, who financed construction of this building as well.

✦   In 1968, the newly formed Historic Landmark Commission managed to thwart developers who sought to build a business tower on this site.

✦   The Portland Symphony Orchestra was launched here in 1882. Five years later, the theater gave its last theatrical production, the victim of competition from uptown.

3 SMITH'S BLOCK 1872

1077–117 SW Naito Parkway, southwest corner of Naito Parkway
and Ash Street
Architect: William W. Piper

The architect of this building was the unfortunate and aforementioned William W. Piper, who designed the New Market Theater. This two-story building lost a corner of itself on First Avenue and Ash Street for . . . you guessed it, a parking lot.

This two-story building was designed to be a warehouse, and an unusually attractive one it is. Floral decorations are bolted onto the columns, and decorations between the first-story arches are nicely wrought. Are those artichokes or pineapples in the keystone sections?

If you like this particular Italian Renaissance style, tough luck; the rest of the several buildings that once sported it in this area have been demolished. Smith's Block almost suffered the same fate in 1965, when a ramp was nearly built from the now-defunct Harbor Drive, over Naito Parkway, through Smith's Block, to Third Street. Try to imagine a blight of that size on this neighborhood; frightening, eh?

✦   During the 1870s, city ordinances were passed in Portland to encourage propriety on the part of its citizens. It became illegal to have an uncollared dog, drag logs through the street, or drive any vehicle on the sidewalk besides a baby carriage. The citywide speed limit was six miles an hour. Hopped-up yuppies *walk* the streets faster than that nowadays.

3 *Smith's Block*

4 FECHHEIMER AND WHITE BUILDING 1885

233 SW Naito Parkway, between Oak and Pine Streets
Architects: Warren H. Williams, Justus Krumbein

A local iron foundry cast the arches for this narrow building in a single piece. The arches are bolted onto the columns, and the windows for the next floor are centered above the arches so that the upper walls are centered above the load-bearing columns.

This building has been restored well, allowing the observer to notice the interplay between the lower floor's iron and the plastered brick of the upper floor. The finials on each top corner served as chimneys.

Justus Krumbein also designed the ballyhooed and lamented Kamm Building (1884), a colossal exhibit of cast iron with Danish carvings and a lack of modesty unrivalled among existing buildings in the area.

5 FAILING BUILDING 1886

aka the Oregon Marine Supply Co. Building
235 SW First Avenue, northwest corner of First Avenue and Oak Street
Architect: Warren H. Williams

An entirely solid and likable building that combines Italian and French influences, the Failing Building is well preserved and conservative, with

5 *Failing Building*

some interesting stuccoed brick detailing above the third story. This building has had a varied series of tenants over the years: cigar importers, Goodyear, rubber-stamp manufacturers, marine suppliers, and architects have all occupied the building at one time or another.

Despite being named as "the father of the public schools" by the *Oregonian* in 1891, Josiah Failing does not have a school named after him in Portland today. No doubt you can guess why. Interestingly, this site is where Portland's first public school opened in 1852. The headmaster was named John T. Outhouse, and his name is also unrepresented in local schools.

✦ The destructive downtown fires of the 1870s were a godsend for architect Warren H. Williams, who got many commissions in this area during the rebuilding of the district.

6 KELLS RESTAURANT 1889

Originally Glisan Building, aka Chown Electric Building
112 SW Second Avenue, east side, between Ash and Pine Streets
Architect: Unknown

The end of an era.

The columns, ornamentation, and general demeanor of this two-story building are noticeably different from the other cast-iron structures that have survived into modern times. Part of the reason for this is that it is the last historic cast-iron building constructed in Portland. This makes it a one-of-a-kind viewing treat, as it combines the traditional cast-iron form with new elements. The general decoration scheme seems more restrained, and the intertwined flower-stem designs on the pillars hinted at the then-latest European design craze, Art Nouveau. These columns do, in fact, support the upper floor and are not merely ornamental pilasters.

✦　Dr. Rodney Glisan (1827–90) hailed from Maryland and became an army surgeon. Moving west, he eventually married into the Couch family, while becoming a widely acclaimed medical practitioner and pillar of the early Portland community.

6　*Kells Restaurant*

7 HASELTINE BUILDING 1893

133 SW Second Avenue, northwest corner of Second and Pine Streets
Architect: McCaw & Martin

This is something of a junior version of the Dekum Building; it is Richardsonian Romanesque, with rough stone on the bottom and brick above. The massive arches are worthy of a Roman aqueduct; some of the stones weigh three thousand pounds. In the interest of safety, its original

7 *Haseltine Building*

8 *Embassy Suites Downtown, originally Multnomah Hotel, photo circa 1920*

cornice was taken off, as in Portland there have been numerous instances of cornice pieces breaking off and falling to the pavement below. This unbalances the building's look, but one supposes this is a small price to pay to avoid being hit in the head and getting a terra-cotta concussion.

8 EMBASSY SUITES DOWNTOWN 1912

Originally the Multnomah Hotel
319 SW Pine Street, north side, between Third and Fourth Avenues
Architects: Gibson and Cahill/Restoration: SERA

The Multnomah Hotel was the largest building in Portland when it opened, and it was the biggest hotel in the city until 1961. Done in a style called "American Renaissance," the light-colored brick hotel has an interesting three-wing design, with accompanying light courts that enabled the hotel to bill itself as "every room an outside room."

The lobby was designed to impress with twenty-four decorated marble columns, which are still marked with "MH" for the hotel's original moniker. The lobby's original terrazzo floor (a mix of cement and marble chips) is beneath the current carpet. The Arcadian Garden in the lower floors is an original room (complete with fountain) that was designed for cabaret entertaining. The wall that divides the space now was installed in the 1990s as part of earthquake-proofing the structure.

The original owner of the hotel went bankrupt less than a year after it opened, and the following owner did so after three years. Western Hotels Inc. ran the hotel from 1931 to 1963, under their company strategy of "Intelligence, Integrity, Intestinal Fortitude." (Urp.) From 1965 to 1992, government offices were in the building, followed by four fallow years. Finally, in 1995, the hotel was purchased and renovated by its current operators in homage to the building's past. The lobby's plaster was even restored by the great-grandson of the original contractor.

Notable visitors here have included Queen Marie of Romania and nine U.S. presidents; John F. Kennedy gave an impromptu speech from a balcony here while campaigning in 1960. Charles Lindbergh was feted at the Multnomah in 1927, after he landed *The Spirit of St. Louis* at Swan Island. Elvis Presley stayed in 1957; one female fan climbed the outside of the hotel to the second floor before being caught. Elvis was on the seventh floor. More tragically, Robert ("the Power Broker") Moses holed up here in the early 1940s, gathering information on how to make Portland "more driveable."

✦ In 1912, as part of a promotion to publicize the Rose Festival, Silas Christofferson built a wooden runway on the roof of the Multnomah Hotel and used it to launch a biplane off from the roof. He landed minutes later in Vancouver. Christofferson would die in 1916 flying a test plane. The flight was replicated eighty-three years later off the same roof to trumpet the hotel's re-opening.

✦ Building alterations over the years have included work by Pietro Belluschi and Richard Sundeleaf.

9 PORTLAND POLICE BLOCK 1912, 1944, 1955

209 SW Oak Street, northwest corner of Oak Street and Second Avenue
Architect: Emil Schacht

Although seemingly aged, this American Renaissance/Georgian building is actually the third Police Block on this site (the first was built in 1859), so it's a relative newcomer. A building with a strong horizontal presence, it has a stone first floor, brick above that, rosette decorations, and a big cornice. Architect Richard Ritz has conjectured that it shares many of its restrained classical elements with the Multnomah County Central Library to the north because its architect was a fan of Doyle's design there.

The Police Block was vacated by the police in 1984 (the Portland Police Headquarters are now in the Justice Center), and the building was restored.

✦ In 1874, this building's predecessor on the site held in its jail five members of the Women's Temperance Prayer League. These criminals were

9 *Portland Police Block*

10 *Charles K. Henry Building*

charged with "disturbing the peace" for having the gall to sing hymns in Portland's serene and meditative saloons.

✦ This building's basement served as a clearinghouse for confiscated liquor during the 1920s; apparently, much of the supply was diverted to City Hall.

10 CHARLES K. HENRY BUILDING 1909

309 SW Fourth Avenue, southwest corner of Fourth Avenue
  and Oak Street
Architect: Francis J. Berndt

This six-story building's exterior walls were made with a unique, enamel-faced "Tiffany" brick from Denver. These white-and-blue bricks were actually glazed, making them highly reflective and eye-catching, although they were apparently selected for the building because they were easy to clean. The building was executed according to the Chicago School of commercial architecture, and its crisp lines and clean, slightly decorated façade make it stand out on this street. (The corner column is wrapped in copper.) Some of its only decorations are the lion's-head cartouches below the iron roof cornice.

Charles Henry was a Liverpudlian by accident; in 1856, his Irish mother bore him in Liverpool while in the process of immigrating to the United States. He liked the enameled brick used on his building for its hygienic quality.

11 SHERLOCK BUILDING CIRCA 1896
aka the Forbes and Breeden Building
309 SW Third Avenue, southwest corner of Third Avenue
and Oak Street
Architect: F. Manson White

The steel frame beneath this building is hinted at in its clean, fresh lines. This building, like the Hamilton Building, has a restrained and elegant but also modern look about it, despite being over a century old. The building combines Romanesque and Chicago School elements, and is one of the first Chicago-style buildings in the city. Its stone and brickwork visible in the arches, capitals, and face are not weight bearing, as the columns and beams take care of that.

A pioneer who came out to the West the hard way, by land, William Sherlock was an Irish immigrant who became successful in the livery business. Records do not confirm rumors that a physician named Watson was his closest confidante. Sherlock didn't finance this building, but rather owned the property it was built on.

12 BISHOP'S HOUSE 1879
219–223 SW Stark Street, north side between Second
and Third Avenues
Architect: P. Heurn (San Francisco)

Something of a local celebrity, the Victorian Gothic front of this building is a real eye-catcher. Originally the Bishop's House contained a church library, the living quarters of Archbishop William Gross, and an insurance agent's office. The archbishop only resided here for a year; he had misgivings about the church's location in such a seedy part of town. The eponymous tenant's faith was reflected in the beautiful cathedral window in the center of the third floor, as well as other equally obvious elements. (The fact that it is shaped like a miter and was next door to a cathedral provided another design tie-in.)

11 *Sherlock Building*

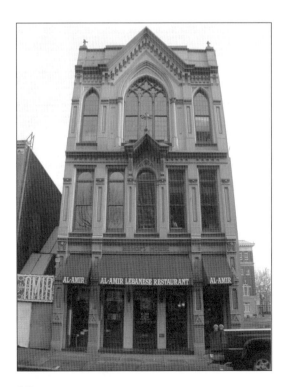

12 *Bishop's House*

This particular building qualifies as "High Victorian Gothic" in that it hails from the correct time period and draws upon German, Italian, and English stylings for its look. The cast-iron columns are apparently a bit of an anomaly for this style. It springs vertically from a narrow width; it was built next to a seventy-foot-wide cathedral that was demolished in 1894.

Between 1911 and 1915, the architecturally oriented Portland Atelier (French for "workshop") met here, with A. E. Doyle and Morris H. Whitehouse presiding over the studio, which focused on teaching craftsmanship and design skills to young architects. The Bishop's House has also functioned at various times as the headquarters for a Chinese tong society, a sign company, and a speakeasy. Currently housing a Lebanese restaurant, the Bishop's House is the only Portland building that has witnessed baptisms, bathtub gin, and *baba ganouj.*

The building was restored in 1965 by William Roberts.

✦ The Portland Atelier was set up by Ellis F. Lawrence (of the firm Lawrence and Holford), the man who founded the University of Oregon School of Architecture.

✦ Historian E. Kimbark MacColl wrote that police vice arrests in the late 1890s were often foiled, possibly due to underground phone wires running from the old Portland police headquarters to the Bishop's House, then a Chinese tong spot.

13 CONCORD BUILDING 1891

208 SW Stark Street, southwest corner of Stark Street and
   Second Avenue
Architect: Whidden and Lewis

This is a genuinely engaging building. It has stone-faced first-floor piers (and a great entryway) while utilizing rusticated Japanese brick with buff sandstone trim for the upper stories. Most interesting about this building is its very conservative and regular rectangular window pattern, typical of what we have come to expect of office buildings today, but at the time of its construction, it must have seemed quite unusual and modern. The top level's arches are an interesting classical touch to what otherwise could be construed as an early precursor to the metal-and-glass office-boxes of Anycity, U.S.A. But it is from the simple juxtaposition between the arches and straight lines that the building derives its strength, synthesizing the classical with the modern. This building may be the first to herald the coming modern age, years ahead of its time.

13 *Concord Building*

✦ Whidden and Lewis, the architects of this building, maintained an office on the sixth floor of the Concord Building. Later, in the 1930s, a beanery operated in the bottom floor here.

14 GRAND STABLE AND CARRIAGE BUILDINGS 1885

*415–521 SW Second Avenue, west side between Washington and
   Stark Streets
Architect: Warren H. Williams*

The cost to create this stately, Italianate cast-iron front, four-story building was $27,000. The buildings were erected by Simeon G. Reed, a noted local businessman who founded Reed College in his will.

✦ The motto of the Carriage Company, the original proprietors of the building: "We Furnish the Most Stylish Turnouts in the City."

14   *Grand Stable and Carriage Building*

15 WALDO BLOCK 1886, 1984
201–215 SW Washington/431–439 SW Second Avenue, north side
    of Washington between Second and Third Avenues
Architect: Unknown/Restoration by Allen, McMath, Hawkins

Just down from the Grand Stable and Carriage Building is the Waldo Block. Another Italianate storefront, this three-story building seems a bit more restrained and elegant than most of its contemporaries, despite the fact that the name "WALDO" is above the main entrance. It's named after Judge John B. Waldo, who served on the Oregon Supreme Court.

15   *Waldo Block*

16   *Spalding Building*

16   SPALDING BUILDING 1911

aka the Oregon Bank Building
319 SW Washington Street, northwest corner of Washington Street
and Third Avenue
Architect: Cass Gilbert (New York)

In the early 1900s, this structure passed for a skyscraper. It is an entirely respectable American Renaissance–style building, with a gray brick façade covering a skeleton made of steel. There is a terra-cotta cornice and some terra-cotta ornamentation visible on it, as well as a painted limestone attic story at the top.

The Spalding follows a pattern sometimes called "tripartite composition," which is also visible on dozens of other downtown buildings. This building pattern mimics the construction of a column: a base and shaft, topped by a capital.

Cass Gilbert's masterpiece was his design of New York's celebrated 792-foot Woolworth Building (he worked on this project while the Spalding Building was constructed). He also designed Washington, D.C.'s Supreme Court Building. The Ohio native worked in conjunction for a time with James Knox Taylor, who designed the Custom House near Union Station.

17 OREGON PIONEER BUILDING/HUBER'S RESTAURANT 1910

Originally the Railway Exchange Building, aka Builders Exchange Building
320 SW Stark Street, south side between Third and Fourth Avenues
Architect: David Chambers Lewis

This six-story building contains Huber's Restaurant (founded 1879), which is Portland's oldest eating establishment, having moved to this "new" location after thirty-one years in business. The proprietors chose wisely; the building is very handsome and has the distinction of being Portland's first major building made of concrete, as well as a pretty good example of Chicago-style architecture. The building also hints at the architectural stylings that lay in wait for Portland in the coming decades; for although it has some classical detailing (I like the arched windows on the top floor), it is essentially a functional-looking commercial structure.

Named for bartender Frank Huber, Huber's had no tables when it opened at this location; patrons simply stood, drank, conversed, and waited for a booth to open up. The manager was a Cantonese chef named Jim Louie, who specialized in shrimp coleslaw and gave away free turkey sandwiches with every drink.

17 *Oregon Pioneer Building/Huber's Restaurant*

18 DEKUM BUILDING 1892

aka "The Dekum"
519 SW Third Avenue, southwest corner of Third Avenue and
 Washington Street
Architects: McCaw, Martin and White

The Dekum Building cost $300,000 to build, a sizable sum in its day, and the investment still pays dividends today. It is a very powerful Romanesque structure with great presence, although this type of building went out of vogue not long after its completion.

While cast-iron was the rage in the rest of Portland, and the columns on the Dekum emulate cast-iron fashion, this building was made from solely Oregonian materials. The floral terra-cotta friezes and patterns were another major departure from the conventions of the time, although they seem to match nicely with everything else now, deriving somewhat from Art Nouveau form. Rough-cut sandstone makes up the first three stories; take note of the extraordinary design on the Third Avenue entranceway. The top five floors of the Dekum are redbrick and glazed terra-cotta with floral designs, with the Richardsonian Romanesque features of the building shining through in the seventh-floor window arcade tops. If you look at the very top of the building, there are spaces known as *machicolations* in places in the parapet. Their original architectural usage was to allow the dropping of unfriendly items such as burning pitch, rocks, or a dead cat upon attackers below.

The alteration of the ground-floor piers took place during an exterior renovation after World War II. The building was later restored by Bill Naito.

Frank Dekum (1823–94) came to Portland from Germany in 1853, and with Fred Bickel opened a small confectionary shop, Portland's first. Very successful in finance and building, he eventually lost his substantial banking investments in the financial panic of 1893, which probably contributed to his death a year later.

✦ As president of the hugely influential German Song Bird Society, Frank Dekum was instrumental in the importation of goldfinches, nightingales, and our beloved starlings to Portland.

✦ In true Teutonic fashion, the masons on this job supposedly drank beer instead of coffee while working.

18 *Dekum Building*

19 HAMILTON BUILDING 1893, RESTORED 1977

529 SW Third Avenue, west side of Third Avenue, next to
   Dekum Building
Architects: Whidden and Lewis

You could walk past this building and never notice it. (Perhaps you have already done so.) Nevertheless, it anticipated the direction of commercial architecture decades ahead of its time. Commercial constructions during the Hamilton Building's timeframe tended to be ornate, even overdone, affairs, but this structure has very geometric and precise windows, and an unpretentious design with just enough decoration to avoid being soulless. It is brilliant in an understated way, a terrific compositional balance between the overly ornate and the entirely unadorned.

This six-story office structure has a cast-iron post bottom, with pink, black, and gray granite columns. Above, the spare ornamentation of the windows with cable moldings and the Japanese-brick face make for an understated, even classy building, which looks good near the complementary Dekum Building.

19 *Hamilton Building*

20 POSTAL BUILDING 1900
Originally the Failing Building
310 SW Third Avenue, between Washington and Alder Street
Architects: Whidden and Lewis
Restoration: Allen, McMath and Hawkins

If you like terra-cotta decoration, you should enjoy this building's classical detailing all over its boxy exterior.

20 *Postal Building*

21 ODS TOWER 1999

601 SW Second Avenue, west side between Alder and Morrison Streets
Architect: ZGF Partnership

Named for ODS Health Plans, this twenty-four-story, 395,303-square-foot office tower's east face is slightly curved to give a better view of the river below, with a special floor design that allows six corner offices at each end. This, and its layered green-glazed glass and white pattern catches the eye, although according to some, not necessarily in the best spirit of the phrase. (Those unhappy with the building choose to call it the "Odious Tower.")

As noted in the introduction, contemporary architects working in Portland seem to want to compensate for their buildings' lack of intrinsic ornamentation by commissioning large works of art to prominently feature in front of their structures. In an attempt to make it stand out more, there is a huge cedar tree carcass bolted to the modern high-rise. The promotional literature for the piece trumpeted that it would "call attention to the state's majestic trees both in terms of natural beauty and economic vitality." Although the wooden hulk has been bronzed (at the bottom) and covered in aluminum (at the top), it still serves as an expensive reminder ($380,000) of the perils of combining the beauty of natural wood with the sterility of a modern glass-and-metal building.

21 *ODS Tower*

22 Bank of America Financial Center

22 BANK OF AMERICA FINANCIAL CENTER 1987

Originally One Financial Center
121 SW Morrison Street, between First and Second Avenues
Architect: ZGF Partnership

This eighteen-story building has a granite-and-glass exterior in a nearly plaid pattern, and a great skylight. The green neon hat was added in 1995, giving the structure a bit of Los Angeles kitsch and making it an object of vituperation. Although the building apparently has its advocates, architectural writer Randy Gragg has noted "among other architects [it is] the most loathed building in downtown . . . ."

23 VAN RENSSELAER BUILDING/LOVE BUILDING/ HARKER BUILDING 1878–80

65–73 SW Yamhill Street, 730 and 728 SW First Avenue, northeast
corner of Yamhill Street and First Avenue
Architect(s): Unknown

Here are three buildings in a row, originally built at the same time, with a unifying style. The top two floors of the Van Rensselaer were added six years after the initial construction, resulting in the odd phenomenon of a cast-iron building with differences in style easily spotted from one story to

23   *Van Rensselaer Building*

the next. The projecting masonry brackets at the top give it an extra air of lordliness. This structure served as a J.C. Penney warehouse sometime in the early 1900s.

The Love Building (730 First Avenue) was renovated in the mid-1960s; none of its original iron remains. At 728 First Avenue, the Harker Building, while not as imposing as the Van Rensselaer, possesses some similar features. A music conservatory originally existed on its second floor.

24 NORTHRUP BLOSSOM AND FITCH BUILDING 1858
731–737 SW Naito Parkway, between Morrison and
*   Yamhill Streets*
Architect: Unknown

Portland's oldest surviving masonry structure that is still as it was originally designed, the older section of the building is the south side, originally known as the Northrup and Blossom Building. This brick Italianate edifice was originally one-story; the second floor was probably added in the early 1870s. Three large arches in the front show the site of the original doors.

The Fitch Building was built in 1873, also originally as a one-story building. Efforts were made to make it resemble its older neighbor, although eventually its front got cast-iron columns as well. The two buildings were joined together and raised to their present three floors sometime before 1894.

✦ The original part of this structure is the only survivor of the Great Fire of 1873 in the Yamhill Historic District.

25 POPPLETON BUILDING 1867

aka Seges Artbar, Sharff Furniture
818 SW First Avenue, east side between Yamhill and Taylor Streets
Architect: Unknown, possibly E. M. Burton

One block south of the previously noted Van Rensselaer/Love/Harker triumvirate is yet another trio of buildings. These three (the Pearne, Poppleton, and Patrick buildings) do not share the same similarity in style and date of construction, but they are all right next to each other, helping one visualize the cast-iron thoroughfare that First Avenue once was.

The energetic Poppleton Building really jumps out at the observer, and it owes much of that life to the district's huge fire in 1873. Only the iron columns and piers were saved, and work began anew on the building. The first two stories were completed in the mid-1870s, with the third story and roof added five years later. One assumes that the fire damage inspired the designers to be extremely bold in their remodeling of the building.

25 *Poppleton Building*

The roof is the Poppleton's most striking feature. Apparently added in 1890, it has a dramatic pediment flanked with a finial on each side. From the central bull's-eye window, an Italian woman's head looks calmly down, flanked by rather perverse satyrs in support brackets. Elsewhere, there are dense patterns of medallions, scrolls, and ornamented columns. All in all, a dramatic show, and a worthy neighbor to the Patrick Building's orderly presence to the south.

The Pearne Building (1865) was designed by Absalom B. Hallock and E. M. Burton. Hallock, a Quaker from New York, came to Portland in 1850. He was the first surveyor Portland ever had, and its first architect— a potent combination. Hallock was instrumental in the creation of many buildings in Portland, including the first ones to use cast-iron fronts.

26 MIKADO BLOCK 1880

117 SW Taylor Street, northwest corner of Taylor Street and
  First Avenue
Architect: C. E. Smith

This building was remodeled six years after its construction. At that time, Gilbert and Sullivan wrote a highly successful operetta called *The Mikado, or The Town of Titipu*. On the basis of that work's popularity, and for the fact that the name "Titipu Block" would sound foolish at best and inappropriate at worst, the structure was named Mikado.

26 *Mikado Block*

The Victorian Italianate's rather simple first-floor exterior gives way to rich detailing on the upper two stories, including exotic detailing on the cornice. Tenants over the years have included a Civil War veterans' organization (the Grand Army of the Republic) and Goodwill Industries. In 1971, thieves took wooden carvings from the heraldic crest at the top of the building and a cast-iron head from the arched entry.

✦ C. E. Smith, the original owner, was a member of a dreaded group who called themselves *Savoyards*. This fraternity was distinguished by their feverish dedication to community theater, and the works of Gilbert and Sullivan in particular. The horror!

✦ This area was once the site of a number of flophouses, from which unwary sailors would find themselves shanghaied onto ships leaving Portland.

27 *Ancient Order of United Workman Temple*

27 ANCIENT ORDER OF UNITED WORKMEN TEMPLE
1892
aka Tourny Apartments
915 SW Second Avenue
Architect: Justus Krumbein

This mysterious Richardsonian Romanesque building was originally built as a club; it has masonry on the ground floor, brick throughout. Its red massiveness and impressively mossy Ionic columns on the fifth and sixth stories make for a nice contrast to the antiseptic federal courthouse looming behind it.

✦ Military and secret societies became very popular after the Civil War and by 1900, there were over seven million members of various clubs like the AOUM.

28 LOTUS CARDROOM AND CAFÉ 1906

Originally Hotel Albion
932 SW Third Avenue
Architect: Unknown

A worthy weathered sidekick to the temple next door, this utilitarian brick building with the pronounced keystones gives card sharks a flavorful place to hang out while waiting for their court times.

29 AUDITORIUM BUILDING AND MUSIC HALL 1894

920–928 SW Third Avenue, west side between Salmon and
  Taylor Streets
Architect: F. Manson White

Designed by the same architect who created the Imperial Hotel, this energetic Romanesque four-story building has a redbrick face and some nice capital carvings on it, as well as interesting arches and decorations that vary from one story to the next. The terra-cotta friezes below the strongly projecting cornice give it an extra flair, as does the botanical theme one sees throughout. The arched windows on the fourth floor have their own columns with terra-cotta capitals, a nice touch.

This building was originally designed for a wholesale liquor company, which was on the first floor. The second floor was a dance hall, and from the third floor to the top of the building was a concert hall. In the early 1900s, the concert hall was eradicated by the addition of apartments in a newly added fourth floor. High-density housing does have its costs.

✦ Emil Jorgenson, the director of the 1905 Lewis and Clark Expo, owned this building.

29   *Auditorium Building and Music Hall*

30   THE GILBERT BUILDING 1893

319 SW Taylor Street
Architects: Whidden and Lewis, most likely

The decorative use of brickwork throughout this building distinguishes it, making some people think it should probably be situated right where the monstrosity known as the Wells Fargo Tower currently sits. That way, this building could provide a nice companion to City Hall. The roofline of the Gilbert echoes the Romanesque arches in the inset window bays on the top floor. The yellow brick patterns are fascinating, and for once, a building has quoining that does not stand out in colossal blocks of contrasting texture.

YAMHILL DISTRICT BRIDGES

Before these bridges existed, folks either took ferries across or simply stayed on their side of the river. Historian Percy Maddux relates the refrain of a local poem from 1870: *"They're going to build it, I feel it yet, / A bridge across the Willamette!"*

Yet some opposed bridge construction for fear that they would prohibit shipping and hurt business. An injunction against the construction of the Morrison Bridge went all the way to the Federal Supreme Court before it was struck down. Because of this, Maddux suggested an alternate couplet: *"In spite of all, we'll get it, damn it! / A bridge across the Willamette."*

✦ HAWTHORNE BRIDGE 1910

Designer: J. A. L. Waddell of Waddell and Harrington (Kansas City)

The Hawthorne Bridge is the oldest operating *vertical lift bridge* (a bridge that moves up in a horizontal position) in the U.S. It is also the oldest remaining highway structure bridging the Willamette River. The Hawthorne is an industrial-looking bridge, but its size and historicity lend it a certain charm. It has two 165-foot steel towers that house red 888,000-pound concrete counterweights. These are used for lifting the bridge at each end of the lift span.

✦ MORRISON BRIDGE 1958

Designers: Sverdrup, Parcel of St. Louis/Moffat, Taylor and Nichol (Portland)

Located at the site of the oldest regular transportation route across the Willamette River, the Morrison Bridge is raised with two 900-ton concrete counterweights in the bridge's main piers, allowing maritime traffic to pass beneath, and defining the span as a *bascule* (French for "seesaw") bridge. It is undoubtedly the least visually interesting of the five bridges downtown. The Morrison is named for John L. Morrison, a Scottish immigrant who came to Oregon in 1842. Morrison served as an officer in the Oregon Rangers, sustaining three arrow wounds in his adopted state's service. No records are available on how many bullet wounds he inflicted in retaliation.

✦ BURNSIDE BRIDGE 1910

Designers: Gustav Lindenthal, Joseph Strauss
Design Engineer: Chester A. Houghtaling

The Burnside Bridge is an exercise in concrete; its lift span deck is solid concrete and steel, and two huge concrete counterweights (1,700 tons each) in the bridge's main piers swing the 133-foot spans vertically. Like the Morrison Bridge, the Burnside is of the bascule type. (Technically, it is a *steel double-leaf Strauss bascule*.) The Burnside boasts some architectural flourishes, as its two cantilevered control turrets have decorated roofs and bottoms that add pizzazz to the structure. Designer Joseph Strauss also worked on the Golden Gate Bridge. The "dean of American bridge engineers" (although he was from Czechoslovakia), Gustav Lindenthal was commissioner of bridges in New York City. Among many others, he designed the Hell Gate (the world's highest arch bridge) and the Manhattan Bridge.

CHAPTER 5

BROADWAY BRIDGE.

WILLAMETTE RIVER

STEEL BRIDGE.

(14)

UNION
STATION

(13)

(11)
GLISAN ST
(12)

FLANDERS ST

8TH AVE

BROADWAY

6TH AVE

5TH AVE

4TH AVE

EVERETT ST

3RD AVE

2ND AVE

(9)

(8)

1ST AVE

(10)

DAVIS ST

(7)

(6)

COUCH ST

(4) (3)
(2)
(1)

(5)

BURNSIDE ST

N
W   E
S

OLD TOWN/CHINATOWN

5a   *Chinatown Gate bronze lion*

CHAPTER 5

OLD TOWN/
CHINATOWN

"Do not let us deceive ourselves in this important matter; it is impossible, as impossible as to raise the dead, to restore anything that has ever been great or beautiful in architecture." –John Ruskin, *The Seven Lamps of Architecture*

Old Town is bordered roughly by Hoyt Street to the north, the Park Blocks to the west, and Burnside Street to the south. In 1843, city founders Asa Lovejoy and William Overton marked the site of the first claim in what is now Old Town with a tomahawk. (Don't try this technique now; it's a felony.) As this was once the commercial center of Portland, many of the city's oldest buildings survive here, untouched by the demolitions that happened all around them.

Old Town suffered the same neglect that the Yamhill District did, although its descent did not begin as quickly, as out-of-town sailors and lumbermen lodging their families in town kept money flowing into the area. By the 1930s, though, Old Town also became a locale frequented more by ne'er-do-wells than respectable folk, while the next decade brought the nefarious widespread demolitions.

The Skidmore Design zone, created in 1959, established architectural parameters over new construction and remodeling in the area. In the mid-1970s, a variety of groups persuaded the city to establish a historic district around Skidmore Fountain. This done, financial incentives kept existing property owners happy and encouraged outside investors to the area, resulting in a dramatically successful upgrade to the district.

1 "MADE IN OREGON" SIGN/HIRSCH-WEISS BUILDING
1907/1941
67 W. Burnside Street
Architect: Unknown

While this building is not very interesting, the celebrated sign atop it is. This massive neon sign was originally an ad for White Satin Sugar, and showed sugar pouring into a bag. It was converted to White Stag in the late 1950s. Although White Stag moved to Van Nuys, California, in 1973, the sign remained and was designated an official landmark in 1975. It remained in place afterward, but problems arose when White Stag discontinued rental payments on the sign in 1988. Warnaco, Bill Naito, and Ramsay Signs maintained the landmark, which underwent a switch in advertising to "Made in Oregon" (with the stag still in place) in 1997.

✦　Elizabeth Blair Hirsch, wife of the building's owner, had the idea for lighting up the stag's nose with red in December.

2 OLD TOWN WATER TOWER
Northwest Naito Parkway, on top of the old White Stag building,
*　north of the "Made in Oregon" reindeer*
Architect: Unknown

The genesis of the name "Old Town" in lieu of Skid Row came about in the 1970s, when Bill Naito had the words painted on the highly visible water tower. Essentially a wood barrel on a steel platform, it was used to store water for the fire department's emergencies. The original was dismantled in 2000, after the City of Portland declared the old tank a dangerous structure. The hope is that a new, nonoperational tank will eventually be installed here. Such measures may not be cost effective, as the tower has no means to recompense such an investment, but it would help to preserve a part of the city's original skyline.

✦　At least six other water towers exist in the Northwest in various stages of disrepair.

3 BICKEL BLOCK 1883

Southwest corner of Naito Parkway and NW Couch Street
Architect: Justus Krumbein

Across from the Japanese American Historical Plaza is the somewhat Gothic Bickel Block. (Say that fast.) It was owned by candy maker Frederick Bickel, a native of Germany who immigrated to St. Louis in 1848. Bickel was business partner with Frank Dekum, and the two opened their first confectionery shop in Portland on Front Street in 1953. Built thirty years later, and in the same year as Bickel's retirement from the business, this building has some interesting and complex geometric patterns in its detailing, though it is showing signs of wear and tear.

3 *Bickel Block detail*

4 BLAGEN BLOCK 1888, RESTORED 1980–83

78 NW Couch Street, on the southeast corner of First Avenue and
*   Couch Street*
Architect: Unknown

Near the Bickel Block is the Blagen Block. A real treat to behold, this Italianate building is the most recent surviving example of the cast-iron columns and arches that once dominated this neighborhood. Try to imagine storefronts like these going down the street as far as the eye can see.

The top three floors of this building are brick, with cement-plaster facing and some wood and iron detailing. Each floor has a different win-

4   *Blagen Block detail*

dow design for maximum variety. The manifold embellishments include metal scrolls at the top of the building that bear the owner's name and the date of construction. Women's heads can be seen at the roof and at the fourth floor. As the Statue of Liberty had been put in place two years earlier in New York, their spiked crowns may be an homage to Lady Liberty. Below the women are gaping lions' heads two-thirds of the way up the second-story windows. At the side corners and center of the building are columns that also have lions' heads, in addition to scrolls, arrows, laurel and acanthus leaves, stars, and stripes.

This building was constructed to house a sail- and tent-making business and was deemed an especially sturdy building, withstanding heavy machinery and steam-elevator vibrations. Part of the restoration of the building involved removing many layers of paint to reveal the original blue-gray colors.

5 CHINATOWN GATE 1986

North side of Fourth Avenue and Burnside Street
Architect: Yu Tang Wang

Two mammoth bronze lions flank this nearly forty-foot gateway, frightening the timid and delighting children. Above them are the five roofs and sixty-four dragons of the China Gate, dedicated in 1986, in memory of

Portland's Chinese residents. Keep in mind that Portland's historical Chinatown existed to the south of Burnside Street, not on this side of the street, as far as Washington and Alder Streets.

At the end of the Civil War in 1865, Portland's total population of 6,168 included 2,000 Chinese residents, with eight thousand more Chinese immigrants joining them over the next fifteen years. Revolving around Alder Street south of Burnside Street, a traditional Chinese culture (complete with music, art, trade, and celebrations) flourished in Portland. Outsiders were drawn to Chinatown's food and gambling. But as job competition increased in the 1880s for menial labor that white settlers had previously been only too happy to give the Chinese, anti-Chinese sentiment in Portland resulted in arson and beatings. Portland still qualified as a relative haven for the Chinese compared to the prejudicial fever that swept through Seattle, Tacoma, and California.

Most of these Chinese immigrants anticipated a return to their homeland, and so they did not construct new buildings but rather decorated and remodeled existing ones. With the increasingly rickety buildings in the district being demolished, this centralized exotic influence began to fade, leaving behind little in the way of a historical architectural heritage.

✦   In the 1850s, a new paper called the *Oregonian* referred to people of Chinese descent as "Celestials."

5b   *Chinatown Gate*

6 *Simon Building from back*

7 *Merchants' Hotel*

6 SIMON BUILDING 1892

West side of Third Avenue, between Couch and Davis Streets
Architect: Unknown

This modestly sized building's interior was gutted in a fire. Destined to become a parking lot, it was saved by preservationists—and became a parking lot. The façade of this must-see building remains, while the interior is paved and awaits your vehicle.

7 MERCHANTS' HOTEL 1884

aka Merchant Block
123 NW Second Avenue, southwest corner on Davis Street
Architect: probably Warren H. Williams

The cast-iron columns for this building are more than sixteen feet tall, with blank-faced women's heads bolted on about twelve feet up. It was renovated in 1968 with no change in the ladies' demeanor. Be sure to look at the Davis Street side of this building.

In 1868, three brothers named Louis, Theodore, and Adolph Nicolai moved to Portland to begin a sawmill. They did well for themselves, and invested in this building (which took four years to build), which occupies a full half-block.

This building has also housed a bar, brothel, billiards hall, and most notoriously, a cracker factory.

✦ In addition to other Japanese-American businesses that have been housed in the building, the *Japanese Oregon Weekly* was printed here after World War I.

8 NORTHWEST NATURAL GAS BUILDING/ ONE PACIFIC SQUARE 1983

aka R2D2
223 SW First Avenue, west end of Broadway Bridge
Architect: Campbell, Yost and Grube

This hexagonal tower succeeds in becoming an entirely reflective surface for its surroundings. Given its prominent setting in an interesting architectural milieu, this is a successful strategy, if not a very imaginative one.

8 *Northwest Natural Gas Building/One Pacific Square*

9 LAN SU YUAN ("GARDEN OF THE AWAKENING ORCHID") 2000
aka Classical Chinese Garden
Between NW Second and Third Avenues, Everett and Flanders Streets
Architects and Garden Design: Kuang Zhen Yan, Suzhou Institute of
*   Landscape Architectural Design, He Feng Chun (landscape architect),*
Robertson Merryman and Barnes Architects, KPFF Engineering
*   Consultants*

Behind the tile-roofed pavilion, beautiful pond, and carefully framed views of this garden is an interesting melding of yin and yang; a mix between an ancient culture and, well, Portland. This constitutes the largest Suzhou-style Chinese garden in the world outside of China. Suzhou-style gardens are a thirteenth-century urban Chinese design derived from a merchant class trying to bring the country into the city. They are intended to be refuges for thoughtfulness amid a combination of architectural and natural elements.

Every aspect of the garden, from every angle, has been meticulously laid out to create the most auspicious spatial harmony. All parts were made in China with manual tools, then imported; the symbolism of each part is sometimes obvious (the mountain in the center) and sometimes more complex (the winding path one can take through the garden.)

Design challenges included linguistic barriers, as well as how to construct a culturally accurate garden of interlocked timbers and unfixed stone that lives up to current seismic standards; the solution was to hide the steel reinforcing rods within them. Feng shui, the Chinese concept of energy routing, does not do well with square shapes like a city block; the problem was partially solved by the usage of staggered walls. Some problems were less complicated but more aggravating; the wood columns were inundated with moisture when they arrived. Upon drying, they cracked, and had to be patched with epoxy and then bored into to allow the insertion of steel bars to make the structures seismically safe.

City commissioner Mike Lindbergh came up with the idea of this garden as a cultural exchange in 1985, when he was in one of Suzhou's famed gardens, and Bill Naito and Mayor Vera Katz were instrumental in making it happen.

✦   An ancient city of canals fifty miles west of Shanghai, Suzhou is something of a Chinese Venice, though it is 1,700 years older than its Italian counterpart.

9 *Lan Su Yuan*

10 U.S. CUSTOM HOUSE 1901

220 NW Eighth Avenue
Architect: James Knox Taylor/Supervisor: Edgar M. Lazarus

The Army Corps of Engineers currently occupies this unusually designed French-Renaissance building. It has granite facing, terra-cotta walls, and is currently federal-government property, so watch your step. There are a lot of steps to watch out for, as the infill for this building was huge; the pilings for the building go down eighty to one hundred feet, and the Custom House was substantially built up on its site to avoid the flooding problems that plagued this part of town during the early twentieth century.

If you look at the terra-cotta lentil stones over the window arches, you'll find interesting governmental symbols like the staff of Aesculapius and the dreaded glove on a stick. The ornamentation of weighing scales is interesting, as they reflect both the weighing of goods inspected for customs and the traditional scales of justice. Courthouses were originally intended for the top two floors of the Custom House, and although it is easy to forget in modern times, the revenue of customs duties was once hugely important to the Portland City coffers. This helps to explain the presence of the forbidding ironwork on the windows of the first floor; this is original to the building and was designed to protect the goods in the building that were going through customs.

10 *U.S. Custom House*

The two towers visible from the front (west) side of the building are for ventilation, and do not contain bells. While on the west side, note that the impressive balcony is, sadly, inaccessible.

✦ James Knox Taylor was the supervising architect of the Treasury Department.

✦ The federal government would not mind unloading this property if it could, but its unusual shape, inaccessibility, and seismic instability disqualify it from many usages. The open courtyard on the west side could make a delightful spot for dining *al fresco,* however.

UNION STATION AREA

Captain John Couch, 28, in command of the brig *Maryland,* sailed on his first trip to Oregon from the east coast in 1839. He made note of a spot north of Ross Island as a site where he could safely bring ships year-round. Subsequent voyages convinced him of the worth of this spot, and, in 1845, Couch claimed a square mile of land just north of Portland, to be called "Couch's Addition." An influential man, Couch's vote of confidence in the area was instrumental in diverting commerce away from Oregon City and other maritime commerce rivals on the river and to the newly born Portland.

Portions of this area, especially close to the river, were a quagmire at the time. An early visitor remarked, "The streets . . . are just mud and water, mixed up into a very good batter," and this was particularly true in Couch's Addition; a small, shallow lake covered what is now the railroad yards. (To the west of it was the Couch home.) Landfills facilitated construction, although major floods came as recently as 1948. As the blocks filled in, the area became known as the "Alphabet District," because it (unlike the rest of Portland) had alphabetized street names intersecting with the numbered avenues.

With the opening of Union Station in 1890, commercial and industrial construction went up in the portion of the Alphabet District closest to the river, and many of the city's oldest and best brick warehouses can still be found in this area. More recently, with the dismantling of the Lovejoy ramp leading up to the Broadway Bridge, there has been an expansion of condominiums, townhouses, and apartments in the area that show some interesting color and design choices, if not historically sympathetic architecture. Particularly exciting is the news that world-renowned architect Frank O. Gehry (Guggenheim Bilbao, Experience Music Project) will be working on a project in the area.

11 FEDERAL BUILDING 1918

aka the U.S. Post Office Building
511 NW Broadway
Architects: Lewis P. Hobert and James A. Wetmore

A solid Italian Renaissance building, but not one that screams "federal government!" the way many ostentatious government buildings from this era do. Its ornamentation makes it a solid architectural lynchpin in its domain. Although the Immigration Service is the current occupant of this building, it was originally a post office; if one inspects its entrance columns, the lettering is still visible.

The building features federal motifs such as eagles above the main entrance, and the limestone exterior gives it a properly sober and gray demeanor. Above, the Chicago-style windows contribute to the building's seriousness, though if one carefully inspects the window decoration on the ground floor, the unexpected appearance of small human nudes lessens the building's primness.

Inside is much of the splendor one would expect of a federal building of its era: marble floors, travertine walls, and decorated plaster ceilings with gold trim and peacock motifs. Although there was a public outcry at the time of the building's opening for its ornateness, it does not appear to be overly decorated at all; its external simplicity is a nice balance to its internal décor. Although it once had bronze inserts lining the main hall, it has been infilled to an unfortunate degree with drywall.

✦   To see how far "drop-down" ceilings containing fluorescent lights have dipped into the building's first floor, simply examine the arched windows on the first floor from outside. From the blackened area up is wasted space.

12 OREGON CRACKER COMPANY BUILDING 1901

aka Portland Biscuit Company Building
616 NW Glisan Street, southwest corner of Glisan Street and
*   Sixth Avenue*
Architect: Unknown

The Pacific Coast Biscuit Company.

Robber barons trembled in fear at its name. Evildoers shook in their shoes contemplating its fine products. And well they should have. The Pacific Coast Biscuit Company was a titan in its field, ranking third in the

11 *Federal Building*

country in terms of total biscuit and cracker production. The honest people of Portland, good and true, ate their crackers in the knowledge that they probably had passed through the Oregon Cracker Company Building. Chew a few saltines and appreciate the nicely arched window features, fine brick-work, and the blocky, stolid appearance of this structure. Now try to whistle.
✦ The name of the Keebler Elf was uttered with hatred hereabouts. In 1927, several bakeries decided to join forces to form the United Biscuit Company of America, which featured the products of Godfrey Keebler (among others). To avoid confusion, the network decided to adopt one brand for all its products. The Keebler mascot, created by a Chicago adver-tising firm, helped to make the Keebler company one of the top sellers of cookies and crackers in the country.

13 *Union Station*

13 UNION STATION 1890–96
800 NW Sixth Avenue
Architect: Van Brunt and Howe (St. Louis)

This is one of the most handsome of Portland's landmark symbols. The Italian Renaissance Union Station's 150-foot redbrick clock tower and prominent positioning at the base of the Broadway Bridge combine to make it perhaps the most visible building of Portland's Old Town district. The train station holds something in common with similar towers in northern Italy with its stucco, molded brick, and overhanging tile roof. The structures are of pressed brick, with gray sandstone trimmings and panels of stucco.

Interior remodeling courtesy of Pietro Belluschi occurred in the 1930s, with Italian marble sheathing being added to the walls and floor and columns being subtracted. Union Station almost fell victim to Robert Moses's 1943 rehabilitation plans for Old Town ("Railroad stations should be as modern as airports," he wrote of this "obsolete facility"), but it survived to be substantially renovated in the mid-1980s and restored in the late 1990s. The landmark neon signs on the tower reading "Go By Train" were installed after World War II and were almost removed in the station's remodel forty years later since they weren't original to the building.

The man responsible for Union Station was German-born Henry Villard (1835–90). Acquiring the financial properties of the bankrupt Ben Holladay in 1876 enabled Villard to build the first transcontinental rail line into Portland.

Villard went bankrupt in 1883, and his financial interests were taken over, including his completed plans for the train station, which had an estimated construction price of $1.5 million for a "Grand Union Depot," where the Central Post Office now resides. The front of the building would have been toward the south, with the tracks where the North Park Blocks are now.

The inheritors of Villard's business interests did not use that site. The St. Louis firm of Van Brunt and Howe was brought in, and they made modifications to the existing plans, including the relocation of the station to its present spot and the addition of the station's tower. Flooding and money problems made this a long and nasty construction. The initial building investment exceeded $300,000, $60,000 of which was expended on underground work in piling and foundation. The tower was almost not constructed because of these financial difficulties, but the architects insisted on its inclusion to maintain the integrity of their plans.

✦ Famed African explorer Henry M. Stanley passed through Union Station in 1895.

14 ALBERS BROTHERS MILLING COMPANY BUILDING
1909–11
1118–1130 Naito Parkway
Architect: Unknown

Time was, if you were looking to buy flapjack flour in bulk, this was the place. At one point, the Albers Brothers were the largest grain and cereal manufacturing company this side of, well, Nevada. This brick building is the oldest feed mill still in Portland (it contained a dog-food factory at one time), and it is enjoyable for its painted artwork on the silos, which are nicely visible from the Broadway Bridge. The old building went through a dramatic recycling/renovation to waterfront office space in 1989, and is now home to the Wheat Marketing Center Museum.

During World War I, J. Henry Albers, mill president, was arrested on suspicion of treason for singing in German on a train ride from San Francisco. Sentenced to three years in jail, he successfully appealed but was expelled from his Elks Lodge and died shortly thereafter.

14   *Albers Brothers Milling Company Building*

OLD TOWN BRIDGES

✦ STEEL BRIDGE 1912

Designer: Waddell and Harrington (Kansas City)

What's not to like about the Steel Bridge? Admittedly, the name isn't very imaginative, but still, it's fashionably black, it has a complex network of steel trusses, and it's a one-of-a-kind vertically telescoping bridge. A *vertically telescoping bridge* is one that can raise a portion of its span vertically and evenly. The Steel Bridge qualifies as the *only* bridge in the world that is a *"double-deck telescoping vertical lift bridge."* That is, both of its levels can be raised vertically. Trains use the lower deck, which when raised, fits nicely into the bottom of the upper deck.

About that name—the precursor to the Steel Bridge was an 1888 double-deck bridge made of steel. It was called "the Steel Bridge." Old habits die hard.

✦ BROADWAY BRIDGE 1913

Designer: Ralph Modjeski

Another bridge that keeps drivers honest with its open-grating steel deck, the Broadway is the most northerly of the Waterfront Park downtown bridges. The longest of the drawbridges in Portland (297 feet), it originally included trolley tracks, which were removed in 1940. Like the Burnside and Morrison Bridges, the Broadway is a *bascule* bridge. The particular fashion in which it works is more complicated than that of the other two bridges. The portion of the span which is counterweighted going through a combination of an upward swivel and a horizontal slide. One of only three bridges in the world of this variety (a *double-leaf-Rall bascule*), it is an expensive bridge to maintain. New parts have to be machined especially for it, and because the counterweights roll *on* the bridge itself, there is a lot of stress on the structure.

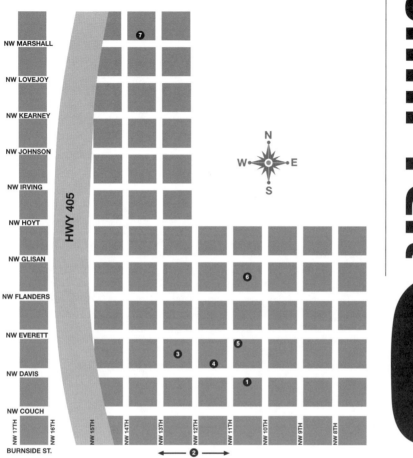

NW MARSHALL
NW LOVEJOY
NW KEARNEY
NW JOHNSON
NW IRVING
NW HOYT
NW GLISAN
NW FLANDERS
NW EVERETT
NW DAVIS
NW COUCH

HWY 405

NW 17TH
NW 16TH
NW 15TH
NW 14TH
NW 13TH
NW 12TH
NW 11TH
NW 10TH
NW 9TH
NW 8TH

BURNSIDE ST.

PEARL DISTRICT (AKA "THE PEARL")

1 *Portland Armory Building*

CHAPTER 6

PEARL DISTRICT
(AKA "THE PEARL")

"The architectural profession gave the public 50 years of modern architecture and the public's response has been 10 years of the greatest wave of historical preservation in the history of man."

—George E. Hartman, architect

This area was once composed primarily of industrial buildings and warehouses, some of which dated to the opening of the railroad line to Portland. Trucking began to cut into the railway's shipping, and the warehouses became increasingly abandoned for wider roads and easier access outside the city in the 1960s and '70s. As the area has zoning that allows for both residential and industrial usages, warehouse "rehabbers" began a gradual (then in the 1990s, accelerated) transformation of the district into an unusual neighborhood. The Pearl District is now a melange of disparate elements: wholesale stores, art galleries, automotive shops, train tracks, high-density housing, cafés, conventional warehouses, and antiques shops create a unique whole.

The name of the Pearl District is relatively recent and promotional, the mid-1980s invention of an art dealer who contrasted the area's hoary old buildings containing treasures with oysters and their pearls. (The area was previously known by the less flattering nickname of "Slabtown.") The 1999 destruction of the Lovejoy Ramp, which was originally built in the 1920s to accommodate rail traffic below it, markedly opened up the district. With the decline of train activity, the ramp's removal opens up a substantial area for housing. A variety of condominiums, townhouses, and apartments are springing up to fill the void, and one could almost hear the slavering of developers when they found that they might be able to build as high as 175 feet north of the ramp, as opposed to the seventy-five-foot restriction on the south side.

1 PORTLAND ARMORY BUILDING 1891

aka the First Regiment Armory Building
West side of NW Tenth Avenue between Couch and Davis Streets
Architect: McCaw, Martin and White
Remodel: GBD Architects

The Armory has been a locale for wrestlers, military brass bands, gunpowder storage, and flying hockey pucks. Although it looks like a medieval stone fortress with arrow loops and turrets, the Portland Armory Building is in fact a glib facsimile of a fort; it is constructed of masonry and wood. The tradition in the nineteenth century was to make armories look classically military in style, and this (the oldest armory in the state) certainly followed in its era's fashion. The arched entranceway and powerful presence of this building are somewhat adulterated by the fact that the exterior brick was painted white in the 1970s, which ruins the effect of the stonework in the base of the building contrasting with the brick above.

The National Guard eventually moved their armory to Marine Drive in the 1930s, and the 249th Artillery Group left in 1968, leaving the huge, cathedral-like space (supported by hundred-foot trusses) inside this building available for Portland State University basketball games, Saturday-night professional wrestling, and even ice-hockey matches. Word has it that in 1960, John F. Kennedy spoke to a crowd inside here during the course of his presidential campaign.

Blitz-Weinhard purchased it in 1968 for $302,600 and used it as a bottling plant until 1999. Its later purchase by the same development company that got Weinhard's five-block parcel has led to a revision of the building with retail shops and offices. There may even be a condominium tower and open plaza on the south side.

✦   Portland hosted the nation's first professional hockey game in 1912.

2 a *A.B. Smith*
Automotive Building

2b   *Blitz-Weinhard Brewery*

2 BLITZ–WEINHARD BREWERY 1908
1133 W. Burnside, between Burnside and Couch Streets
Architect: Unknown/Remodeling: GBD Architects

A. B. SMITH AUTOMOTIVE BUILDING 1929
1207–1235 W. Burnside
Architect: Charles Ertz

Henry Weinhard (1830–1904) learned brewing techniques in Germany and came to the Columbia River in 1856. (The "Blitz" was added to the name in 1928, when Arnold Blitz joined the company.) Although the brewery has been sited here since 1864, this medieval Tuscan brick building was built later. The then-popular style became the local template for many warehouses and industrial buildings in the area.

Often a controversial resident, Prohibition-era attitudes brought about a cloud of controversy for the brewery. Politician Oswald West stated that "there isn't a brick in the brewery down here that doesn't represent a broken heart." Oregon became nonalcoholic in 1916, years before Prohibition was enacted nationally. The brewery continued beverage production, making beverages like Luxo, a "cheery, beery drink," as a substitute for alcohol.

The Blitz-Weinhard Brewery's brands were sold to the Miller Brewing Company in 1979, and the multiple-block site was purchased by a local development company for about $20 million. As of this writing, the intended plan is to develop a mixed-use site for the colossal five-block area (the largest contiguous piece of property holding in the city) that would include retail, residential, and business uses. Theoretically, there are about 1.7 million square feet of property that could be developed. Plans for the original brewery building include offices on the upper floors with a restaurant and (surprise!) a brewpub on the bottom. All are on line for 2002 completion. Because of the unique interior layout of the Weinhard building, with its different ceiling heights designed to accommodate various brew vats, the remodel proves to be a bit of a challenge.

The shell of the A. B. Smith Automotive Building (a former Chevrolet/Ford auto dealership), with an Art Deco air and fascinating cast-stone eagles, will be retained, expanded upwards, and turned into a specialty grocery store with parking or offices above it. The insertion of a "para-building" (a glass building within the walls of the older structure) is the intended treatment.

✦   The last bottle of Weinhard's beer was capped here on August 27, 1999.

✦   Plans call for the Weinhard Brewery building's main smokestack to remain in place and serve as the underground parking garage's ventilator shaft.

3 WIEDEN + KENNEDY HEADQUARTERS 1910

Originally Fuller Paint Co. Building, later the Ice House
224 NW Thirteenth Avenue, between Twelfth and Thirteenth Avenues,
   Davis and Everett Streets
Architect: Unknown
Renovation by Allied Works

For years, pedestrians walked past this five-story building, rarely giving the gray monstrosity a second look. One $36-million renovation job later (and $10 million over-budget), it is a major concrete architectural lynchpin of the Pearl District. Even in its heyday, this structure was at best a stalwart if drab affair. The building suffered extensive wood-rot in its incarnation as a cold-storage building (when the interior was lined with six inches of cork). Upon its purchase by the advertising firm Wieden + Kennedy, the intent was to remake the structure in a way that would recall the atmosphere of Andy Warhol's infamous "Factory," where a free exchange of ideas could

3 *Wieden + Kennedy Headquarters, central atrium*

occur between artists of widely ranging mediums without the building getting in the way.

For the 1999 renovation of this factory, the architects kept only the exterior shell of the building, choosing to use the strength of a central atrium to uphold the building and provide its social nexus. The structure was originally built as four square buildings with joined masonry walls. The former juncture of those structures is now a substantial sky-lit amphitheater/central civic space. The impact of this open center stretching upward is felt throughout the entire building, as space opens onto space horizontally and vertically, creating a phenomenal open-air layout that facilitates a sense of unity throughout the building. It also divides the building's floors into quadrangles, just as it once was.

There are virtually no architectural flourishes or decorations; rather, the building is businesslike, with concrete-tile floors and exposed concrete and beams. Many posts and beams are original, showing cracks beneath their white paint, and recycled wood is used throughout. By all reports, the concrete work on this building was the most exacting and precise to date in Portland, as the imported Chinese cement was carefully poured and smoothed to the consistency of gray pudding.

✦ The price of this building's renovation was $16 million more than the purchase price of the five-block Weinhard complex to the south.

✦ In order for Weiden + Kennedy employees to feel more at ease inside the building, a water-balloon fight was staged inside the building. As the building's electrical system was wired beneath the concrete slabs of the structure's floors, this led to a few problems. This isn't the only water problem the building has had; the exterior walls sank up to eighteen inches in spots due to water leakage from the Tanner Creek aqueduct running underneath it.

4   *Portland Cracker Factory*

4 PORTLAND CRACKER FACTORY CIRCA 1890

aka Portland Biscuit Company
1101 NW Davis Street, between Eleventh and Twelfth Avenues
Architect: Unknown

This is a notable brick warehouse in the region, with a corbeled brick edge at the cornice and a bull's-eye window in the original design at the gable's peak. Anecdotally, some people remember a brick swastika design under the gable, which was removed once that symbol was no longer associated with its original Hindu meaning of good luck.

5 BEARING SERVICE COMPANY 1944

1040 NW Everett Street, southeast corner of Everett Street and
*   Eleventh Avenue*
Architect: Richard Sundeleaf

Standing on the corner opposite this wonderfully rounded building, one is presented with a great juxtaposition between the low-lying, organic Art Deco contours of the Bearing Service Company, providing a foreground for the straight-edged and gleaming U.S. Bancorp Tower behind it.

The most recognizable feature of the Bearing Service Company is the entrance; an inward-curving, glass-blocked portal overhung by a coin-shaped marquee that rests on one column, dead center. Whether or not this is intended to be an axle and wheel (Roadside Thematic!), it makes for one of the city's most distinctive street-corner fronts.

6 THE GREGORY 2001

Between NW Flanders and Glisan Streets, Tenth and Eleventh Avenues
Architect: Ankrom Moisan Associated Architects

The Gregory warrants mention, as the streamlined Art Deco giant will be the largest modern development in its immediate area at twelve stories high in places and covering a full city block. The building holds significant promise of curved corners and futuristic detailing, all right next to a trolley line that will already be operational when the building is complete.

5 *Bearing Service Company*

Courtesy of Kieran, O' Brien, Ozymandius

6 *The Gregory*

7 *BridgePort Brewery Building*

7 BRIDGEPORT BREWERY BUILDING CIRCA 1888

1313 NW Marshall Street, northwest corner of Marshall Street and
  Thirteenth Avenue
Architect: Unknown

One of the oldest industrial buildings in Portland still in use, this brewpub also takes the city award for being the building most covered in extensive vegetation. Virginia Creeper has begun its takeover of the structure, and it is right up against the surface of the building, not on some carefully hidden trellis; although doomsayers claim it will destroy the mortar, the building seems okay so far. This rough-hewn structure was originally home to a cordage company that made ropes for Portland's many sailing ships. In the mid-1980s, a new law allowed small, or "micro," breweries to sell to the public. Micro-seconds later, a brewpub was in business here.

MONTE VISTA TER

RAINIER TER

ARIEL TER

RAPIDAN TER

SUMMIT AVE

MAYWOOD DR

MAYWOOD DR

WESTOVER RD

BURNSIDE ST

EVERETT ST

FLANDERS ST

IRVING ST

JOHNSON ST

LOVEJOY ST

MARSHALL ST

RALEIGH ST

VAUGHN ST

HWY 30

25 TH AVE

24 TH AVE

23 RD AVE

22 ND AVE

21 ST AVE

20 TH AVE

19 TH AVE

18 TH AVE

17 TH AVE

16 TH AVE

HWY 405

W

S   N

E

CHAPTER 7

NORTHWEST

1 *Temple Beth Israel*

CHAPTER 7

NORTHWEST

There have been hundreds of subdivisions created within Portland's city limits. Portland's old residential neighborhoods were mostly established before World War II by middle- and upper-class families eager to raise their children away from metropolitan Portland's high ratio of single men. They generally feature traditional urban designs, with a variety of styles following the basic template of large front windows, front porches, and a garage often recessed or hidden behind the house.

There has been limited pressure on Portland housing markets until recently, which has helped to ensure that many of these older neighborhoods have stayed intact. Some have had to deal with a measure of creeping condominiums and gentrification issues, but there are still a number of well-maintained or restored homes in the area. One can trace the more recent neighborhood developments by the garage's role. The beginning of America's automobile frenzy in the 1950s led to the garage creeping forward on the lot, gaining size and proximity to the street. The final result is the "snout house," in which a blank garage door becomes the foremost feature of a home. (This design also cuts homes off from each other, minimizing social contact.) In 1999, Portland's Bureau of Planning began considering guidelines for homes that would outlaw "snout" houses and require that 15 percent of a home's front be devoted to windows.

In terms of residential architecture, only about 5 percent of any relatively modern homes built in the Portland area are designed by architects; developers and contractors create the majority. As a result, the finer sensitivities of home design are more likely to be offset by profit margins. Another feature of current housing trends in the late twentieth century has led to any number of "McMansions" (oversized mansions of bastardized architectural form) mushrooming throughout the Portland area.

NOB HILL

"Nob" is British slang for a wealthy or important person, which explains this area's name, since Nob Hill was once considered a prestigious place to live in Portland. This was part of John Couch's 1845 land claim (see "Union Station.") Couch extended his district's street pattern to Nineteenth Avenue, and from there he expanded the blocks westward to twice Portland's usual block size to accommodate palatial family homes. The base of Portland's wooded west hills thus formed a setting for an affluent residential neighborhood.

In some areas, Victorian homes are crammed in on top of each other in cheerful claustrophobia. The construction of streetcars in the area, as well as the commercial explosion of building after the 1905 Lewis and Clark Exposition, resulted in the construction of apartment buildings and commercial developments in and near Nob Hill. By the 1940s, virtually all of the original families had moved out, and their huge homes were either razed or converted to apartments or offices. The historic preservation movement in Portland in the 1960s and '70s managed to stop the piecemeal destruction of Nob Hill houses; although many of the most ornate specimens have been torn down, some original homes still exist. Many of them were designed by Whidden and Lewis, Portland's most distinguished architectural firm at the turn of the century. And while the architecture isn't anything to write home about, the bustling retail strip on Twenty-third Avenue (aka "Trendy-third") gives the neighborhood a real vitality.

1 TEMPLE BETH ISRAEL 1927

1931 NW Flanders Street, between Nineteenth and Twentieth Streets
Architect: Herman Brookman, with Whitehouse and Church, Harry
Herzog, and John V. Bennes

For a taste of Asia Minor, visit this impressive Byzantine synagogue. Made of reinforced concrete, sandstone, salmon-colored Willamina brick, and terra-cotta, the plans for the temple were reportedly reworked fourteen times before they were considered complete. The result is a building utterly unlike anything else in Oregon.

If one is fortunate enough to travel to Essen, Germany, one can see in that city's main synagogue the inspiration for Temple Beth Israel. The distinctive dome of the temple is topped with terra-cotta shingles, and its shape defines the whole building with a powerful, organic motif. The motif is repeated in the turrets of the domed corner towers that flank the entrance, as well as in the smaller columns between the towers and the entryway. Inside, the stained-glass roof at the top of the massive, octagonal-shaped auditorium crowns what may be the most profound spiritual space in the city.

✦   The sculpted, bronze doors, with a depiction of the burning bush, were crafted by Frederic Littman. To see another example of his spiritually inspired work, go to the "narthex" doors of Zion Lutheran Church (1015 SW Eighteenth Avenue).

✦   Architect Morris Whitehouse's nickname was "Molly."

2 NORTHWEST NEIGHBORHOOD CULTURAL CENTER
1909

Originally First Church of Christ Scientist, aka Northwest
   Service Center
1819 NW Everett Street
Architect: S. S. Beman (Chicago)

Across the street from the impressive stone splendor of Trinity Episcopal Church is this charming wood and stone building. Although three stories high, it seems gracefully lower than that; the domed roof is tasteful but modestly curved, and its detailing is commendably restrained.

2 *Northwest Neighborhood Cultural Center*

3 SAINT MARY'S CATHOLIC CHURCH 1924

1716 NW Davis Street, corner of Couch Street and Eighteenth Avenue
Architect: Joseph Jacobberger
Renovation by Thomas Hacker and Associates

This simple yet impressive Romanesque/Byzantine cathedral was commissioned by Archbishop Alexander Christie to be a symbol and flagship of one of the nation's oldest archdioceses. The architect chosen for this job was Joseph Jacobberger, a man who created many designs for the church in the early twentieth century. Jacobberger also oversaw the layout of the University of Portland. (See his 1924 Monastery of the Precious Blood/Saint Andrews Care Center in the Southeast chapter.)

A mid-1990s, multimillion-dollar remodeling went beyond renovation and into the realm of finishing the job that was begun seventy years before. Murals painted by a Flemish artist and stained glass (which had been taken from another cathedral) were already present in the interior, and these were respectively restored and revealed, the latter through the removal of balconies. The motif of the rose (important to both Portland and Saint Mary) was echoed throughout the interior of the church in the form of light fixtures, glasswork, and other design elements. Ultimately, it doesn't matter if you've been through the sacraments or not; if you want to see a beautiful spiritual and architectural space, visit this church.

✦ The proper Latin terminology for the Portland area is *Archidioecesis Portlandensis.*

✦ Historians believe that Archbishop Christie may have been inspired to build this cathedral because of the Compulsory School Bill of 1922, a bill sponsored by intolerant anti-foreigner types who wanted to divert youth away from Catholic private schools. This structure was intended to impress the heck out of potential voters.

4 MISSION THEATER 1912

1624 NW Glisan Street, south side between Sixteenth and
*   Seventeenth Avenues*
Architect: Unknown

This brick building has seen changes over the years, ranging from lutefisk to Longshoremen to local lager. Although it looks like a warehouse and currently functions as a pub and theater, this blocky building was originally constructed as a church by members of the Swedish Evangelical Mission Covenant Church of America. It was the second church the group built on this site, and its design was intended to be practical so that the property could be converted to non-spiritual uses if the congregation relocated. The Swedes left in 1953, to be replaced by the Longshoremen's Union for the next two decades, and it was eventually obtained by the McMenamins in 1987.

Although the series of crosses on the roof are now missing, the interior still boasts some of its original plaster decoration, as well as a U shaped balcony.

5 THE WINSLOW B. AYER HOUSE 1903

811 NW Nineteenth Avenue, northwest corner of Nineteenth Avenue
*   and Johnson Street*
Architects: Whidden and Lewis

THE GEORGE GOOD HOUSE CIRCA 1895

829 NW Nineteenth Avenue
Architects: Whidden and Lewis

Modeled after a manor house from another era, this Jacobean brick home is big and relatively plain. Distinguished-looking to some, but a bit too much like an English private school's crematorium for others, any severity of style is softened by its variously arched and projecting windows. At one time, large shade trees in the front and real shutters on the windows existed, and if the observer can imagine these features reconstituted, the house benefits mightily. If you can imagine a landscaped front yard where the parking lot currently is, the re-creation will please you.

If you've been looking for a Good House, you'll find it next door to the Ayer. The bricks on the front of the home were made in England and shipped

5 a   *The Winslow B. Ayer House*

5 b   *The George Good House*

here specifically for this home. (Richard Marlitt theorizes they came as ballast on grain ships.) Reminiscent of an English country home, the split front of the roofline and double gables give it personality. Unlike the Ayer house next door, there are still a few trees left in the front yard, which almost makes up for the stupid little box that's been tacked onto the front entrance in a remodel.

6 ABBOTT L. MILLS HOUSE 1908

733 NW Twentieth Avenue, southwest corner of Twentieth and Johnson Street

LEWIS MILLS HOUSE 1916

2039 NW Irving Street
Architects: Shepley, Rutan, and Coolidge (Boston)

Abbott L. Mills was the president of the First National Bank. He and his wife had resided in Philadelphia before coming to Portland, and it was there that Mrs. Mills took a fancy to Georgian Revival homes and Philadelphia townhouses. Their brick Georgian home on Twentieth Avenue took the place of an earlier wood structure designed by Whidden and Lewis to the rear of the property.

The presidential-sounding architect Jefferson Coolidge was a family friend of the Millses, and when Abbott Mills's son, Lewis, married into the Coolidge family, a new Mills house was built facing Irving Street, so the two Mills domiciles could share a garden. This home was more of a New England Colonial (or Colonial Revival, Second Phase, if you prefer) with a wood exterior. In 1936, Lewis Mills thought enough of the interior detailing to have the millwork (paneling, mantels, exterior trim, doors, stair rails, etc.) taken out of this house and moved to his new home in Dunthorpe.

7 THE WILLIAM TEMPLE HOUSE 1892

aka the K. A. J. MacKenzie House
615 NW Twentieth Avenue, northwest corner of Twentieth Avenue and Hoyt Street
Architects: Whidden and Lewis

You've got to like a stone house. When the tract houses in the sprawling masses of Tigard and Beaverton begin to collapse in one hundred years, the

William Temple House will still be standing proudly. The stonework alone is worthy of admiration, not to mention the conically roofed and powerful turret. There are numerous arrow loops, peepholes, huntsman dormers, and windows, including an interesting bowed window over the arches facing Hoyt Street and a little eyeball window peeking out of the roof, just to the left of the turret.

This home has been described as both a Shingle-style and Richardsonian Romanesque home, but the more evocative term of Scottish Baronial seems to suit it best; this house certainly would not be out of place on a foggy hill, nestled in thistles (which show up in the original front entryway's woodwork). Another dramatic feature is the cast-iron stag's head in the window recess on the Hoyt Street side. The woodwork and detailing within are remarkable; be sure to note the stairway and fireplace features.

Be respectful of the fact that the building is now the William Temple House, a social service agency named for an archbishop of Canterbury of the 1940s. Founded by the Reverend C. T. Abbott in 1965, the program moved into this home six years later.

Dr. K. A. J. MacKenzie was the original denizen of this home. He was born in Saskatchewan and studied medicine in Edinburgh, Scotland, a factor that probably influenced this home's design. The good doctor moved to Portland at the suggestion of a trusted family friend and went on to almost single-handedly create the University of Oregon Medical School (now known as Oregon Health Sciences University).

✦   The contractor of the house was Archibald MacKenzie, no relation to the doctor.

7 a *The William Temple House*

7 b   *The William Temple House*

8 SAINT MARK'S ANGLICAN CHURCH 1924

aka St. Mark's Episcopal Church, the Cathedral Parish of Saint Mark's
1025 NW Twenty-first Avenue, west side between Lovejoy and Marshall
   Streets
Architect: Jamieson Parker

The arched windows, geometric embellishments, and the large, spoked, stained glass window give this brick Romanesque church an organic look quite different from the Colonial Unitarian Church, also designed by Parker. For instance, compare its squared-off bell tower with the Unitarian Church's slender spire.

◆   *Two Copies from Verona:* Interestingly, this is a copy of a Philadelphia church, which was a copy of one in Pisa, Italy, which in turn was a copy of the Basilica of San Zeno in Verona, Italy.

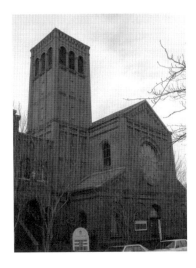

8   *Saint Mark's Anglican Church*

9   *Saint Patrick's Roman Catholic Church and Rectory*

9 SAINT PATRICK'S ROMAN CATHOLIC CHURCH AND RECTORY 1891

1635 NW Nineteenth Avenue, northwest corner of Nineteenth Avenue and Raleigh Street
Architect: Otto Kleeman/Restoration by George McMath

The cornerstone for this church was laid on Saint Patrick's Day, 1889. Two years later, the church was open for spiritual business and has been ever since, making it one of the oldest churches in Portland still being employed as its creators intended at its original location. Its only significant change was the front entrance, which was once a pyramidal stairway. German-born architect Otto Kleeman didn't realize that his Renaissance Revival dome would later be so close to passing motorists on Highway 30's ramp, but at least commuters can admire his work up close. Kleeman moved to Portland in 1880 and worked for Justus Krumbein before striking out on his own. He designed many of the Mount Angel Abbey's original buildings, almost all of which subsequently burned down.

10   NATHAN LOEB HOUSE 1893

726 NW Twenty-second Avenue, east side, south of Johnson Street
Architect: Rudolph Becker

The Nathan Loeb House is an impressively maintained, narrow, tall, and ornate Victorian with a sunburst pattern around a second-floor window. There is a high density of embellishment on this home between the porch columns and on the projected gable and decorative shingles.

✦   Nathan Loeb helped found the Temple Beth Israel down the hill.

11   ALBERT H. TANNER HOUSE 1883

2248 NW Johnson Street, south side between Twenty-second and
*   Twenty-third Avenues*
Architect: Unknown

Another of the few Stick-style houses in Portland, its highlights are the decorated gables and sweet wraparound porch. Next door to the west is the 1906 Mary Smith House (architect unknown). Its projecting, bowed portico has a bow window on the second floor above it, and a dormer above that, making for an unusual symmetry.

11   *Albert H. Tanner House*

12 *Arenson Court Apartments*

WILLAMETTE AND KING'S HEIGHTS

12 ARENSON COURT APARTMENTS 1930
2533 NW Marshall Street
Architect: Elmer E. Feig

This is a brick apartment building masquerading as a faux castle. Most interesting are the turrets; an examination of the sides of them reveals them as fakes! Architect Feig designed so many of the apartment houses east of Twenty-third Avenue within a three-year span that his corner-cutting, turret-gutting ways are almost understandable.

13 MONTGOMERY PARK BUILDING 1922, 1936
Originally Montgomery Ward Building
2741 NW Vaughn Street
Architect: W. H. McCaully

If you are well traveled, this reinforced-concrete building may look familiar to you, as there are seven others like it in the country. This was Montgomery Ward's first west coast warehouse, and that's what it looks like from afar: nine spacious stories of Montgomery Ward merchandise. A closer look belies this, as the building went through what was supposedly the biggest renovation project west of the Mississippi in 1986. The old warehouse became the spacious home to an atrium, convention/event areas, and office space.

The building was originally built in an **L** shape, with the final wing being added in the 1930s. The steel-framed roof sign is the largest in Portland and can be read by the naked (or clothed) eye from the other side of the Willamette.

14 DR. RALPH FENTON HOUSE 1918
1940 NW Summit Avenue
Architect: Wade Hampton Pipes

The March 1919 issue of *The Architect and Engineer of California* recognized ten notable Portland buildings, including the Portland Hotel (McKim, Mead and White), the Central Library (Doyle), the University Club (Whitehouse and Fouilhoux), and this home. This stucco-and-stone home has the flavor of an English cottage with the sensibilities of an Arts and Crafts home. Its prominent feature is a geometric, three-story bay/turret. To quote the magazine's tribute: "Although a small house, it was . . . more successfully handled than any other domestic building [the jury] viewed, including a great many which cost as much as ten times more than this building."

13 *Montgomery Park Building*

15 D. C. BURKES HOUSE 1948

700 NW Rapidan Terrace
Architect: Pietro Belluschi

Designed to take advantage of the site's view while maintaining its privacy, the resulting L-shaped residence is probably Belluschi's finest and a pioneering work of northwest regionalism as well. A flat, overhanging roof, lots of wood, horizontal massing, open interior layout—it's a local twist on International style. The accent on the home's layout is not just the view of Mount Hood to the east, but more so on the Japanese-style enclosed garden; it doesn't have a lot of street presence, because it is oriented from the back of the structure.

Belluschi himself ended up moving into this understated home twenty-four years after its completion, and he maintained residence in it until his death in 1994. Its natural woods, open interior layout, and masterful design are still admired today.

16 CLARISSA INMAN HOUSE 1926

aka Ariel Terraces
2884 NW Cumberland Road, junction with Winchester Terrace
Architect: David L. Williams

This lavish Mediterranean home was designed as a showpiece; it sits at a prominent location on Cumberland Road, where its impressive stairway (complete with lily pond) steps up to huge Ionic columns upholding the portico. Many of the architectural details found here (such as the extended eaves with dentils) were used by the same architect in a 1911 Irvington home in which Clarissa Inman also lived.

✦ Clarissa Inman invented the electric curling iron.

16 *Clarissa Inman House*

Photo © Michael Henley, Courtesy of Portland Parks and Recreation

17   *The Pittock Mansion*

17   THE PITTOCK MANSION 1909–14

or the Henry L. Pittock House
3229 NW Pittock Drive, follow the signs off of West Burnside going
   out of town
Architect: Edward T. Foulkes (San Francisco)

The uncontested kingpin of homes in the Portland area is the French Renaissance Pittock Mansion. Built by Henry Pittock (1835–1919), publisher of the city's beloved daily newspaper, the *Oregonian,* the cost of the mansion is uncertain, but given the five years of construction and the imported woods, stones, and marble, the figure must have been colossal. (While on the topic of large numbers, it should be mentioned that Henry Pittock moved into the house at the age of seventy-nine.)

One thousand feet above the city, the mansion, with its reinforced concrete walls with cut Bellingham sandstone facing, resembles a combination of a chateau and a fortress. Because of its remote location, transportation to and from the house as well as maintenance of the home were problems.

The idea was to have the two main wings of the house meet where the large drawing room looks out on the view to the east between two turrets. Dormers and the turrets break up the red-tiled roofline above the terrace, scrolled cornices and ornamented entablatures fill the middle space, and a stone balustrade greets the pedestrian at the bottom.

Inside, marble stairs with bronze rails flow upstairs, and beautiful paneling, friezes, crystal chandeliers, and oak or marble floors vie for your attention. A favorite area is the round Turkish smoke room, where Henry Pittock would perhaps go to enjoy watching others smoking exotic tobaccos (Pittock himself did not smoke). Upstairs are three suites and a gallery appointed in a smug Edwardian sumptuousness that never fails to impress the gawking hoi polloi traipsing through the mansion.

The mansion fell into serious disrepair until 1964, when news leaked out that the building and its property were to be sold to a private developer and razed. Private, city, and federal funds were pooled, and the Parks administration soon had itself a mansion and its forty-six-acre estate. The groundswell of grassroots support to "save the Pittock" provided momentum for the 1965 derailing of the Ash Street Ramp project, a roadwork that would have wiped out historic buildings in the Skidmore Historic District.

Henry Lewis Pittock was born in England but immigrated to Pittsburgh with his family while still a child. He came to Portland as a sixteen-year-old printer's "devil," an employee lower than an apprentice. If there was a job nobody wanted to do, the master printer would cry out, "The devil take it!" Henry would then get moving. Eight years later, he gained control of the paper in lieu of back wages owed him. He converted the *Oregonian* to a daily and went on to become one of Portland's wealthiest and most influential private citizens. His home is evidence that devilish work can eventually pay off.

18 TO DR. FRANK KISTNER HOUSE

14 TO AUBREY WATZEK HOUSE

HEWETT BLVD

FAIRVIEW BLVD

13 KINGSTON DR

OREGON ZOO

KINGSTON DR

17

PATTON RD

FAIRVIEW BLVD

12

26

KINGSTON DR

JAPANESE GARDEN

11 PARADISE LN

WASHINGTON PARK

VISTA DR

16

19

BURNSIDE ST

VISTA AVE

GREEN ST

20

HIGH ST

HAWTHORNE TER

21

18 TH AVE

15

ST CLAIR AVE

9 10

KING AVE

16 TH AVE

8

HALL ST

MONTGOMERY DR

7

6

PORTLAND CIVIC STADIUM

LINCOLN HIGH SCHOOL

OREGON HEALTH SCIENCES UNIVERSITY OHSU

23

22

4 5

2 3

1

PORTLAND STATE UNIV.

24 TO LEWIS & CLARK COLLEGE

405

10 TH AVE

WEST PARK AVE

BROADWAY AVE

6 TH AVE

5 TH AVE

405

BURNSIDE ST

W

S — N

E

SOUTHWEST

1 a *Tiffany Center*

CHAPTER 8

SOUTHWEST

"I believe . . . that there is not much new that is good that is not based on something old that is good."—Portland architect A. E. Doyle (from a 1925 letter written to fellow architect Donald J. Stewart)

1 TIFFANY CENTER 1928
Originally the Neighbors of Woodcraft Building
1410 SW Morrison Street
Architect: Sutton and Whitney Architects; Frederick Fritsch, designer

The Tiffany Center is attractive, if a bit monolithic in construction; it is one big brick-faced building, and one can see the hand of Frederick Fritsch (the Masonic Temple) in its massiveness. The style is Italian Romanesque, with a dash of Art Deco, and just for kicks, stone grotesques extending from the structure's north front. (The grotesques are an odd touch for the building, but one that works.) Its current name comes from the daughter of the building's 1993 buyer. There is also a stained-glass window honoring her at the entrance to the Emerald Room auditorium, in case anyone misses the connection. Also note the speakeasy-style sliding peepholes in the doors leading to this auditorium.

✦ The Tiffany Center's Crystal Room has small balconies embedded in the north wall; these were designed so that chaperones could keep a discreet but wary eye on youthful proceedings.

✦ Woodcraft Insurance (the original owner) was an insurance group that catered to fraternal-organization members, including carpenters.

1 b   *Tiffany Center gargoyle*

2 THE MALLORY HOTEL 1912

729 SW Fifteenth Avenue, northwest corner of Fifteenth Avenue and
  Taylor Street
Architect: H. Hanselmann

Designed as a "strictly modern, high-class eight-story fireproof structure,"
the Mallory is a welcome sight on the west side of Highway 405. Although
marooned from the rest of downtown by the construction of the highway,
it projects its architecturally modest but beneficent presence into this area.
Its light brick is reminiscent of the Embassy Suites, constructed at the same
time downtown.

Rufus Mallory (1831–1914) was Oregon's most colorful member of
the U.S. House of Representatives. A New York native, he taught in
Roseburg, Oregon, and there met and married the daughter of Aaron Rose,
after whom the town was named. Mallory entered politics, and perhaps the
highlight of his career was an incendiary speech he gave in favor of the
impeachment of Andrew Jackson. (It obviously didn't work since Jackson
went on to get his face on the twenty-dollar bill.)

✦   The Mallory is one of the only hotels in town that provides dog bis-
cuits for canine trip companions.

3 SCOTTISH RITE CENTER 1906

Originally the Scottish Rite Temple
709 SW Fifteenth Avenue
Architect: Richard Martin Jr.

This powerfully built, classic Greek building is the only one in Portland
still owned and maintained by a Mason group. Stained-glass windows that
once graced the exterior have been brought into the building's lounge and
backlit, creating a room with significant ambience.

2 *The Mallory Hotel*

3 *Scottish Rite Center*

4 LAFAYETTE APARTMENTS 1930

730 SW Sixteenth Avenue
Architect: Luther Lee Dougan

This is another unique apartment house in the district; huge human heads project from the top of the building to express their outrage at the use of artificial turf in Civic Stadium to the west. Decorated Greek panels are at the bottom and top of the apartment building, illustrating a classical variety of dramatic, debauched, and Dionysian events. Architect Dougan designed many distinguished structures in town, including the Princeton Building.

5 COMMODORE APARTMENTS 1927

Originally the Commodore Hotel
1621 SW Morrison Street
Architect: Herman Brookman

One of the finest Art Deco apartment buildings in Portland, this pleasant four-story structure was originally constructed by the oldest daughter of Aaron Meier (of Meier and Frank) as an investment. This well-maintained building has floral arrangements below the roofline, and Louisiana natives will be pleased to see their official state bird, the pelican, adorning the pillars.
✦ Recruited to move to Portland by Lloyd Frank, New York–native Herman Brookman also designed the Temple Beth Israel and the Frank Estate at Lewis and Clark College.

4 *Lafayette Apartments*

5 *Commodore Apartments*

KING'S HILL/GOOSE HOLLOW

This area was originally claimed by Daniel Lownsdale, but he sold it in favor of obtaining land closer to the Willamette, and an investor named Amos Nahum King ended up buying the property. King is remembered for selling the city forty acres that were the beginning of Washington Park.

A group of large, even huge, homes, built primarily between 1890 and 1910, sometimes took up double blocks of land in this area. Streetcar development began to gentrify the lowlands—the quaintly-named Goose Hollow—from the higher elevation, higher-class area—the lordly King's Hill. Although house lots have become smaller and denser over the years, the higher reaches are still patrician, although residents have had to survive rampant apartment and condominium development, heavy traffic, and even an aborted attempt to bring a major-league-sized baseball stadium to the area.

✦ PGE Park (1926, aka Multnomah Stadium, Civic Stadium) was the site of a 1923 speech by President Warren G. Harding on the perils of indiscriminate immigration to the U.S. He died four weeks later, leaving behind the Teapot Dome Scandal.

6 *Zion Lutheran Church*

6 ZION LUTHERAN CHURCH 1950

1015 SW Eighteenth Avenue, between Salmon and Main, south of the Civic Stadium
Architect: Pietro Belluschi; design assistant: Ken Richardson

At first glance, this church recalls a rural New England design. To be sure, it does have the usual steep-steeple design, deep porch, and wooden construction characteristic of this type of prayer place. But this church makes its own distinctive statement. Following the redwood-shingled roofline down from the copper-covered spire, one finds that it continues right into the angled porch area. This gives the structure an overhanging, cloaking top, which unifies it and makes it appear "secure," for lack of a better term. The roof of the church is also interesting in that the first two proposals for it were rejected by the church as too flat and industrial.

Against Belluschi's wishes, the congregation insisted on a spire. The copper material of the spire is also used inside, on the porch doors, altar, cross, and even in the slight recesses of the glass blocks embedded in the non-load-bearing walls. Light flowing through the rose and amber windows highlights the space around the altar very effectively. While inside, one cannot help but notice the distinctive laminated arches that seem ubiquitous in West Coast churches today, but were considered innovative in Belluschi's use of them in 1952.

✦   The narthex of a church is the entry between the main entrance and the church's primary interior space. The copper narthex doors of this church were sculpted with angels by Frederic Littman, the Hungarian artist who also sculpted the doors of the Temple Beth Israel.

7 MORRIS MARKS HOUSE 1883

1501 SW Harrison Street
Architect: Warren H. Williams

The dramatic two-story bays projecting from all sides of this building are attention-getters, and the Italianate Victorian house's detailing (keystones in the windows, decorative portico, cornice bracing, etc.) holds one's eye. Many of the features here are wooden, not cast iron, despite their appearance and the era.

Warren H. Williams arrived in Portland in 1872, an auspicious year for an architect given the fire that had just occurred and the monstrous one that took place the following year. He was noted as a master of cast-iron architecture and high-rises. This house is a good example of his style, and it would be easy to picture it in San Francisco, his hometown. Williams also designed the original Temple Beth Israel (1888).

✦   This home was sawed in half and dragged by horse from 321 SW Ninth Avenue to its present wretched location in 1910.

7 *Morris Marks House*

8 JACOB KAMM HOUSE 1873

1425 SW Twentieth Avenue, between Jefferson and Market Streets
Architect: Justus Krumbein

A somewhat daunting structure, the Jacob Kamm House may qualify as the city's first real mansion. Built for a Swiss immigrant who was previously an engineer on Mississippi River steamboats, it has dramatic quoined corners, arched and elongated windows with keystones, and expressive baroque dormers in the mansard roof. Alone on a dead-end street, it seems to look reproachfully at an area developed in a hodgepodge manner.

Properly termed a "French Second Empire" structure (the oldest of this type in Oregon), the inspiration for the layout of this home was found in a period of jingoistic fervor in mid-nineteenth-century France. French architects rushed about restoring and adding on to national monuments in a style that was a bit self-important. Fortunately, the Kamm House avoids most of the excesses of that era and remains restrained and impressive, even substituting wood in lieu of masonry.

✦   This home was originally constructed on a thirteen-acre site where Lincoln High School is now located. It was moved to make way for the school in 1950. The building housed a restaurant at one time.

✦   Justus Krumbein had arrived in America from Germany the year before he designed this home. He later designed Oregon's original state capitol building, which burned down in the 1930s.

9 THEODORE B. WILCOX HOUSE 1893

931 SW King Avenue
Architect: Whidden and Lewis

The Wilcox House is a strong, upstanding citizen of a house, with a sandstone first-story and a beautiful carved entry. The double dormers at the top are done in an interesting style, but the home's true charms are reportedly inside, where it is fashioned with mahogany and marble. This home had a whiff of conspiracy during World War II, when it was inhabited by Soviet "purchasing agents."

8 *Jacob Kamm House*

9 *Theodore B. Wilcox House*

10 STRATTON-CORNELIUS HOUSE 1894

aka the Howard Stratton House
2182 SW Yamhill Street, Yamhill and St. Clair Avenue
Architect: Unknown

This is a colorful Queen Anne/Arts and Crafts hybrid of a house. It's open to debate as to whether the geometric lines of the top floor mesh with the curves on the pediment above the front columns. There is a neat mini-balcony right above there, though.

The significance of the golden scallop above the portico is unknown at this writing; along similarly mysterious lines, an apartment building across the street features a colorful bowl of fruit atop a ram's head. For more excitement, walk west on Park Place from here, and you will encounter some nicely done residential architecture in the block preceding Lewis and Clark Circle.

ARLINGTON HEIGHTS

The residential zone twines into Washington Park, Hoyt Park Arboretum, the Japanese Garden, and the Portland Zoo.

11 AARON H. MAEGLY HOUSE CIRCA 1915

226 SW Kingston Street, just north of Parkside Drive on the right
Architect: John V. Bennes

Although this tile-roofed home resembles other Mediterranean-villa knockoffs in the area, the young Frank Lloyd Wright might have looked fondly upon its derivation of his Prairie School style. The low-slung, overhanging roof, narrow windows, and horizontal layout of the home are vintage Prairie, and the porte cochere in front reflects the house's lines. Decorative elements have crept in, however, including protruding bay windows and Romanesque ornamentation. Interestingly, this home was originally designed with twelve porches, and the interior woodwork reportedly all came from a single mahogany log.

✦ A decade after this home's completion, John V. Bennes would begin designing local buildings in Art Deco variations, notably the Hollywood Movie Theater.

12 J. O. FRYE HOUSE 1930

aka the Ferris House
2997 SW Fairview Boulevard
Architect: Jeter O. Frye

Yes, it's a stone English cottage, and one look at it makes a convincing case that this style is a natural for Portland. Forget the Mediterranean-villa copies and Colonial knockoffs found elsewhere in these hills; Italy has less in common with our local environment than merry old England. Portland has the right flora and climate, as well as many local citizens' interest in gardening.

In this home's case, the architect was also the carpenter. While the use of dark clinker bricks in the chimney and sides of this home to give it a peppery look was not unorthodox, the twisted and unusual nature of some of them was. The spiderweb windows are another interesting and original touch. The bull's-eye window on the right side of the house, in conjunction with the downwardly sloped roofline, gives the house the look of a Cyclops with a Beatles haircut.

✦　Jeter Frye went bankrupt after building the Canterbury Castle, which he was unable to sell.

12 *J. O. Frye House*

13 WORLD FORESTRY CENTER 1971
Formerly the Western Forestry Center

CHEATHAM HALL
Formerly Forest Hall

THE MUSEUM (MAIN EXHIBIT HALL)
4033 SW Canyon Road, by the zoo
Architect: John Storrs

If you want to get a splinter, this is the place to do it. For many years, the largest log building in the world was Portland's Forestry Building, designed for Portland's Lewis and Clark Expo in 1905. When it burned down in 1964, a new facility was needed to showcase Portland's lumber treasures. Two buildings were designed to highlight the role wood can play in construction, and there is a lot of the hard, fibrous substance used in these mushroom-roofed, octagonal buildings.

Since wood is the name of the game, let's talk lumber. In the museum/main exhibit hall, one finds redwood, cedar, white fir, teak, Douglas fir, western red cedar, ponderosa pine, sugar pine, western hemlock, pecan, white oak, birch, and everybody's favorite, *damar min yak* (a tropical species). Despite their different characteristics, somehow the combination of woods doesn't go against the aesthetic grain. Cheatham Hall is designed similarly, and in addition to some of the above-mentioned woods, it has black-walnut paneling in the lobby.

Merlo Hall (1989) is an obvious and somewhat daring departure from the earlier buildings with its Japanese winged-roof entrance and wing-shaped roof apparently made of plastic (shudder). Actually, the roofing material is a semi-translucent substance called Kalwall, two layers of white fiberglass sheets with a bit of insulation between. The interior paneling of the structure includes imbuia (a yellow-olive-streaked Brazilian wood), alerce (a Chilean wood), mahogany, and chanul (a chocolate brown Ecuadorian wood with interesting grain patterns).

✦   John Storrs is noteworthy for his mastery of the Northwest Regional style; one of his trademark touches was the use of cork floors.

✦   To get a firsthand description of the pleasures of photosynthesis, be sure to visit the seventy-foot, multilingual Talking Tree.

13a   *The Museum*

13b   *Merlo Hall*

14 AUBREY WATZEK HOUSE 1936

Proposed John Yeon Center for Architectural Studies
1061 SW Skyline Boulevard; take Fairview Boulevard west to
*   Skyline Boulevard and turn right*
Architect: John Yeon

This home is a pioneering work of Northwest Regional architecture, which
is wide open to natural views and is composed of local wood. Its landscaping alone was revolutionary, seeming to arrive at a unique aesthetic without
overt references to any previous styles . . . well, except for Modernism. The
garden façade facing the view is where the real action is, so don't pull a
drive-by and be disappointed by the greenery facing the entrance. Just read

about it until the proposed center opens. Inside, the way in which the interior of the house interrelates and interconnects with the garden and view is what makes this home phenomenal.

Despite his acclaim as an architect and designer, John Yeon was never officially certified as an architect. John Yeon was twenty-six years old when he designed this house, as well as its furniture, landscaping, and interior design. He even went so far as to lay stones in the yard himself. As to the landscaping, all plants used were native Oregon flora, and as no nurseries at the time could supply the variety needed, many trips to the coast and mountains were in order.

✦ This house was donated to the University of Oregon's School of Architecture and Allied Arts in 1995, a year after Yeon's death.

✦ Nearly across the street at 1100 Skyline Boulevard is Belluschi's Jennings R. Sutor House (1938), his tribute to the emerging style the Watzek House had pioneered.

PORTLAND HEIGHTS/COUNCIL CREST

The key to enjoying the homes in this impressive residential district is to take a slow drive or a long walk through it. An 1898 cable-car line facilitated its development, and twenty years later, the views of the city had lured much of Portland's elite to the area.

The grid of blocks that Vista Avenue passes through (the six intersections north of Spring Street) are eminently explorable, and further discoveries await anyone willing to venture up the winding lanes and roads off of Vista Avenue and Montgomery Drive. The range in architectural styles is fascinating, and gawking is appropriate.

Council Crest was supposedly found by an early settler in the region looking for a lost cow. Accounts vary as to how the area got its name, but it was topped by an amusement park for some time before being made into a city park proper in 1937. Riding a trolley car one-thousand feet above Portland and looking west, one can see the glory of Tualatin, an area once noted for its farming and now for its housing tracts.

15 JOSEPH R. BOWLES HOUSE 1924

1934 SW Vista Avenue
Architect: A. E. Doyle

Mediterranean villas sprinkled throughout the west hills of Portland were inspired by the social elite's trips to Italy. This home was built for nearly a million dollars by Joseph Bowles, president of the Northwest Steel Company. Ironically, there is not any steel visible in the construction of this beautiful, tile-roofed, two-story home with an unusual gray combed-stucco surface. The original sumptuous, even decadent, interior was once complete with its own temperature-controlled fur vault.

Joseph Bowles was a somewhat unsavory local character who was found in contempt of court during a trial in which he was accused of bribing a government inspector.

Up the street, at 2030 Vista Avenue, is the three-story Nicholas-Lang House (1885). It is notable for the chimney that comes thrusting up through the center of its front, with interesting designs evolving on the brickwork. Horace Nicholas was a Portland attorney who purchased fifteen blocks in this area for just under one hundred dollars. He lost it all, including this house, in a court settlement ten years later.

16 FRANK J. COBB HOUSE 1918

aka the J. D. Cobb House
2424 SW Montgomery Drive, east of Montgomery Drive,
*   west of Vista Avenue*
Architect: A. E. Doyle

One of the best-known homes in the state, this Jacobean behemoth is one of the handful of residences that A. E. Doyle worked on, and his work achieved landmark status here. (In 1919, an AIA jury recognized this home as one of the ten best examples of architecture within ten miles of City Hall.) Primarily stone-dressed brick, with a slate roof and an assortment of strong chimneys, this is a huge, stalwart, somewhat Gothic, and frighteningly large home, one of the biggest estates within city limits at fifteen thousand square feet and a couple of acres.

The view of the grounds is good from Vista Avenue, though you'll have to park at the base of the hill. The tower visible from Vista contains the library; one imagines it to be an idyllic spot for reading or napping.

16 *Frank J. Cobb House*

✦ Maybe you don't really want to live here; 1999 property taxes were over $36,000. Besides, think of all the dusting.

17 SAINT THOMAS MOORE CATHOLIC CHURCH 1939–40

3525 SW Patton Road, corner of Dosch Road, Talbot Road, and
Humphrey Boulevard
Architect: A. E. Doyle and Associates; designer, Pietro Belluschi

As a purveyor of the newborn Northwest Regional style, Pietro Belluschi was interested in creating modern expressions of architecture that were not shackled to past fashion. This church was the first of many that Belluschi designed (he had two chapels to his credit), and it was this sort of commission that gave him the greatest personal and professional sense of accomplishment. This is not a traditional Catholic church by any means. The pastor requested that the new church be a harmonic addition to its natural landscape, a prime tenet of what is sometimes referred to as Northwest Regionalism. The natural look of the church's wood, as well as the fact that Belluschi designed or approved all interior furnishings, is reminiscent of the "architect-as-unifying-artist" tenet of the Arts and Crafts movement.

Inside, decoration was held to a near-Protestant minimum. Diamond-patterned translucent windows (a pattern echoed in the main doorway) illuminate the interior walls, which are lined with vertically mounted cedar boards. These draw the eye upward to geometric Douglas fir trusses. On the exterior, horizontal pine boards give the building a low profile. Red cedar shingles originally topped the roof, with a discreet spire over all.

✦   This church came in over budget. The original project fund was $12,000. The final billing: $12,500.

18 DR. FRANK KISTNER HOUSE 1930

5400 SW Hewett Boulevard, southwest corner of Hewett Boulevard and Fifty-fourth Avenue
Architect: Wade Hampton Pipes

This house is done in the style of an English cottage that aspired to become a mansion. It shows the influence of master Arts and Crafts architect Edwin Luytens in the home's "butterfly" plan and in the almost bewildering array of various overhangs, windows, recesses, geometric angles, and oculi. There are nearly 11,000 square feet of genuine Arts and Crafts charm (including mahogany woodwork) inside.

17 *Saint Thomas Moore Catholic Church*

19 MAUD AND BELLE AINSWORTH HOUSE 1907–18

2542 SW Hillcrest Drive
Architect: William C. Knighton

A Craftsman house, this brick-and-shingle building has massive gables and unusual features. Lots of twists, turns, triangles, and even some smooth curves make up the outline of this asymmetrical home. One particularly interesting feature is the polygonal bay capped with a dormer on the front of the house. The architect, William C. Knighton, delighted in the unexpected structural flourish, as visitors to the Governor Hotel downtown can attest.

This house was built for two of local notable Captain John C. Ainsworth's daughters, one of whom, Maud, was a photographer. A darkroom was custom-built for her, which may help explain why this house took so long to develop.

19   *Maud and Belle*
     Ainsworth House

20 MARKLE–PITTOCK HOUSE 1889, 1928

1816 SW Hawthorne Terrace
Architect: Unknown
Remodel by Jacobberger and Smith

This is the *other* Pittock mansion. George Markle Jr., the man responsible for reviving the foundations of Willard's Ruins into the Portland Hotel, lived here when it was "the most prominent house on the Portland skyline," according to E. Kimbark MacColl. Markle went on to face arrest for misuse of public funds within two years; he slipped out of town, never to return. Originally a Queen Anne-style home, Frederick Pittock (the only son of newspaper kingpin and real-estate investor Henry Pittock) remodeled this house to suit his Jacobean fancy.

21   *Edwin Burke House*

21   EDWIN BURKE HOUSE 1926

1707 SW Hawthorne Terrace
Architect: Wade Hampton Pipes

Despite its open front, and because of its limited window space, this Arts and Crafts home seems to look into itself. An interesting note: follow the roof down below the dormer above the front door to see how low it drops from gable tops on the flanking sides.

Wade Hampton Pipes was a Portland native who studied architecture in England, and it shows in his designs for homes like this one and the house to its direct west, the Ida Catlin House (1927), a home with an interesting bay window/turret design. Inspired by English cottages, these homes apparently engaged in some carbo-loading in their drafting to reach their sizable dimensions. The two make a unified pair with their matching roof pitches and gables.

22   PIGGOTT'S CASTLE 1892

aka Charles Piggott House
2591 SW Buckingham Terrace
Architect: Unknown

This house is straight out of a fairy tale with an unhappy ending. Once upon a time (1877, to be exact), a man name Charles Piggott came to Portland. He worked a lot of jobs before becoming a lawyer. (That's not the unhappy ending.)

22 *Piggott's Castle*

Piggott built himself a castle with bricks from a brick company he owned. He called it "Mount Gleall Castle." (The name was an anagram for his children's names—Gladys, Earl, and Lloyd.) Piggott liked to sit in his Romanesque-Moorish castle's tower and look down at the river and city below him. He wanted to build an observatory on the top of his tower.

Then about a year after he moved into the castle, the Panic of 1893 hit. Piggott was broke, and he moved out. Now his castle was called "Piggott's Folly."

23 OREGON HEALTH SCIENCES UNIVERSITY
aka Pill Hill
3181 SW Sam Jackson Park Road

A nonprofit public corporation, OHSU has been engaged in medical care, research, and education since the nineteenth century. From its spot high on the hill, it casts a large shadow on the Portland area in terms of employment and prestige. The particular shapes of these shadows are dictated by the buildings themselves, and there are a nearly bewildering variety of them, from terra-cotta-decorated old-guard structures to more-brutal International styles and some very distinguished modern buildings. As to the location and placement of the buildings, it is a scenic though impractical site, with some creative architectural solutions taking place as a result.

✦ The area above and behind OHSU between SW Ninth Avenue and Fairmount Boulevard is part of the original land claim of John Donner (1790–1879), brother of famed early explorer George Donner of Donner's Pass notoriety.

24 DOERNBECHER CHILDREN'S HOSPITAL 1998
Architect: Zimmer Gunsul Frasca Partnership

A hospital can be a scary place, especially for children. The challenge for the architects of this building was twofold: first, to make a healing space that contained design elements to set children at ease—or to make them feel "cozy," in Frasca's words—and second, to build a hospital where there was no actual physical site.

This building's creation was dictated by the air rights of the hospital as much as by actual land-holdings. The plain yet powerful hospital somehow manages to occupy virtually no actual land, instead stretching like a bridge across a steep ravine and, with near magic, connecting the north and south parts of the hospital. The stated objective of the architectural firm was to "play big" with the exterior space while "playing small" with the interior, giving it a low-key feel and scale for the patients within. Described by architectural critic Allan Temko as "probably the best children's hospital ever built," its curving, metal-paneled exterior, beautiful tableaus, inner courtyards, and playful design elements make it a first-class addition to Portland's buildings.

While the exceptional "suspended curvilinear" exterior is noteworthy, it is the inside of the building that astounds. Flocks of birds fly down halls, bright colors surge, and natural themes are illuminated by waves of natural lighting. The central courtyard is rife with copper animal life by sculptor Wayne Chabre.

23 *OHSU Sculpture, by Larry Kirkland, 1992*

24   *Doernbecher Children's Hospital*

25   VOLLUM INSTITUTE 1987
Architect: Zimmer Gunsul Frasca Partnership

This structure fits between two other looming, pre-existing buildings, but the shape of the Vollum Institute is unique enough to make it stand out separately even under such crowded circumstances. Squeezed between two other structures, the building is bright enough and has enough classical influences to make it notable, and its glass-topped rooftop greenhouse is perhaps a first evolutionary step towards OMSI's later glass pyramid lobby.

The southwest side of the building is busy, full of angles, and reflects bright light from its terra-cotta facade onto the courtyard below. Opposite it, on the northeast side of the lab, is a very different view. Visible to downtown Portland, it is brick, with a curved architectural feature (called a *belvedere*) to allow for an appreciation of the vista below. If you need a steady hand to play Operation, this is the building; portions are "vibration isolated for delicate instrumentation."

26   "FLEXURAL" BRIDGE 1993
Campus Drive between Terwilliger Boulevard and Sam Jackson
  Park Road
Designer: Mike Walkiewicz

This remarkable 660-foot bridge links Oregon Health Sciences University with the Veterans Hospital. Constructed in accordance with building codes, it was designed in twenty-four-foot sections because of the limited physical space available for installation. This was made possible by repeated bracing and having the sections cantilevered out from the two structural towers.

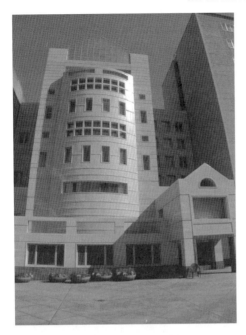

25 *Vollum Institute*

26 *"Flexural" Bridge interior*

CORBETT-TERWILLIGER-LAIR HILL

This is close to where early settler William Johnson came with two Native American slaves and a distillery to make a liquor encouragingly called "blue ruin." Later, Kentucky native Elizabeth Caruthers and her son, Finice, laid claim to the 640 acres south of the original Portland site in 1847, about where the Ross Island Bridge is currently located. The two left no heirs, and a series of parties laid claim to their property, most notably a man who went by the moniker "Wrestling Joe."

As Portland evolved into a shipping hub, a rail line and Macadam Avenue turned this area into a transportation corridor for the Willamette farms to the south. When the Harbor Drive project widened Front Avenue (connecting Harbor Drive to Barbur Boulevard/Highway 99) in 1943, it effectively split the neighborhood into two zones. This was followed by the estrangement of Corbett from downtown Portland by the Interstate 5 interchange and the South Auditorium project in the 1960s, which razed the northern part of Corbett for urban-renewal purposes.

The result: the semi-hodgepodge of confusing streets and isolated neighborhood groupings one finds today, as well as one of the first communities to form a neighborhood group to voice their own interests in civic affairs.

27   LEWIS AND CLARK COLLEGE
0615 SW Palatine Hill Road

"Every time a student walks past a really urgent, expressive piece of architecture that belongs to his college, it can help reassure him that he does have that mind, does have that soul."

—Louis Kahn, *Fortune,* May 1963

Lewis and Clark College is a smallish, liberal-arts institution with a good academic reputation and impressive landscaping in a stunning location. It began life as a Presbyterian college (chartered 1867) in Albany. Making the move to Portland, the college rented rooms from the Temple Beth Israel School downtown before moving to the former Fir Acres in 1942 at a purchase price of $46,000. This was a real deal, as the original manor house and gardens cost $1.3 million to build nearly twenty years earlier. While the present-day campus cannot compete with Reed College for having an architectural cohesion to its parts, it does possess some outstanding local highlights, notably the Frank Manor House.

FRANK MANOR HOUSE 1926
Also Odell Manor, aka "Fir Acres"
Architect: Herman Brookman

Anti-Semitism was a contributing factor to the presence of this beautiful building, which was once the city's most impressive private estate. The Frank family (of Meier & Frank) sought to make their own cultural oasis in lieu of

27 b   *Gallery of Contemporary Art*

the Portland clubs that snubbed them because of their Judaism. Herman Brookman (who also designed Portland's Temple Beth Israel) was commissioned for the job, and this building was the dramatic result. Although the style of this building is markedly different from the Byzantine Temple Beth Israel, the similarity in the two buildings is the extraordinary quality of work and attention to detailing that both display.

This lavish residence, which is equal parts English Tudor and French chateau, is eminently well suited for its Portland location. Two wings are angled for garden viewing in the back; a delightful turret to the north can be found where the wings meet in the front. It was designed to look as if it were constructed over a long period of time, although it actually was built relatively quickly. Inside, there are seven fireplaces and some nice carved stone and wood. Check for plaster ceiling animals, carved oak over the

27 a   *Frank Manor House*

doorways, excellent metalwork, and a silverware drawer in the twelfth step up to the second floor of the grand staircase. Take time for a slow walk through and around this building; this one is sure to reward your eye—and your eye is sure to notice the relationship of Mount Hood to this view spot. The undulating slate roof alone is worthy of contemplation as one delays cramming for those final exams.

Be sure to walk east to the symmetrical formal garden. Portland's view of Mount Hood has perhaps been overly ballyhooed over the years by locals, but this is the best spot to view it from. The garden's central focus on the mountain makes it actually look like it does in hyperbolic promotional city artwork. One should continue to the Gallery of Contemporary Art (Thomas Hacker and Associates), a worthy brick building that is considerably enhanced by John Buck's bronze sculptures that flank its entrance. The two figures balance an assortment of odd and contrasting symbols and items, with an astronomical theme running through the left piece's form (*Music in the Sky*), while the right sculpture (*The Hawk and the Dove*) has a more down-to-earth symbology, denoted perhaps by the fact that the figure's head is still on its shoulders.

AGNES FLANAGAN CHAPEL 1969
Architect: Paul Thiry

This sixteen-sided chapel emerges from the trees in a dramatic rise from its wide base. Northwest architect Thiry (who also designed the Aubrey R. Watzek Library on campus) designed a beautiful building, and its rustic nature is perfectly captured when it is approached from the campus side. Walking to the entrance on the walkway/bridge means a closer look at the chapel's Native American guardian statues, which were done by Lelooska in honor of Christian evangelists. Inside, the chapel resembles an amphitheater as much as a church, with circular seating around the center creating an interactive and yet intimate space appropriate for spiritual or concert purposes.

CHAPTER 9

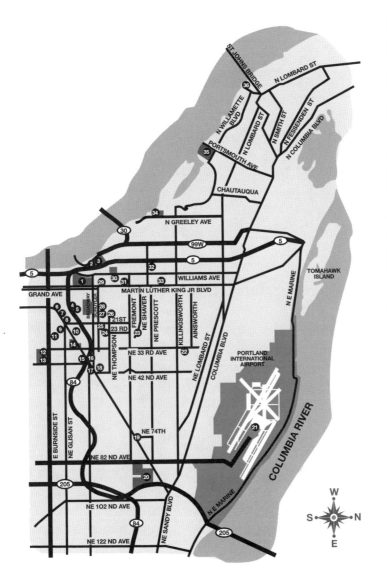

ST JOHNS BRIDGE

N LOMBARD ST

N WILLAMETTE BLVD

N LOMBARD ST

N SMITH ST

N FESSENDEN ST

N COLUMBIA BLVD

PORTSMOUTH AVE

CHAUTAUQUA

N GREELEY AVE

99W

5

5

WILLIAMS AVE

TOMAHAWK ISLAND

GRAND AVE

MARTIN LUTHER KING JR BLVD

BROADWAY

SCHUYLER

21ST

23 RD

FREMONT

NE SHAVER

NE PRESCOTT

KILLINGSWORTH

AINSWORTH

NE LOMBARD ST

COLUMBIA BLVD

N E MARINE

NE THOMPSON

NE 33 RD AVE

NE 42 ND AVE

PORTLAND INTERNATIONAL AIRPORT

COLUMBIA RIVER

NE BURNSIDE ST

NE GLISAN ST

NE 82 ND AVE

NE 74TH

84

NE 102 ND AVE

NE SANDY BLVD

N E MARINE

NE 122 ND AVE

84

205

205

W

N

S

E

NORTHEAST/NORTH

1   *Oregon Convention Center*

CHAPTER 9

NORTHEAST/
NORTH

"Always design a thing by considering it in its next larger context—a chair in a room, a room in a house, a house in an environment, an environment in a city plan."
—Architect Eliel Saarinen, quoted by his son Eero, in *Time,* June 2, 1977

1 OREGON CONVENTION CENTER 1990
777 NE Martin Luther King Jr. Boulevard
Architect: Zimmer Gunsul Frasca Partnership

One of the easiest buildings to spot in Portland is the Oregon Convention Center. Its two 260-foot tinted-green glass towers sprout vertically from the body, creating a distinctive sightline that serves no particular function but still looks great. At a cost of $91.5 million, they'd better. The green towers help to jazz up what is known in the trade as a "limited-use, large-scale facility." In other words, one of those dreadful holding pens full of glad-handing salespeople and marathon foot journeys to get to the restroom.

Writer Paul Goldberger pointed out that the problem in designing a convention center is in figuring how to make the thing look less like a fat behemoth and more attractive. This particular convention center accomplishes these goals with a nicely rounded yellow brick exterior and a user-friendly interior that doesn't intimidate the convention-goer with colossal straight corridors. But let's face it, nobody really cares about this building's "large-scale facility" considerations with those two dramatic towers overhead. The twin towers accomplish something fairly amazing: they are visible from a variety of directions without actually *obscuring* anything. As such, they link the Convention Center to the river and the west side in the best possible fashion. (Part of that link may be attributed to the fact that the convention center's towers appear to emulate the forms of the travertine sculptures in front of the Justice Center.) Although attempts were made to cut the twin towers from the building's plans for financial reasons, they were defended repeatedly by architect Bob Frasca.

Access to the towers is restricted for safety reasons; the highest point one can go to is the Skyview terrace on the fourth floor. Those windows aren't easy to clean either. Crews wash 1,500 panes (53,300 square feet) to get the job done. Interestingly, if you take light-rail past the convention center, take note of the transit shelters there; their ribbed glass is intended to mirror the design of the towers.

✦   The Convention Center's dedication ceremony featured a Tupperware display and a city dump truck.

2 THE ROSE GARDEN 1995

East end of the Steel Bridge. You can't miss it.
Architect: Ellerbe Beckett (Kansas City, Missouri)

Previously a parking lot, the Rose Garden is a 785,000-square-foot arena that was built for $262 million. The design itself is mildly attractive and organic, though not particularly distinctive as giant arenas go. The architect of the Rose Garden specializes in these designs, and he didn't even use a local consulting firm; this made the design review process an antagonistic one, but that's all water under the Steel Bridge now.

The Rose Garden's roof resembles a Belgian ship-captain's cap; its nautical-themed hat fits in with the nearby river and distinguishes it nicely within the surroundings of the convention center, the massive grain silos to the west, and the square International-style Memorial Coliseum. Situating it next to the transit center was an inspired stroke, obviating the need for huge parking lots that gobble up precious riverfront area, as Cincinnati has done with its two sports coliseums.

The Rose Garden holds 21,000 to 23,000 people. Views inside range from great to alpine; one can usually get to one's seat without the giddy vertigo a steeper incline would give, and it is easy to make one's way around inside the arena. It is essentially a well-designed and comfortable interior.

✦   Over 150 adjustable acoustical panels can be "tuned" to the varying needs of Sting, the Trail Blazers, or Motörhead, as the occasion demands.

✦   45,000 tons of construction debris was recycled into the construction of this arena.

2 *The Rose Garden*

3 THE MEMORIAL COLISEUM 1960

It's big and at the east end of the Broadway Bridge.
Architect: SOM

Wood was initially considered as the primary building material for this International-style building, but steel was cheaper, so the Coliseum is primarily made of glass and metal. It's interesting to picture the Coliseum made of lumber; it might redeem its somewhat dated look and less-than-sterling maintenance. Regardless of the look of the building from outside, the view of Portland from inside the Coliseum is sublime; the square building's curtain wall windows look out in all directions in a dramatic fashion. This view may be lost in the near future as city consultants envision new ways to breathe life into the Rose Quarter by gazing longingly at the four city blocks the Coliseum covers.

The greatest moment in Portland sports occurred here on June 5, 1977, when the Trail Blazers defeated the Philadelphia 76ers in game six of the NBA Finals. Nearly thirteen thousand fans rushed out of the Memorial Coliseum to join ranks with the rest of the city in a nightlong celebration dedicated to the spirited revelry that only orange, air-filled spheres can induce.

✦ The first show to play at the Memorial Coliseum did not augur well: it was Holiday on Ice. The Beatles helped to erase that bad taste five years later, playing to the best-behaved U.S. crowd on their national tour.

4 PORTLAND STATE OFFICE BUILDING 1994

800 NE Oregon Street, between Oregon Street, Lloyd Boulevard,
and Ninth Avenue
Architect: GBD Architects

The colors and design of this building obviously take into account the Bonneville Power Administration Headquarters to the east. That's good. But this building seems to be an assemblage of elements that do not flow together, particularly on the south side. The geometric features seem merely stuck on, apropos of nothing, as opposed to massing that flows into the general structure of the building, as exemplified by the Fox Tower.

There are elements that do work in an isolated sense with the State Office Building. One is its dramatic faux-dome at the top. Call it whimsical, call it decorative, but don't call it useless. It's a great spot to fly flags from. Another highlight of this structure is the attractive (though incongruous) Art Deco stairway corner to the east.

As the fashion of cast-iron, plaster, and terra-cotta building ornamentation has long since passed, designers of modern structures in Portland sometimes attempt to make up for the lack of architectural ornamentation by grafting large works of public art onto the buildings. In some cases the results work exceptionally well, as is the case with the sculpture *Ideals* (Muriel Castanis) at this building. Some of the other results range from the queasy *Quest* (Standard Insurance Building) to the controversial *Portlandia* (Portland Building), to the macabre red cedar tree shackled to the ODS Tower.

6 *7-Up Bottling Company Building*

5 BONNEVILLE POWER ADMINISTRATION HEADQUARTERS 1987

905 NE Eleventh Avenue
Architect: Zimmer Gunsul Frasca Partnership

Located in a highly visible spot overlooking Highway 84, the curved span of the seven-story Bonneville Power Administration Headquarters manages to lend an air of dignity to the inauspicious spectacle below it. The white, green, and blue of the bright marble-and-granite façade conceal a courtyard behind, as well as an interesting stepped-back series of terraces on the north side.

✦   From a monograph titled *Zimmer Gunsul Frasca,* this building is described thusly: "The formal architectural idea is that of an oyster; a hard shell cupped around a soft inner core." Blech.

6 7-UP BOTTLING COMPANY BUILDING 1941

Originally Portland Bottling Company
1321 NE Couch Street, just north of Sandy Boulevard
Architect: Arthur Cramer

This building is the first of a series of Art Deco buildings on Sandy Boulevard imbedded amongst its commercial crudeness. If you are headed eastbound, this painted stucco building is the first one you'll see. It has simple horizontal lines that play off of each other nicely; there are smooth lines on the entrance and corner, with harder geometrics around the window and "7-Up" sign; glass bricks line the door. In short: the building gleams with the prospect of a brighter future through bottling soft drinks in fashionable digs. It is très Art Moderne, aerodynamic, and pleasing.

7 *Salvation Army
Divisional Headquarters*

7 SALVATION ARMY DIVISIONAL HEADQUARTERS 1930

Originally Farmer's Insurance Building
1785 NE Sandy Boulevard
Architect: Charles Ertz

The commuters on Sandy Boulevard should consider themselves lucky to have the second of Sandy's terrific Art Deco buildings to ogle. Each is a nice contrast to the others and a good lesson in the range of styles possible within Art Deco. Where the 7-Up Building is horizontal, this structure goes vertical. The unique vertical massing of the structure gives it great lines, and the rounded corner entrance with coin-shaped portico is perfect counterpoint. It serves as an aesthetic complement to its contemporary in time and fashion, the Jantzen Building, which is across the street.

✦ *Confiscating the Trombone Department:* The Salvation Army has been well established in Portland, though not always popular for its vociferous opposition to vice. (Its seal, shown on this building, reads "Blood and Fire.") E. Kimbark MacColl notes that early in the city's history the Salvation Army band often played unsolicited numbers to the city council, until they outlawed the practice and arrested the band.

8 THE JANTZEN BUILDING 1930

NE Sandy Boulevard and NE Twentieth Avenue
Architect: Richard Sundeleaf

This may be the only building in the Pacific Northwest where swimwear and terra-cotta collide.

The Jantzen Organization (originally known as the Portland Knitting Company) got its beginnings by designing swim trunks for the Portland Rowing Club in 1913. By the 1920s, Americans took a greater interest in recreational bathing, and Jantzen became the world's leading manufacturer of swimwear.

During a frenzy of corporate expansion, the company hired Portland native Richard Sundeleaf, a graduate of the University of Oregon School of Architecture, to design the firm's factories, warehouses, and administration offices. The resultant Jantzen Administration Building is an example of what an open-minded architect working in conjunction with an architectural sculptor (Gabriel Lavare) can accomplish in making a company's corporate image delightfully concrete.

The brick building is trimmed in terra-cotta decorated with the Jantzen's trademark "Diving Girl" arched across medallions and interspersed with seashells and briny creatures of the deep. The design of the brickwork, particularly at the front entrance, is stunning. The terra-cotta details are exotic

8 *Jantzen Building*

but tastefully rendered, and the net result is a building that manages to be both stalwart and whimsical at the same time. It is unique, well worth a look.

✦　Architect Richard Sundeleaf worked for local giant A. E. Doyle's architectural firm from 1923 to 1925, whereupon Doyle recommended that Sundeleaf "give up architecture." Thankfully, he didn't, and went on to create a firm with more than two thousand commissions.

✦　The first swimsuit made by Jantzen for the Portland Rowing Club was nearly eight pounds when soaking wet. "Man overboard! . . . Never mind."

9 ALBERTINA KERR NURSERY 1921

424 NE Twenty-second Avenue
Architect: Johnson, Parker, and Wallwork

Alexander H. Kerr, who made a fortune from his invention of the cap for the "Kerr Economy Canning Jar," donated this building for foundlings under the age of three, and named it after his second wife. The respectable-looking redbrick Georgian building has a shallow, two-story portico and lots of dormers.

10 BATTERY KING STATION 1940

North side of NE Sandy Boulevard and the car dealerships
Architect: Associated Oil Company

A beautiful Deco gem, with a mini-tower at the top that looks like pure pottery.

10 *Battery King Station*

11 *Coca-Cola Syrup Factory*

11 COCA-COLA SYRUP FACTORY 1941
2710 NE Davis Street, Davis and Twenty-eighth Avenue
Architect: James M. Shelton (Atlanta, Georgia)

While architect James Shelton was seemingly inspired by the effervescent Art Deco stylings of the 7-Up Bottling Building in northeast Portland, the completion dates of the two streamlined industrial buildings are the same. A drive through the oppressively unimaginative architecture of any modern business park makes one realize how attractive a building like this one really is.

While here, take note of the Laurelhurst Theatre (1923, unknown architect) to the south on Burnside Street. Originally a one-screen movie house, it eventually proliferated into four theaters, but to no avail. The theater could not compete with the multiplexes of the 1980s, and it went to seed until its renovation and reopening in 2000.

LAURELHURST

Laurelhurst straddles both the northeast and southeast. Initially owned by the Ladd Estate Company, it was a 462-acre orchard for a time, and then a ranch. The land was sold to the newly formed Laurelhurst Company in 1909 for $2 million, the largest sale of land in Portland's history at the time. Laurelhurst's meandering streets and rich landscaping (influenced by the famed Olmsted brothers) were meant to create mini-vistas and a bit of the country in the city wherever one turned; today, they discourage through traffic, but are perfect for a walk. Beautiful residences circle Laurelhurst Park (originally a swamp) and its environs.

The statue of Joan of Arc on horseback in the circular park at NE Thirty-ninth Avenue and Glisan Street is the site of the original Laurelhurst sales office. According to some, a horse with one raised hoof denotes that the rider was either injured in battle or died from battlefield complications. Both front hoofs raised may mean the rider was killed in combat. All *four* hoofs raised means that the rider denies the existence of the laws of gravitation.

✦   The Laurelhurst Company promoted this area by advertising that "everything of an objectionable nature will be excluded." That included all nonwhites and apartment dwellers. The major roads into Laurelhurst have impressive sandstone gate pylons, and originally, the main road also had a gate—useful if any apartment dwellers tried to sneak in.

12 *Harry A. Green House*

13 *Mayor H. Russell Albee House*

12 HARRY A. GREEN HOUSE 1928

3316 SE Ankeny Street
Architect: Herman Brookman

From the same man who designed many local homes and businesses in a variety of styles, Brookman here created a one-of-a-kind wonder. It is a Mediterranean/Byzantine marvel with round tower, plentiful chimneys, bronzed iron gates, and Art Deco decorative features utilizing a peacock motif.

13 MAYOR H. RUSSELL ALBEE HOUSE 1912

3360 SE Ankeny Street
Architect: A. E. Doyle

Although designed in the Colonial Revival style, the design elements and brick of this house make it seem "heftier" than other local examples. The Palladian windows give the boxy Colonial form some much-needed curves, and there are rounded bays on the back side of the home as well.

14 NITYANADA INSTITUTE RUDRANADA ASHRAM
1910

Originally Mann Old Peoples Home
1025 NE Thirty-third Avenue, west side, just south of Sandy
  Boulevard
Architect: Whitehouse and Foulihoux

This beautiful Tudor rooming house was built by distinguished architects; presently, its occupants have ensured their peace of mind by enclosing the grounds with steroidal shrubbery. To their credit, they have also renovated and added a wing to the building, and have landscaped the property nicely.

15 EIGHTH CHURCH OF CHRIST SCIENTIST 1926

3505 NE Imperial Avenue
Architect: Charles Ertz/Stanton, Boles, Maguire and Church

This church does a great job of commanding its street corner. It is an interesting hybrid of Byzantine massing, Mediterranean roof stylings and Romanesque details. The octagonal center of the church is surrounded by various attachments; the decorative mini-arch corbelling below the cornice gives the church a noteworthy (if slightly odd) look.

HOLLYWOOD

Named after its theater, regrettably few noteworthy buildings remain in Hollywood from its time of primary initial development from 1910 to 1940.

16 THE STEIGERWALD DAIRY BUILDING 1926

aka the 7-Up Building
3705 NE Sandy Boulevard
Architect: H. L. Camp and Company

As cars became more omnipresent in the 1920s and 1930s, architecture became more assertive in trying to catch the eye of the passing motorist with a style sometimes referred to as "Roadside Thematic." Regardless of the high-falutin' terminology, this style is easily recognizable. This sophisticated approach to building theorizes that if you are going to name your restaurant the Brown Derby, the establishment should be shaped like a brown derby hat.

The Steigerwald Dairy Building once held the distinction of being in the shape of a huge milk bottle, as well as qualifying as the tallest building in northeast Portland. The original milk-bottle shape was covered over with lath and plaster in 1936, and for a short time it took the shape of two Pabco Paint cans before the current 7-Up sign was placed on the top. The discerning observer can still get a sense of the milk jug beneath, trying to proclaim "Steigerwald Milk: Bold on Quality—Never on Price."

15   *Eighth Church of*
      Christ Scientist

16   *Steigerwald Dairy Building*

17   *Hollywood Movie Theater*

17   HOLLYWOOD MOVIE THEATER 1925

4122 NE Sandy Boulevard
Architect: John V. Bennes, Harry A. Herzog

This theater can best be summed up by the term *rococo* Art Deco. Made of stuccoed concrete, the multi-colored terra-cotta ornamentation on the pavilion is elaborate, colorful, and stunning. Details from that incredible tower include shells, theatrical masks, scrolls, fruits, lyre-playing angels, mermaids, bearded men, finials, and even a cleverly disguised kitchen sink. This theater must have been even more impressive at its 1925 unveiling, with produce stands around it and farms in plain sight.

Originally built as one theater with 1,500 seats, it was partitioned into three venues in 1975. This did not prevent it from becoming increasingly dilapidated until its purchase more than twenty years later by a nonprofit group that has been restoring it to its former glory. Note that in the main theater the red drapery to the sides of the screen may be pulled back, revealing the original hand-painted Art Deco designs and fake balconies.

✦   Unfortunately, the currently attached 1960s marquee is ugly, and given its exotically beautiful setting, it stands out even more by contrast.

18 HOLLYWOOD LIBRARY 2002

NE Tillamook Street between Fortieth and Forty-first Avenues
Architect: Thomas Hacker and Associates/GBD Architects

The watchwords of Portland architecture in the new millennium are "mixed use," and here's a good example of it. This proposed four-story building houses a library, with forty-seven rental housing units above it. The corners and penthouse floor will be stepped back, and the sides have a number of bays to make the size of the library less imposing in its nearly residential setting. (The library's large scale will theoretically make it useful until at least the year 2100.) With its brick and cast-limestone detailing and reasonable size, this should be another beautiful library in a city becoming known for them.

FARTHER EAST

19 SANDY JUG TAVERN 1929

Originally the Jug, the Orange Blossom Jug
7417 NE Sandy Boulevard
Architect: Unknown

This windowless bottle squats in the middle of a parking lot in its current incarnation as a topless bar. No doubt the owners thought that painting their establishment brown and titling it in the worst spirit of sophomoric wordplay was a stroke of wit. Call it brash symbolism or merely a bad idea, it is still the only building in town once capped by an eight ball, with simulated pool balls recessed in the roof.

19 *Sandy Jug Tavern*

20 *Marilyn Moyer Meditation Chapel*

21 *Portland International Airport Canopy*

20 MARILYN MOYER MEDITATION CHAPEL 1991
The Grotto, Sandy Boulevard and Eighty-fifth Avenue
Architects: Bob Thompson and Ned Vaivoda

Erected by local developer Tom Moyer for his wife, Marilyn, this $1.9-million memorial commands a beautiful view from a scenic spot. Literally perched on the edge of a cliff and backed by a scenic garden and monastery, the chapel is a still and introspective location. The design of the glass-fronted building takes beautiful advantage of its unique setting.

✦ East of the Grotto lies the Parkrose neighborhood, noted for being part of the original land claim of Vermont native Ebenezer Quimby.

21 PORTLAND INTERNATIONAL AIRPORT CANOPY 2000
Northeast Portland
Architects of Terminal Access Program: ZGF Partnership, KPFF Consulting Engineers

The artistic promotional renderings for this remodel/roof job showed a huge glass canopy enclosing the traffic lanes between the new parking garage and the renovated terminal—resembling a glittering future vision from a 1940s science-fiction pulp.

The results lived up to my expectations, despite the fact that the advertised design was not executed exactly. Hanging nearly a hundred feet high, the 100,000-square-foot roof is practical in that it keeps one dry when approaching the airport from the parking garage. (The new, more closely located parking garage, terminal remodel, and road work were all part of the same project.) But practicality is combined with the sublime in this two-acre umbrella. The space that is created over the roadway is huge, and with its prudent landscaping and white color, it is awe-inspiring and (for lack of better terms) open and friendly. The sun's rays are muted and the rain (or even snow) is kept from one's back in style.

The most notable engineering feat of the canopy may be the steel rod rigging that connects the wide pedestrian access bridges with girders above. These, in turn, are supported by triangular trusses all the way across the canopy. Looking up, across, and down again is a singularly rewarding experience.

22 KENNEDY SCHOOL 1915

5736 NE Thirty-third Avenue
Architect: Floyd A. Naramore/Renovation: Fletcher Farr Ayotte

This schoolhouse was something of an anomaly in its day. Its multi-winged, single-story plan was designed for safety in case of emergency evacuation. Now, the building is a good example of the approach Portland's McMenamin brothers take to their restorations. This school was closed down in 1980, and it remained boarded up until the McMenamins purchased the property from the city and "re-did" it as a community center/restaurant/hotel/movie house, creating a synthesis between the school's history and the company's own psychedelic Olde English interiors.

This building's renovation began with an organic approach, incorporating as many original features of the school as possible. According to Mike McMenamin, the project's spontaneity was reflected in the fact that there was not an architectural rendering of the interior at the outset of the project, only a floor plan.

The results include the still-functional basketball court and the classrooms (with blackboards intact), which now serve as lodging quarters for the hotel's guests. The manifold aspects of the location's art reflect the area's history, as no surface has been left undecorated. Electrical boxes, steam pipes, doors, and even the backboards of the basketball court are all tied together in one grand thematic tapestry, combining with the school's original Renaissance bas-relief panels in the lobby.

✦ Architect for the Portland school system Floyd Naramore impressed so many people with his designs for schools like Couch Elementary and Franklin High School that he was hired away by the Seattle School District in 1919.

22 *Kennedy School*

ALAMEDA

aka The Alameda, The Alameda Ridge

This unusually shaped district runs southeast along the top of the Alameda Ridge for about two miles. While the ridge is relatively low, it stands out prominently on the rather flat east side of Portland.

Developed primarily between 1910 and 1940, many parcels in the area originally went for two-to-three-thousand dollars, and at that outrageous price, one was not even allowed to build stables on the ridge; the Alameda Park development also excluded all "people of undesirable colors and kinds." Alameda coils and winds through some varied and beautiful residential architecture.

23 THOMAS J. AUTZEN HOUSE 1927
2425 NE Alameda Drive
Architect: Kirtland K. Cutter

This house is located on the Alameda Ridge on its own irregular block in such a way that it addresses a lot of street. This Tudor-style house does an admirable feat of solving its problem, though plantings conceal much of the home's charm. The carved wood above the entryway is in a style known as "linenfold" (mimicking the look of folded linen). This style of carving is carried throughout the interior. If the wood gets wrinkled, it's virtually impossible to iron out.

✦ Kirtland K. Cutter (1860–1939) designed a number of homes in Washington, where he tended toward rambling Tudor styles like this one.

IRVINGTON/LLOYD CENTER

This district was initially the 644-acre land claim (1851) of Scotland native Captain William Irving (1816–72). In 1871, Ben Holladay purchased a portion of this claim to create a 271-square block district to the south of what is now Irvington. After changing hands a number of times, a section of the land was purchased by the Prospect Park Company, who began using Irvington as a site for snob-appeal homes. Houses had to be set back twenty-five feet, cost no less than $2,500, and were limited to large plots of land. The area was primarily built up between 1905 and 1930, with a variety of Arts and Crafts bungalows, Victorians, and apartment buildings toward Broadway.

After suffering the typical losses of buildings to parking lots, commercial development, and conversion to apartments in the 1950s and '60s, Irvington has been impressively revitalized. The southern portion of the area was the residential district known as Holladay's Addition. California oilman Ralph B. Lloyd purchased massive areas of east-side property here in the 1920s, with the hope of creating a commercial district to rival downtown Portland. (One of his wishes for the area was a professional baseball stadium.) By the time of Lloyd's death in 1953, he owned 150 blocks, and with most of them cleared, the area was strangely barren until the construction of Lloyd Center (John Graham, architect) between 1958 and 1960. The mall was the largest urban shopping center in the nation, and certainly the only one with a skating rink. It remained open-air until its enclosure as part of a remodel thirty years later.

The Morland Apartments (1530 NE Tenth Avenue, 1931) were built within a decade of the 1922 discovery of King Tut's tomb. It gives some historic symbolism to the rampant materialism of Lloyd Center. Architect Elmer E. Feig also did a number of other apartment buildings in the Northwest. The Manhattan Apartment Building (1930) on 2209 NW Everett Street also pursues an Egyptian theme, though it's not as powerful or well maintained as this building. The Blackstone Apartments on the Portland State University campus share some identical elements with this building.

✦   Architects Ellis Lawrence and A. E. Doyle both lived in Irvington and designed buildings there.

Morland Apartments

24 *William Kennard House*

24 WILLIAM KENNARD HOUSE 1910
2230 NE Thompson Street
Architect: R. N. Hockenberry and Co.

This is a colossal faux Craftsman-style house, in that it utilizes concrete blocks cleverly imitating natural stone. One cannot help but admire this house's powerful horizontal layout and street presence.

Raymond N. Hockenberry (1876–1951) moved to Portland in 1905, a perfect time for an architect, considering the building boom about to explode in Portland. He designed the Crater Lake Lodge (1911–15) and made a career of building personal homes, living in them for a year, and then moving on to a new one. He lived in Irvington for three years; in 1916 he moved his family to New York.

For fifteen thousand dollars in 1912, you could get yourself a cozy Arts and Crafts home like the Michael Brady House next door to the west (1912, Jacobberger and Smith), complete with bay window and double gable. Now you'd have a hard time remodeling one of its rooms for that amount. Smooth stucco and smooth intersections between walls and roof mark this home.

Across the street is a 1910 home done in the same style, also by Jacobberger.

25 CENTRAL LUTHERAN CHURCH 1948–51
2104 NE Hancock Street
Architect: Pietro Belluschi

The congregation of this church wanted a Gothic place of worship.

They didn't get one.

Instead, they received a Scandinavian church with a Japanese flavor and a Pacific Northwest interior. The rectangular-block shape of the church's body is mildly reminiscent of the Portland Art Museum, although the rounded brick north end makes it distinctively its own. (The flat roof of the clerestory resulted in leakage problems for decades, until the church was substantially remodeled in 2000.) This is not a very traditional design for a church; although it has a tower, it is without walls per se, being constructed, in part, only of simple beams. The church's entrance has a Japanese-flavored gateway, which George McMath has noted shows the influence of Belluschi's chief designer at the time, K. E. Richardson.

Inside, the laminated-wood arches are kept in relative dark compared to the ample natural lighting of the chancel. Originally, the simple beam pattern of the tower was repeated behind the cross in a design that, unfortunately, would become clichéd in the following decades. This simplicity is also found in the building materials used: some bricks, wood, stained glass, a few touches of bronze, and there you have it.

26 MARCUS J. DELAHUNT HOUSE 1909
aka the Hoover House
1617 NE Thompson Street
Architect: John V. Bennes (of Bennes, Hendricks and Thompson)

Frank Lloyd Wright did not design this beautiful Prairie-style home, but he may as well have, as it is an excellent example of the form he innovated, and was the first one of the Prairie style built on the east side of the Willamette. Bennes was an office boy in Wright's office and apparently picked up some pointers from the master.

Witness the big porch, huge eaves, and giant support pillars. For another example of the style, see the Smith House (1911) down the street at 2330 NE Thompson.

27 *Westminster Presbyterian Church*

27 WESTMINSTER PRESBYTERIAN CHURCH 1912–14
1624 NE Hancock Street (facing Schuyler Street)
Architect: Lawrence and Holford

A stone Gothic church all the way, designed by Irvington resident Ellis F. Lawrence, and one that shares certain features with the First Presbyterian Church downtown (besides the congregation's denomination.) Both are stone Gothic structures made of locally quarried black basalt sandstone trim. Westminster has a more solid spire than the downtown church's leaping tower, but both churches had high construction costs, with Westminster coming in at $129,000.

✦   Ellis Lawrence is credited with building Portland's first Arts and Crafts home, at 2210 NE Twenty-third Avenue. He excelled at a variety of design styles, including Art Deco, something hard to imagine, looking at this stone behemoth. He is also remembered for founding the University of Oregon School of Architecture.

28 GUSTAV FREIWALD HOUSE 1906

*1810 NE Fifteenth Avenue, northwest corner of Fifteenth Avenue
and Schuyler Street*
Architect: Unknown

The area south of the Freiwald House was a fashionable area for grand houses, and this turreted structure qualifies as an exuberant Victorian-style house despite its late date of construction. In addition, William J. Hawkins and William F. Willingham, in their book *Classic Houses of Portland, Oregon,* argue that with its square proportions, hipped roof, and curved eaves, this structure has many Craftsman features.

Not too far away, at 1312 NE Tillamook Street, is the Povey House (1891, architect unknown). It is a Queen Anne Victorian that, by virtue of its dense decoration yet modest size, stands out from the crowd. New Jersey native John Povey (1867–1917) came from a family that made stained-glass windows for centuries. John came to Portland with his brother in 1888, and they left their legacy in many local buildings.

✦ Gustav Freiwald, the owner of the Star Brewery, was an original Portland microbrewery entrepreneur.

ALBINA

Part of James Loring's 1852 land claim, the old-time east-side town of Albina was created twenty years later. William Page was an attorney who invested in the area, and the town was named after Page's wife, Albina V. Amiraux. Mrs. Page took the fairly unorthodox step of giving herself a "junior" (this type of ego inflation being usually reserved for the male of the species), and named her daughter Albina also.

In 1891, Albina (the city) annexed almost the entire north peninsula and then was consolidated with Portland. It became a rail-oriented industrial community (nicknamed Stringtown) in short order, and was the site for much of the area's industrial growth. Here and to the north, it also became architecturally run-down, a result of segregation and neglect. In a 1992 article on Portland in the *Atlantic,* Philip Langdon wrote that "high unemployment and gang violence afflict . . . the run-down Albina district." By the turn of the twenty-first century, this assessment is no longer accurate, as there are a number of smaller, interesting buildings here, and Martin Luther King Boulevard has become an intriguing urban redevelopment project. Although it was once thought that adding trees on the median strips and removing parking lots to accommodate more traffic would help the area, parking is being put back in to foster the original pedestrian-friendly layout.

✦ Albinism, a condition that results in a lack of melanin in the skin, causes a very white complexion. With 85 percent of its residents white (the highest of any U.S. city), Portland certainly fits this concept. Settled originally by Scandinavians and Germans, Albina originally did as well. Ironically, however, the Albina neighborhood is now one of the most racially mixed in the city.

29 ARNERICH, MASSENA AND ASSOCIATES BUILDING
1936

Originally Williams and Co.
2045 NE Martin Luther King Boulevard
Architect: F. M. Stokes

This is a truly great Art Deco structure, modest in size and bereft of any ornamentation except those that keep it streamlined. It is gorgeous and dignified, with a fantastic tower at its center. This structure was originally built for a potato chip company with good taste.

29 *Arnerich, Massena and Associates Building*

30 IMMACULATE HEART CATHOLIC CHURCH 1890

*2926 N. Williams Avenue, northeast corner of Williams and
Stanton Streets*
Architect: Vernacular building

This is a Carpenter Gothic church that manages to create its effect with
wood and tin in lieu of the traditional Gothic stone. Galvanized tin masquerading as stone makes up much of the church's exterior detailing, while
the arch is made of fir. Even with these unorthodox materials, through the
magic of transubstantiation, the church still presents an impressive Victorian face to the street.

✦   If you look closely, you can see that the steeple leans to the north.

31 RAVEN CREAMERY CIRCA 1955

3303 NE Martin Luther King, Jr. Boulevard
Architect: Unknown

Simple and white, the building's Art Deco marquee looks like something
crafted in a Boeing bakery.

32 JOHN PALMER HOUSE 1890

4314 N. Mississippi Avenue
Architect: Unknown

This elaborately decorated house is perhaps the only genuine surviving example of Eastlake style in the city. It is two-and-a-half stories of fanciful
dynamite. Admittedly, this former home to the Multnomah Conservatory
of Music has pushed its "candy palace" image pretty far, and the stone balustrade doesn't perfectly match up to the window details, but who cares?
Note that the three gables (one on the south, two on the west) are all different; it's not just the large details that vary with this house. Take some time
and take it in.

30 *Immaculate Heart Catholic Church*

31 *Raven Creamery*

32 *John Palmer House*

PIEDMONT

A real-estate investment group formed by Edward Quackenbush named The Investment Company purchased much of the land here in 1888. Quackenbush was a strict prohibitionist who forbade the sale or manufacture of alcohol in Piedmont; violators could have lost their property if found in violation. Homes had to sell for at least $2,500 to $3,000; this high price kept out "undesirables," a lesson not lost in the subsequent development of Laurelhurst and Ladd's Addition. Utility lines and pipes were kept in alleys, and even innocent steam-propelled vehicles were not permitted. This helped Piedmont found its reputation of being a "town of narrow streets and narrow minds."

33 W. F. DONAHUE HOUSE 1909
5125 NE Garfield Street
Architect: Unknown

A beautiful stone treasure. The cast stone on this home, together with its side turret, make it a real Craftsman castle. It has the requisite bounteous side porch and an interesting Japanese-style side roof, which fits the Craftsman style yet is unexpected on a stone home like this.

UNIVERSITY PARK/MOCK'S CREST/ OVERLOOK

Portland University, Columbia University, University of Portland . . . confusing names, considering they're all the same place.

The University of Portland is situated overlooking the Willamette River and downtown Portland from the north. This was previously the site of Portland University, a Methodist institution built in 1891. It went bankrupt in short order, and the Roman Catholic Archdiocese purchased the site and buildings, and reopened it as Columbia University in 1901. Thirty-four years later, it was renamed the University of Portland and women were admitted for the first time.

✦ John Mock came to Portland as a youth with his family in 1852 bearing the name John *Muck*. He eventually donated a portion of his father's land claim of 317 acres overlooking the Willamette River to Portland University. His currently dilapidated Queen Anne home is at 4333 N. Willamette Boulevard.

34 ADIDAS VILLAGE 2002
5055 N. Greeley Avenue
Architect: BOORA

Building a huge company complex in a residential neighborhood is generally frowned upon by civic-minded individuals, but when Adidas proposed remodeling the dilapidated Bess Kaiser buildings as part of their new Portland "urban village," Overlook residents got their hopes up. Adidas went to great lengths to work with the locals to make sure that their plan met with approval by virtue of its open design, community athletic space, and an Olympic color scheme. Best of all, the parking garage is to be buried in a hillside, with a soccer field on top.

✦   *Jab at Local Shoe Giant Department:* "In keeping with the character of this company, we aspire to create a place that will become part of the fabric of the community, rather than separating ourselves from the world around us." Steve Wynn, Adidas America CEO, 1998.

✦   Designer Eric Cugnart (who worked with I. M. Pei on the San Francisco Public Library) also supervised much of the stonework on the Mark O. Hatfield Federal Courthouse downtown.

35 UNIVERSITY OF PORTLAND
5000 N. Willamette Boulevard, southeast of Willamette Boulevard
and North Portsmouth Avenue

WEST HALL 1891
aka Waldschmidt Hall
Architect: McCaw, Martin, and White

This five-story Romanesque brick structure supposedly marks the site of the farthest point reached by the Lewis and Clark expedition along the Willamette River. Described by Wilfred Schoenberg as "ponderous, like a Fort Knox vault," this building has a ground floor comprised of randomly coursed gray stone with redbrick above, while rounded bays and towers

35 *University of Portland Chapel*

anchor the two ends of the building admirably with their own conical roofs.

This was Portland University's original building (actually, the whole thing was Portland University) and it was modeled after H. H. Richardson's Sever Hall at Harvard. (In 1885, *American Architect & Building News* credited Sever Hall [1880] as one of the top ten buildings in the U.S.) Serving as a site for both dormitories and classrooms, it also provided the subsequent university buildings a template of brick color and classic patterns.

UNIVERSITY OF PORTLAND CHAPEL 1986

5000 N. Willamette Boulevard, University of Portland
Architect: Pietro Belluschi; Yost/Grube/Hall

Designed as a religious spot and student center, the challenge for Belluschi was to pursue his own independent vision while taking into consideration the brick Georgian architectural tradition of the campus. What came about was a beautiful cedar and brick exterior with an overhanging roof, a church that Belluschi considered one of his finest efforts. The interior space of the chapel is intimate, clean, innovative, and impressive. The striking entrance features the wood carving of Leroy Setziol; it gives the chapel a powerful rustic personality. For material, Setziol used four tons of wood in the doors and lintels, taken from three black walnut trees that washed up on the Oregon coast.

✦ Wood carver Leroy Setziol took up his art as an adult, after having survived military action in World War II. He completed his first major commission nearly twenty years after the war and is considered by some to be the "father of woodworking in Oregon."

ST. JOHNS

James Johns (also sometimes spelled "James John") came to Oregon from California's Sacramento Valley in 1843. He established his land claim in 1847 and platted his eponymous town site five years later. James Johns hoped that his town would become a great port city; St. Johns had the modest ambition of becoming the "Manhattan of the West."

St. Johns encouraged industrial development of its waterfront, and a commercial district sprang up to serve it along North Lombard Street. Today, St. Johns' earthy nature can still be seen in its high ratio of shirtless guys patrolling around on warm days.

✦ A reclusive man, James Johns was also a bachelor, leading perhaps to his sobriquet as a "Saint," although mere avoidance of other people can hardly be considered a virtue—unless they are shirtless guys on warm days.

36 WATER POLLUTION CONTROL LABORATORY 1997

6543 N. Burlington Avenue, south of the bridge's base
Architect: Miller/Huller Partnership/Sera Architects

Landscape architect Robert Murase should be justifiably proud of the riverside plantings around the Water Pollution Control Lab. From the ground level, the tall grasses and reeds frame the laboratory beautifully, while from the St. Johns Bridge, the pond on the north side of the building provides an organic counterpoint to the building's angles.

The laboratory and its office space have an industrial look to them, but it is leavened by an inventive color scheme and a simple sloped roof. The building and its grounds are a true synthesis of planning and aesthetics, yielding the area's most significant modern structure.

36 *Water Pollution Control Laboratory*

NORTHERN BRIDGES

✦ ST. JOHNS BRIDGE 1929–1931

Designers: Holton D. Robinson, David B. Steinman (New York)

In the 1920s, a wiseacre remarked about the prospect of a bridge at this location that it would "start from nowhere and lead to limbo." Nonetheless, it is unquestionably the most beautiful of the Willamette Valley bridges. Not only is it the only cable-suspension span in the area, for a number of years, was the largest bridge of its type in the world. Try to envision this stately bridge painted in black and yellow stripes; that was the color scheme originally recommended by city and Swan Island aviation officials.

There is a religious theme going on with this bridge. Designer David Steinman wished to "preach the gospel of beauty in steel," and the bridge does so with its cathedral-like shapes. It has two Gothic arches that bestow classical elegance to the span's two 408-foot towers, and this motif is also visible below the bridge in the concrete piers that support it. The suspension cables exert a pull of 8,500 tons, which anchorages on both sides of the bridge resist.

Despite its charms, given its historically low traffic flow and cost of $3.9 million, the St. Johns Bridge was a construction boondoggle. A special interest group called the Peninsula Bridge Committee rammed the project to approval just as the Great Depression began. Bad timing.

✦   David B. Steinman worked on more than 400 bridges in his career, including stints assisting the designer of the Burnside, Sellwood, and Ross Island bridges, Gustav Lindenthal. Steinman later worked on the design of the Golden Gate Bridge. His words: "If you asked me which of the bridges I love best, I believe I would say the St. Johns Bridge. I put more of myself into that bridge than any other."

St. Johns Bridge

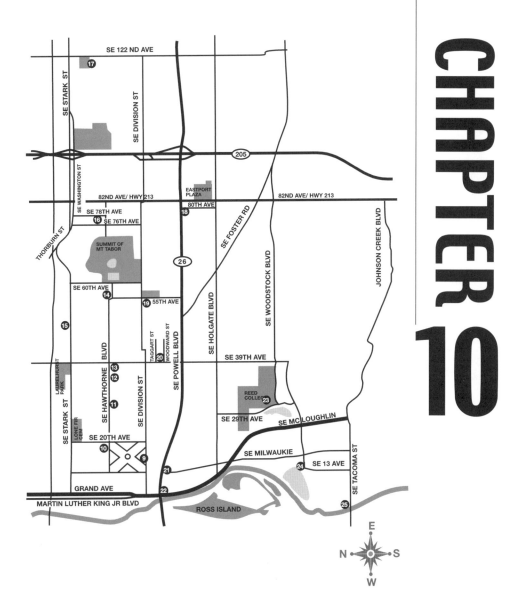

SE 122 ND AVE

17

SE STARK ST

SE DIVISION ST

205

SE WASHINGTON ST

EASTPORT PLAZA

82ND AVE/ HWY 213   82ND AVE/ HWY 213

80TH AVE

SE 78TH AVE   18

THORBURN ST

16 SE 76TH AVE

SUMMIT OF MT TABOR

SE FOSTER RD

SE WOODSTOCK BLVD

JOHNSON CREEK BLVD

26

SE 60TH AVE

14

19 55TH AVE

SE HOLGATE BLVD

15

TAGGART ST

WOODWARD ST

20

SE POWELL BLVD

SE 39TH AVE

LAURELHURST PARK

SE HAWTHORNE BLVD

13

12

SE DIVISION ST

REED COLLEGE

23

SE STARK ST

11

LONE FIR CEM

SE 20TH AVE

SE 29TH AVE

SE MC LOUGHLIN

10

9

SE MILWAUKIE

21

24 SE 13 AVE

SE TACOMA ST

GRAND AVE

22

MARTIN LUTHER KING JR BLVD

25

ROSS ISLAND

E

N   S

W

SOUTHEAST

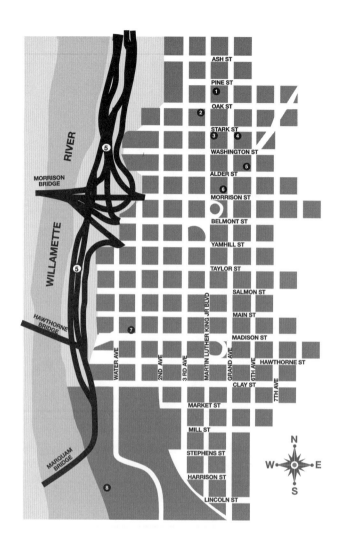

ASH ST

PINE ST
①

OAK ST
②

STARK ST
③ ④

WASHINGTON ST
⑤

ALDER ST
⑥

MORRISON ST

BELMONT ST

YAMHILL ST

TAYLOR ST

SALMON ST

MAIN ST

MADISON ST

HAWTHORNE ST

CLAY ST

MARKET ST

MILL ST

STEPHENS ST

HARRISON ST

LINCOLN ST

RIVER

WILLAMETTE

MORRISON BRIDGE

HAWTHORNE BRIDGE

MARQUAM BRIDGE

WATER AVE

2ND AVE

3RD AVE

MARTIN LUTHER KING JR BLVD

GRAND AVE

6TH AVE

7TH AVE

⑤
⑤
⑦
⑧

N
W — O — E
S

1 *Miller Paint Company*

CHAPTER 10

SOUTHEAST

" . . . The city's inner east side is Portland's dead zone, the riverbank where dumpsters go to die. The warehouses slump like aging whores, flashing a little loading dock, insisting they're available, proud that they're cheap."

—Steve Duin, columnist for the *Oregonian*

The east shore of the Willamette is less favorable as a port because it has a much shallower bank. This, along with inconsistent economic development in the area, caused the southeast riverfront to evolve into a district of warehouses and wholesale marketplaces. Historian Carl Abbott likens East Portland and Albina to "Jersey City and Hoboken, secondary industrial centers built around docks, sawmills, flour mills, and railroad yards." Farther east, independent plats and spotty development patterns sometimes resulted in streets that didn't even line up with each other. But East Portland grew quickly with the arrival of a controversial millionaire to the area.

Kentucky-native Ben Holladay (1826–87) created the nation's largest stagecoach business. Selling the business to Wells Fargo (giving them a great theme for subsequent advertising campaigns), he moved to Portland as a millionaire, in an era when that was a meaningful designation.

Described as "rampaging, rapacious, ruthless" (and a Republican), by an alliterative opponent, Holladay was a much-reviled individual in his time. Eager to transform East Portland, he constructed the first rail line on the east side, which helped to spur the growth of mills, lumberyards, and warehouses. The Holladay Addition, built where Lloyd Center currently is, was his attempt to relocate Portland's business center to the east side of the Willamette. (Holladay accurately predicted that grass would one day be growing along the Willamette's west side, although the grass grows not from the disuse he anticipated, but rather from Waterfront Park.) However, Holladay's would-be empire crumbled beneath poor management.

East Portland was consolidated with the City of Portland in 1891, making it the city's wholesale distribution center. Marshes and gullies were filled in and industrial space took over. Although it is fortunate that Portland's

mayor in 1917 did not make good on his campaign promise to make factory smokestacks "as numerous as trees in the forest" in the district, it has a
decided industrial flavor.

Farther east, one journeys to the terrors of Eighty-second Avenue, where
urban growth boundaries have failed to ensure that actual neighborhoods
would evolve. Instead, one finds sprawl and unwalkable corridors of fran-
chises and car dealerships.

1 MILLER PAINT COMPANY 1936

317 SE Grand Avenue, west side between Pine and Oak Streets
Architect: Edmund Bidwell

Given the product sold herein, this structural design is perfect. Essentially a
commercial warehouse building, sharp angles spruce up the top of this
brightly painted structure on the west side.

2 B. F. GOODRICH BUILDING/A–N–T TIRE AND WHEEL 1930

437 SE Martin Luther King, Jr. Boulevard, west side between Oak and
*   Stark Streets*
Architect: Goodrich-Silverton

Vertical steel Art Deco sheets reach for the sky in geometric precision at the
top half of this shop's street front. While at this location, note the converted
gas station across the street now functioning as a Mexican restaurant. Also
noteworthy is the fruit motif on the west side of the street. The Sheridan
Fruit Company has three fruit billboards on its storefront, and to the south,
at 711 SE Martin Luther King, Jr. is an even larger one.

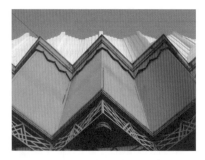

2 a, b   *B. F. Goodrich Building*

3 LOGUS BLOCK CIRCA 1895

523–535 SE Grand Avenue, west side between Stark and
  Washington Streets
Architect: Unknown/Restoration: Allen, McMath and Hawkins

A strong, deep red color denotes this building; it cries out to blue-collar men to eat undercooked beef and arm wrestle. Named for prominent meat-packing businessman Charles Logus, this Romanesque Revival block features carved stone capitals and a rough-hewn rock face on the first floor, as well as some decent terra-cotta designs, finials, and pilasters higher up.

4 BARBER BLOCK 1890

532–538 SE Grand Avenue, east side from Logus Block
Architect: Unknown

This is one of the oldest commercial buildings on the east side of the Willamette. It is a bit of a mix of different styles, including Gothic and Italianate, but instead of trying to classify the building, it's much more fun to simply look at and enjoy the excellent color choices, ornate decoration, protruding window bays, and the old-time east side. The great roofline has designs laid out in stucco and tin. It was restored in 1979.

✦ Diners at the restaurant on the premises are happy to learn that prominent mortician Henry Barber housed his mortuary here.

3 *Logus Block*

4   *Barber Block*

5 a, b   *Volunteers of America
Velma Joy Burnie Memorial Center*

5 VOLUNTEERS OF AMERICA VELMA JOY BURNIE MEMORIAL CENTER 1930

Originally East Side Funeral Director's Building, aka Eastside Mortuary
537 SE Alder Street, northwest corner of Alder and Sixth Avenue
Architect: Thomas and Mercier

This is a beautiful Art Deco building composed of cast stone with botanical embellishments and multi-shade tan brick. The building's corner entrance and vertical panels around the windows give it a street presence. Gideon Bosker and Lena Lencek exuberantly described the building's hip appearance as "a classic in Deco death palaces."
✦   It is mere coincidence that the stonework has what appears to be a series of V markings; these do not stand for Velma or Volunteer.

6 WEST'S BLOCK 1883

701–707 SE Grand Avenue

NATHANIEL WEST BUILDINGS 1892, 1896

711–727 SE Grand Avenue, west side between Alder and
   Morrison Streets
Architects: Unknown

The somewhat plain-looking Italianate cast-iron front of West's Block is the oldest remaining building left from old East Portland. The adjacent buildings are commercial structures that were built shortly after the consolidation of East Portland and Portland.
   Nathaniel West promoted the construction of the original Morrison Street Bridge, which was also the first bridge over the Willamette River. The new bridge encouraged trade in West's buildings on the east side.

7 OREGON PORTLAND CEMENT BUILDING 1929

111 SE Madison Street, north side, just west of Madison and Second
   Avenue
Architect: Richard Sundeleaf

The gargoyles on this building may presage the nautical nightmares that appeared on Sundeleaf's Jantzen Building the year after this structure's creation. Created by architectural sculptor Gabriel Lavare, the three leonine figures, together with the more prosaic dentils, create a homage to classical forms while engaging in an Art Deco atmosphere. With the construction of the Hawthorne Bridge ramp, the front of this building was reconciled to a shadowed, troll-like existence.

✦   In 1866, the area between Taylor and Madison bounded by Ninth to Twelfth Avenue was the Lunatic Asylum Grounds, with the Oregon Hospital for the Insane at the southeast corner of Tenth Avenue and Salmon Street. Vestiges of this legacy still linger in the area today.

8 OREGON MUSEUM OF SCIENCE AND INDUSTRY 1992

aka OMSI
1945 SE Water Avenue, south of the Clay Street intersection
Architect: Zimmer Gunsul Frasca Partnership

In an unlikely location with a great view, OMSI set up camp. The east side of the Willamette River has been littered with unfortunate industrial wreckage in plain view (look to the southeast side of the Fremont Bridge), and the bottom of the Marquam Bridge with its abandoned power plant on this site fits right in with the theme.

What the architects did was remarkable. They incorporated the main smokestack from the power plant (now red) into the new overall structure, retaining the turbine building to the west. (Gazing down into the turbine's workings in the north wing, you'll get a good view of the machinery of power production as well as where the building floods when the Willamette runs high.) Thus, OMSI maintains a stylistic link with the industrial themes

7   *Oregon Portland Cement Building*

8   *Oregon Museum of Science and Industry*

of the east side, while whimsically combining them with new structures that look like a children's toy set. Laid out in what the architect called a "modified bow-tie" arrangement, the simple geometric shapes used in the cluster of buildings gratify both young and mature visitors.

The colored fiberglass in the central lobby is a perfect complement to the dense brick on either side of it. The variegated patterns of the brickwork recall some of Portland's finest west-side buildings. Upwards, the translucent pyramid roof of the lobby is counterbalanced by the copper dome of the Omnimax theater to the east and the verticality of the smokestack to the north.

✦ OMSI began life as the Portland Free Museum, an institute dedicated to sharing with the local citizenry important artifacts such as an artificial cucumber and a spoon from Armenia. In 1957, the core of the Free Museum's collection was transferred to OMSI, which was built on the site of the West Hills golf course, near the Portland Zoo. At this location, OMSI featured new and improved displays, including a Portland Chicken Farmer Hall of Fame and a stuffed, two-headed sheep.

LADD'S ADDITION

Originally occupied by fir forests, the Ladd subdivision was created in 1891 by William S. Ladd. Developed between 1903 and 1925, Ladd's Addition can be something of a shock for the uninitiated. The usual residential block pattern of a neighborhood layout has been transmogrified into a radial street network. The "spokes" of these streets lead inward to one primary circular park and four diamond-shaped rose gardens. Confusion turns into pleasure as the pedestrian realizes that the neighborhood turns in upon itself, in order to focus on a natural "hub." It forms a clearly distinct neighborhood that is utterly unique, even insular. (The inspiration for this design supposedly came from a trip Ladd made to Washington, D.C., which has an enlarged version of radial streets.)

Ladd was a New Hampshire native who came to Portland in 1851, at the age of twenty-four. He set up shop as a liquor dealer and was successful enough to build Portland's first brick building in 1853. He later branched out into other business ventures, notably real estate. Strangely, when Ladd's Addition was being developed, Ladd made provisions excluding bars from the subdivision for all time, and disallowing the sale of liquor anywhere in it. Perhaps his early experiences in commerce had taught him that demon alcohol and social utopianism don't mix. Ladd died ten years before the first house was built in the area.

9 SAINT PHILIP NERI CATHOLIC CHURCH 1949–52

SE Eighteenth Avenue and Division Street, north side of Division Street
Architect: Pietro Belluschi/SOM

With this commission, the Italian-American community in this area was interested in getting a traditional church that would recall their homeland. What they got was a neo-traditional design with a lot of brick and the most no-nonsense bell tower in the Pacific Northwest. This church is serious; it eschews fripperies such as spires or external ornamentation. Belluschi avoided the decorative excesses of traditional church architecture by using an early Christian basilica as his inspiration.

Before the trees matured in front of this church, it appeared to be a tad stark and crematorium-like, as well as somewhat overwhelming for the compact neighborhood it butts up against. Now, the church's formerly severe front (with the rounded corner tower, imposing entrance, and very nearly detached bell tower) seems bold, assertive, and powerful.

One thing to notice with this church is its usage of elemental forms to create a strong message—a message repeated elsewhere in the district. From left to right, there is a round turret, peaked entrance, and monolithic bell tower for verticality. Now think of the church's southeast neighbor, OMSI: from left to right, a rounded dome, glass pyramid entrance, and red smokestack for a vertical element and the perfect foil to the dome. Coincidence?

9 *Saint Philip Neri
Catholic Church*

✦   Studies for the church were begun in 1946. By the time the church was finally finished, Belluschi had sold his practice to Skidmore, Owings, Merrill and was on the east coast serving as dean of architecture at MIT.

10 PORTLAND BUDDHIST TEMPLE 1926

*Originally Third Church of Christ, Scientist
1722 SE Madison Street, one block north of Hawthorne Boulevard
    between Seventeenth and Eighteenth Avenues
Architect: William Gray Purcell*

Given the year of this building's construction, its lack of decoration is unique. It is a strongly geometric structure, focused on rectangular forms in its composition; even the windows are squared off, an unusual touch for a church built in the 1920s. The architect, William Gray Purcell, once worked in the noted Chicago firm Purcell and Elmslie, which specialized in commercial buildings in the Chicago style. Unfortunately, that style isn't particularly suited to a building with spiritual intents. Viewed from the outside, this cube-like temple could be mistaken for a bottling plant, or perhaps a Prairie-home design that got left in an industrial furnace, but nonetheless, it is a landmark building and a useful structure.

✦   William Gray Purcell also worked with famed American architect Louis Sullivan.

10 *Portland Buddhist Temple*

11 *Holman Funeral Service*

11 HOLMAN FUNERAL SERVICE 1901

Originally the Walter F. Burrell House
2610 SE Hawthorne Boulevard, southwest corner of Twenty-seventh
*   Avenue and Hawthorne Boulevard*
Architect: Whidden and Lewis

Purchased in 1920 by the present funeral service operators, this Prairie-style structure (with elements of Mediterranean style) was originally intended as a residence, and a grand one at that. Architects Whidden and Lewis (who are strongly represented in the Northwest's traditional residential architecture) ventured outside even their wide repertoire of styles to create a home with a strong horizontal element. This is reflected in the lines of the porte cochere's roof and in the third floor's eaves. Take note of the interesting Prairie turret to the east of the porte cochere; the roof's eaves are shown to dramatic effect there.

12   BAGDAD THEATRE AND PUB 1927

3702 SE Hawthorne Boulevard, southeast corner of Thirty-seventh Avenue and Hawthorne Boulevard
Architect: Lee Thomas

Perhaps the best legacy an architect could hope for is that his work would not just survive but be used as originally intended for a long time. That being the case, Lee Thomas must be particularly pleased up in Architects' Paradise. Originally billed as an "Oasis for Entertainment," Universal Pictures helped to finance this theater, and the well-kept Mediterranean-style building with a stucco finish, ornamental plasterwork, and red clay-tile roof still pays off on that investment. In 1991, the McMenamins picked up the property that Universal had let go and funkified it in their own inimitable fashion.

The distinctive Middle Eastern neon marquee matches up with the theater's original interior features, although it was added decades after the theater opened. Gurgling gawkers still enjoy staring at the hip historicity of

12 *Bagdad Theatre and Pub*

the theater's innards, though regrettably, the Arabian-style uniforms originally worn by theater employees are no longer part of the show. Architect Lee Thomas was employed by Albert Mercier at an office in the U.S. National Bank Building.

✦   Notable premieres at the Bagdad: Jack Nicholson at the 1975 premiere of Ken Kesey's *One Flew over the Cuckoo's Nest;* in 1991, local son Gus Van Sant premiered *My Own Private Idaho.*

13   SUNNYSIDE MASONIC TEMPLE 1919

*3862 Hawthorne Boulevard, southwest corner of Hawthorne
   Boulevard and Thirty-ninth Street*
Architect: O. F. Sunde

The substantial white columns on this former temple are wooden, and along with the decorative brickwork and strong portico, the exterior of this building is still strong and crisp. The high ceilings inside can provoke awe, though not of the social club/mystical variety for which the building was originally designed.

13   *Sunnyside Masonic Temple*

14 *Western Seminary*

14 WESTERN SEMINARY 1906
Originally Philip Buehner House
5511 SE Hawthorne Boulevard, at the east end of the boulevard
Architect: Whidden and Lewis

While Whidden and Lewis did the bulk of their residential work in the northwest area of Portland, their crowning achievement in that style may be this home. It is yet another of their Colonial Revival houses (and one of the last the firm designed) with extremely tall, stately columns and an elegant simplicity. The portico was originally designed as a porte cochere.

In the mid-1800s, a farmhouse was built on this site that later served as a stagecoach stop for travelers between Oregon City and Vancouver. It fell victim to dry rot, and its stables are long gone now, but if one listens carefully, a whinny can still be heard on the wind . . . although it may well be emanating from one of Hawthorne's ubiquitous hipsters getting a tattoo.

15 *Wilbur Reid House*

NORTH OF HAWTHORNE DISTRICT

15 WILBUR REID HOUSE 1914

4775 SE Stark Street, northwest corner of Stark Street and
* Forty-ninth Avenue*
Architect: Francis Brown (California)

Although there were a large number of bungalows built in East Portland (mostly between 1900 and 1925), this particular example of the style is probably the best one in the city, and possibly in the entire Pacific Northwest.

It is enjoyable to visit a well-crafted bungalow with a knowledgeable woodworker, as they are able to point out the degree of difficulty in wood joinery that a home like the Wilbur Reid House represents, particularly in an era without power tools. For a look at how rustic, non-metal materials are used in the construction of a bungalow of this type, one can inspect this home's double-pitched gables, veranda roof over the carriage area in front, protruding roof beams, and shingled and stone walls. The architect, Francis Brown, was supposedly linked with the architects Greene and Greene, and it's easy to believe. The cantilevers of this roofline betray the bungalow style's Japanese influence, and all in all, the various layers of horizontal detail make this a very rich bit of architectural pastry. Recent sightings have shown some wear and tear in need of repair on some parts of this local treasure.

✦ Wilbur Reid was apparently taken with the many bungalows he saw in southern California on his honeymoon (the Pasadena area is particularly rife with them), and commissioned his home in the same style.

NEAR MOUNT TABOR

16   SAINT ANDREW'S CARE CENTER 1923

Originally Monastery of the Precious Blood
1208 SE Seventy-sixth Avenue, east side of Seventy-sixth Avenue
  between Salmon and Main Streets
Architect: Jacobberger and Smith

This monastery is a good example of the Spanish Colonial construction that is widespread in California but rarer in Oregon. This building stands out with its cupola, tiled roofs and archways. View the west side of the building to appreciate its detailing.

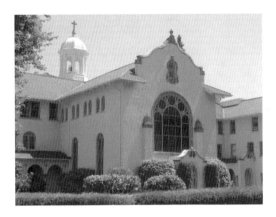

16 *Saint Andrew's Care Center*

FARTHER EAST

17   MIDLAND REGIONAL LIBRARY 1996

805 SE One Hundred Twenty-second Avenue, west side at Morrison
  Street (south of Stark)
Architect: Thomas Hacker and Associates

This redbrick library is decorated with simple botanical-themed concrete medallions. But what gives the library street presence is the gargantuan clock sitting astride its front. The library's surroundings include four lanes

17 *Midland Regional Library*

of heavily traveled asphalt, an adult dancing establishment, and car dealerships up and down One Hundred Twenty-Second Avenue. Yet the smallish Midland Park to the north of the library provides the perfect viewpoint to forget about one's surroundings and get some reading done, thanks to the simple and ingenious design of this structure. Laid out as a long, high-ceilinged hallway, the library opens a glass wall to the bucolic idyll of the park and at the other end, turns a blind eye to the monstrosity of One Hundred Twenty-second Avenue with artwork.

18 SAINT ANTHONY VILLAGE 1999

3600 SE Seventy-ninth Avenue, between Rhine and Center Streets, south of Powell Boulevard
Architect: Robertson Merryman and Barnes Architects

Piazza: a place for the community to be together in an environment that has fountains and pleasant landscaping. Amid the generica of Eighty-second Avenue, Saint Anthony Village has a church, day-care center, and more than a hundred units of senior housing, and this planned community is designed around its central piazza.

The church itself is modestly sized, in perfect proportion to the area around it. A tower (sans bell) creates a symbolic focus to the building. Dramatic stained glass is used throughout the church, but there is also ample clear glass that allows patrons to interact with the piazza outside. The design, location, and appearance of the church create a well-composed tableau in this village.

✦   This is the first church in the state designed by a firm owned by women.
✦   Father Michael Maslowsky used yogurt cups to model his notions for how the church should look.

19 FRANKLIN HIGH SCHOOL 1914

*5404 SE Woodward Street, south of Division Street between
Fifty-second and Fifty-eighth Avenues
Architect: Floyd A. Naramore*

This school is widely acknowledged as the epitome of fine secondary-school architecture. Architect Naramore liked to situate his schools so that they would dramatically address themselves to the street. View Franklin High from Division Street to see how the school makes a strong and dignified statement, majestically rising over its fields. Admittedly, the large and slightly goofy statue of the school's namesake ameliorates the effect a bit.

18   *Saint Anthony Village*

19   *Franklin High School*

20   *Joseph Kendall House*

20 JOSEPH KENDALL HOUSE 1889–94

3908 SE Taggart Street, southeast corner of Taggart and
Thirty-ninth Avenue
Architect: Joseph Kendall

This interesting home has a rustic Romanesque stone turret, with a style that is really more Queen Anne. It is an uneasy alliance. Whether the fish-scale shingling pattern meshes well with the rounded stone wall and brick is a matter of taste. The foundation of this home is comprised of Belgian stone faced with brick.

Joseph Kendall came to Oregon from Missouri in 1881. An architect, cabinetmaker, and builder, he acquired six hundred acres around this property and constructed an earlier wood-frame home on this site. He died before he could implement all his plans for this home (although he did put busts of his son's and wife's likenesses at the tops of arches).

✦   This modestly sized home was designed with five fireplaces.

BROOKLYN

21 ALADDIN THEATER 1928

3017 SE Milwaukee Avenue, southeast corner of Milwaukee and
Powell Boulevard
Architect: Edward A. Miller

The stucco and tile Aladdin's neon marquee is a landmark, but it achieved true celebrity in 1975 when the police raided the theater and seized the adult film *Deep Throat* as a violation of anti-obscenity laws. During the trial, a jury was treated to a screening of the film (though not at the Aladdin), and they were apparently impressed enough to label it "not obscene." Stringed-instrument master Paul Schuback bought the establishment in 1991 and turned it back into a real theater of which the area could be proud.

22 JOHAN POULSEN HOUSE 1890

3040 SE McLoughlin Boulevard; try parking on SE Brooklyn Street
Architect: Unknown; probably vernacular

The Queen Anne–style Poulsen House looks out over the Willamette River with perhaps the best tower turret of any residence in Portland, although it has had two local copies. A replica of this house formerly existed to the house's north: Poulsen's business partner had an identical home built across the street, but it was destroyed in 1958 to make way for a parking lot. The tower and its finial are also the same as the one found on the Officers' Quarters at Fort Vancouver.

The home is pleasingly asymmetrical with lots of wood detailing, which is unsurprising, as Poulsen was a builder and lumberman. His lumber mill was located approximately where OMSI is now. Poulsen lived in this home less than a year, apparently because his wife did not like it.

✦ *Bridge tale:* In 1889, after having taken out a life insurance policy, Johan Poulsen walked across the old Steel Bridge in the dark. As the "draw" was open, he fell into the Willamette River. After swimming to shore, he doubled his insurance policy the next day.

22 *Johan Poulsen House*

EASTMORELAND/WESTMORELAND

These neighborhood names stem from Julius Caesar Moreland, a real-estate magnate who gained control of some of the area's property. Separated by a golf course, parks, and a modest lake, Westmoreland and Eastmoreland's plats were completed in 1909 and 1910. Eastmoreland grew around Reed College between 1912 and 1940, and probably has the best residential architecture in town. The neighborhood feels insulated against its environs by the aforementioned obstacles, as well as Reed College and the off-kilter arrangement of its tree-lined streets.

✦   An early promotional pamphlet for Eastmoreland stressed nearby Reed College's influence: " . . . refining influences . . . will radiate from (Reed), out, over and beyond Eastmoreland, thus lending its power to sway the life of man . . . throughout the state and the Northwest."

23 REED COLLEGE

3203 SE Woodstock Boulevard

First opened in 1911, Reed College was established by the estate of Portland businessman Simeon Gannett Reed (1830–95). Simeon Reed began his business career by working for William S. Ladd in the liquor business.

He went on to become a prosperous local citizen, profiting particularly from his real-estate investments.

Reed's first campus president, William Foster, stated that "hallowed traditions are petrified errors," and the initial architectural plan was definitely not traditional; it called for the construction of forty-nine buildings on the campus. After consideration, the college trustees instead chose to concentrate their efforts on three permanent (and "petrified-in-their-error") buildings. The result of this is that the college has a variety of Tudor-style buildings (a form of the Gothic style often applied to university buildings), dating from 1912 to 1930.

Architect Pietro Belluschi led the way for some less-distinguished structures designed by SOM from 1956 to 1970. In the mid-1940s, Reed was interested in promoting its science department, which had contributed to the technical aspects of World War II. Belluschi was interested in symbolizing the cutting-edge modernism of the sciences with a structure behind the library then called the Science Building (1949, design by Warren Weber), but he had to form some sort of thematic architectural link with the already present and traditional campus buildings that he had helped design. In the end, the only acknowledgement of the college's past were the bricks used in this flat-roofed, glass-and-brick structure. Belluschi argued to his client that this was a cheaper and more forward-thinking direction to take instead of yet another Tudor Gothic.

Richard Ritz has pointed out that there is a continuity of architecture at Reed that runs from A. E. Doyle's original buildings through Belluschi's and up to the more recent Zimmer Gunsul Frasca creations. Just as Reed

23 a   *Eliot Hall Main Entrance*

College has a vastly disproportionate number of Rhodes scholars and Ph.D.s among its alumni, so too has it attracted the finest talent in the field for its buildings.

✦   In 1950, thinking it unseemly for Belluschi to take on the dean's chair of architecture at MIT without an advanced degree of any kind, Reed president E. B. MacNaughton bequeathed him an honorary doctor of law degree. Upon Belluschi's arrival at MIT, his feet were dipped in red paint, and he was turned upside down so that he could leave his footprints on the ceiling of the president's office, next to those of renowned architects such as Buckminster Fuller and Walter Gropius.

✦   The college's one-time unofficial student body credo was "Communism, Atheism, Free Love." One possible source of this philosophy may have been that from its start, Reed College had no denominational religious institution backing it, an unusual thing in its day.

ELIOT HALL 1912

Originally the Arts and Science Building

THE DORMITORY 1912

3203 SE Woodstock Boulevard
Architects: Doyle, Patterson, and Beach, A. E. Doyle designer

Eliot Hall was named after the Unitarian Reverend Thomas Lamb Eliot, the first president of the board of trustees and the man who promoted the idea of the college to Reed in the first place. This distinguished building looks older than it actually is, perhaps because of its emulation in form of various historical English churches and abbeys.

Based on Saint John's College in Oxford, projecting windows with arched frames and gables periodically stick out of the brick-and-stone face of the hall. The bricks (from Spokane) were selected by Doyle for their variety of colors. Giving the building more local flavor are the carvings of Oregon's beloved roses in the stonework over the arched main entrance, and the brotherhood of upper education is symbolized in the seals of fifty-two other colleges in the window bays. Also, keep your eyes peeled for native fauna, represented in subtle fashion in the building.

The dormitory shares an obvious lineage with Eliot Hall, although in its own right, it has a fortified entryway, which may come in handy if Reed is ever besieged by the unlettered throngs of the Brooklyn neighborhood. It is topped with a sundial called a "sallyport," which is a delightful feature of the building.

23 b, c   *The Dormitory*

ERIC V. HAUSER LIBRARY 1930

Reed College Campus
Architects: A. E. Doyle and Associates, Pietro Belluschi, designer
1960s expansion by Harry Weese and Associates (Chicago)

UNIFIED SCIENCE LIBRARY ADDITION 1989

Architects: Zimmer Gunsul Frasca Partnership

This rectangular, brick and limestone-trimmed building matches up nicely with Eliot Hall, thanks to Belluschi's careful observance of the Tudor Gothic precedent that had already been established on the campus. The battlements on the central tower are okay, although they look a little odd on the rest of the building, given the pitch of the conventional roof behind them. There's a nice arched entranceway with a bay window above it.

The nearly 42,000-square-foot addition to the original Hauser Library was connected to the venerable original in a most creative fashion. Attached to the east side of its precursor, this library (deemed Post-Modern Gothic by Richard Ritz) uses the same brick and limestone as the older buildings, and successfully emulates their style (even including gargoyle heads inside and out) while staying fresh and modern. Even more fun is the fact that the reading room at the center of the library retains the original brick

23 d   *Unified Science Library Addition*

exterior wall of the old library inside, lending a nice "inside/outside" atmosphere to the place. It does an excellent job of being a contemporary building on campus that pays direct homage to the original architectural styles of the school.

24 PORTLAND MEMORIAL INDOOR CEMETERY 1946

*6705 SE Fourteenth Avenue; Fourteenth Avenue and Bybee Street,
   overlooking Oaks Bottom Wildlife Refuge*
Architect: Fred T. Weber

"Harrow the house of the dead; look shining at
New styles of architecture, a change of heart."

—W. H. Auden, "Sir, No Man's Enemy"

Though one does not think of a cemetery as a likely destination for a pleasant sojourn, if one is in the properly reverential mood for the perusal of some interesting architecture, this sprawling indoor mausoleum is the place. It boasts a wide variety of well-executed architectural designs (beginning with the Mediterranean style facing the road), and has more marble in different varieties inside than in perhaps any other Portland-area building.

The cemetery was first designed as a crematorium and as a place to store "cremains" but later expanded to whole-body interment as well. Begin in the Rose Room (the original building) and explore the hallways lined with names and dates of yesteryear. From there, the necropolis expanded architecturally over the decades (including work by Richard Sundeleaf), and with stained glass casting its light inside and lots of skylights, it makes for a fascinating experience. Highlights include a six-story spiral marble staircase rising up to a skylight and a multi-floor cutout looking down upon a fountain.

✦   Local luminary John B. Yeon is buried here, as is Mayo Methot, who preceded Lauren Bacall as Humphrey Bogart's wife.

✦   This locale has been advertised as the largest indoor cemetery west of the Mississippi.

SELLWOOD

This area is named after English immigrant John Sellwood, an Episcopal minister, pioneer, and real-estate baron who bought 321 acres in this area for $5,400 in 1866. He later sold the parcel to a real-estate company seeking to create a market for Portland's increasing housing needs. The first homes, designed for blue-collar workers, were unexceptional; the area was intended as a suburb, and (barring the industrial development on the waterfront) a suburb it has remained. Sellwood became its own town in 1887, only to merge with Portland six years later.

24 *Portland Memorial Indoor Cemetery*

25 OAKS PIONEER MUSEUM 1851

Originally Saint John's Episcopal Church
455 SE Spokane Street, northwest of Spokane and SE Grand Avenue
Architect: Unknown

Oregon pioneer, shipbuilder, and steamboat captain Lot Whitcomb partially constructed this church, which was originally intended as a residence and now qualifies as the state's oldest church in continuous usage. Destined to be torn down in 1961, the wood frame building was transported by river barge to its present location. It originally had square windows, as opposed to the Gothic arched ones present today.

✦   In keeping with this building's nautical heritage, the church's belfry bell came from one of Whitcomb's ships.

FAR SOUTH

26 MOUNT ANGEL ABBEY LIBRARY 1970

Take I-5 south to exit # 271 (Woodburn/Silverton). Follow signs to
    Mount Angel. The monastery is east of the town of Mount Angel.
Architect: Alvar Aalto
On-site Architect: Erik T. Vartiainen
Architects of Record: John Wells, Vernon Demars

Although hardly a structure within the Portland metropolitan area, this building may be the most architecturally significant in the Pacific Northwest. The Mount Angel Abbey (founded in 1882) was created by Benedictine monks from the Abbey of Engelberg in Switzerland. Having lost an earlier library to fire, the library's director wrote to Alvar Aalto (1898–1976) in 1963, asking the world-famous architect to design a structure for the rural monastery that fit in with the existing buildings, hillside, and the Benedictine order's traditions. While Alvar Aalto ranks among the twentieth century's greatest architects and designers, his work is found primarily in his home country of Finland (this library is one of only two Aalto buildings in the United States). Because of this, he does not have the instant name recognition of, say, Frank Lloyd Wright. Interestingly, despite his substantial accomplishments, Aalto was not licensed in the United States, and he is not the legal architect of record for this building.

Aalto designed the entire building in Finland, a country not noted for its topography. Using maps and photos, he managed to create this building with only one visit to the site in 1967, a trip which did virtually nothing to change the plans he had made a hemisphere away. In order to keep the building's (and its occupants') attention turned inward, no view windows were designed in the original blueprints.

One enters the library on its main floor, where its white brick subtly brings one in from the courtyard. This floor is built up to be on a level with the rest of the hilltop monastery. Below are two more floors that go down the hillside. The circular/fan-shaped building is something along the lines of an auditorium-style structure, or perhaps an amphitheater that has gone through a black hole and been marvelously transformed. In the library's central space, where the mezzanine balcony looks down upon the spoked design, one can appreciate the organic, rounded curves and the light woods and shades awash in ample natural light. A famous designer as well as architect, Aalto also designed all of the building's furniture, the largest such collection in the world. The building is a significant work by a master of architecture; it is an understated, undulated masterpiece.

✦ This library won a Presidential Citation from the American Institute of Architects in 1995, essentially the group's Medal of Honor award for a building.

Photo © Nathan Good, courtesy of the Mount Angel Abbey

26 *Mount Angel Abbey Library, central light well*

27   *Gordon "Usonian" House*

27   GORDON ("USONIAN") HOUSE 1963

Oregon Garden, Silverton
Architect: Frank Lloyd Wright

This is the only Oregonian structure designed by the world's most famed architect.

In 2001, this famed home was moved twenty-six miles from its original location in order to escape the destructive intent of its new owners. The house had been sited on a concrete pad south of Wilsonville, but when the property was purchased by individuals with little interest in the structure, the Frank Lloyd Wright Conservancy stepped in. It was relocated in three pieces to its current position in a sixty-acre garden.

The 2,133-square-foot home is known as a "Usonian house," a design that Wright initiated in the 1930s for middle-class homeowners. (The term "Usonian" was an adjective Wright used to refer to the United States. It never really caught on.) The Usonian house was intended for working-class people who wanted something affordable, rustic, and private, with a sense of connection between interior and exterior space. This home exhibits Wright's trademark horizontal design elements. It is made of cedar and cinder blocks, and sports twelve-foot floor-to-ceiling windows. Adding to its unique nature is the fact that out of the five Wright homes existing in the general Pacific Northwest area, this is the only one open to the public.

✦   When the American Institute of Architects selected the "Top Ten" buildings of the twentieth century, four were designed by Frank Lloyd Wright. He was the only architect with more than one listing. Wright died four years before this home's completion.

✦   In 1938, *LIFE* magazine commissioned Wright to design "A House for a Family of $5,000–$6,000 Income." One was built in Wisconsin the following year. This home was the second (and last), and it was finished over twenty years later.

BIBLIOGRAPHY

Abbott, Carl. *Portland: Planning, Politics, and Growth in a Twentieth-Century City.* Lincoln, Nebraska: University of Nebraska Press, 1983.

—. *Portland: Gateway to the Northwest.* Tarzana, California: American Historical Press, 1997.

Adamy, Janet. "U.S. Bank seeks bids to buy its pink tower." *Oregonian.* 24 July 1999.

Allen-McMath-Hawkins-Architects, Huntington, Wallace K. "Skidmore Old Town Historic District." Portland: Portland Development Commission, 1976.

Bjorhus, Jennifer. "Beware of those intersections." *Oregonian.* 2 July 1998.

Bosker, Gideon and Lena Lencek. *Frozen Music: A History of Portland Architecture.* Portland: Western Imprints (The Press of the Oregon Historical Society), 1985.

Brandon, Steve. "It's not a pipe dream." *Oregonian.* 18 May 1995.

Brewster, Elizabeth. *Portland Sketchbook.* Oregon Printing Plates, 1968.

Carlo, Jake. "Walk this way." *Willamette Week.* 8 September 1999.

Christ, Janet. "Central Library: The next chapter." *Oregonian.* 6 April 1999.

—. "Report points way to dynamic west end." *Oregonian.* 23 July 1999.

—. "Benson House on the move." *Oregonian.* 23 August 1999.

—. "Church celebrates 125th anniversary by moving ahead." *Oregonian.* 9 September 1999.

—. "Lewis & Clark honors priceless gift." *Oregonian.* 1 October 1999.

Clark, Rosalind. *Oregon Style: Architecture from 1840 to the 1950s.* Portland, Oregon: Professional Book Center, 1983.

Clarke, Ann Brewster. *Wade Hampton Pipes: Arts and Crafts Architect in Portland, Oregon.* Portland, Oregon: Binford & Mort Publishing, 1985.

Clausen, Meredith L. *Spiritual Space: The Religious Architecture of Pietro Belluschi.* Seattle: University of Washington Press, 1992.

—. *Pietro Belluschi: Modern American Architect.* Cambridge, Massachusetts: The MIT Press, 1994.

Cuneo, Alice Z. "From warehouse to hothouse: A virtual tour." *Advertising Age.* May 15, 2000.

Curtin, Cáit. *The Grand Lady of Fourth Avenue: Portland's Historic Multnomah Hotel.* Portland, Oregon: Binford & Mort Publishing, 1997.

Delahanty, Randolph. *Preserving the West.* New York: Pantheon Books, 1985.

DeMarco, Gordon. *A Short History of Portland.* San Francisco: Lexicos, 1990.

DeWolfe, Fred. *Portland West.* Portland: Press-22, 1973.

—. *Portland Tradition in Buildings and People.* Portland: Press-22, 1980.

Dietsch, Deborah K. "Postmodern ruins." *Architecture.* July 1997.

Doyle, Brian. "Doorway to Heaven." *Preservation.* January/February 2001.

Duany, Andrés. "Punching holes in Portland." *Oregonian.* 19 December 1999.

Duany, Andrés, and Elizabeth Plater Zyberk, Jeff Speck. *Suburban Nation: The Rise & Sprawl & the Decline of the American Dream.* New York: Farrar, Straus & Giroux, 2000.

Duin, Steve. "Gaining a little altitude." *Oregonian.* 21 November 1996.

—. "East side offers more than just a river view." *Oregonian.* 21 March 2000.

Edwards, Thomas G. "Six Oregon Leaders and the Far-Reaching Impact of America's Civil War." *Oregon Historical Quarterly.* Spring, 1999/Volume 100, Number 1.

Farrell, Peter. "Ironworker plunges to death." *Oregonian.* 28 February 1996.

Bibliography

Ferriday, Virginia Guest. *Last of the Handmade Buildings: Glazed Terra Cotta in Downtown Portland.* Portland, Oregon: Mark Publishing Company, 1984.

Fleming, John with Hugh Honour, Nikolas Pevsner. *The Penguin Dictionary of Architecture and Landscape Architecture.* London: Penguin Books, 1998.

Foden-Vencil, Christian. "Vision is architect's thing." *Oregonian.* 7 March 1995.

Frank, Ann Wall. *Northwest Style: Interior Design and Architecture in the Pacific Northwest.* San Francisco: Chronicle Books, 1999.

Frank, Gerry. "From Hatfield to Harding . . ." *Oregonian.* 18 August 2000.

Freedman, Adele. "Creative Space." *Architecture.* June 2000.

Freeman, Judy. "Mike McMenamin: On pub art and historic preservation." *Oregonian.* 29 October 1999.

Friedman, Elaine S. *The Facts of Life in Portland, Oregon.* Portland, Oregon: Portland Possibilities, Inc., 1993.

Gamarekian, Barbara. "New Game in Town: Façademanship" *New York Times.* 31 August 1983.

Gantenbein, Douglas. "Frozen Music: A history of Portland architecture." *Architectural Record.* April 1987.

Gelernter, Mark. *A History of American Architecture: Buildings in Their Cultural and Technological Context.* Hanover, New Hampshire: University Press of New England, 1999.

Gibney, Frank, Jr., and Belinda Luscombe. "The Redesign of America." *Time.* 20 March 2000.

Goldberger, Paul. "Busy Buildings." *New Yorker.* September 4, 2000.

Gordon, Walter. "Mural will overwhelm Park Blocks' architecture." *Oregonian.* 22 March 1989.

Gragg, Randy. "On the Waterfront." *Oregonian.* 25 October 1992.

—. "The Rose Garden's Urban Thorns." *Oregonian.* 15 October 1995.

—. "Architect Yeon's legacy to live on as UO Center." *Oregonian.* 22 October 1995.

—. "Aalto's modest masterpiece." *Oregonian.* 10 December 1995.

—. "St. Mary's Full of Grace." *Oregonian.* 11 February 1996.

—. "Connoisseur of buildings." *Oregonian.* 13 April 1996.

—. "Outstripping the neighborhood." *Oregonian.* 15 September 1996.

—. "Underground parking floated for downtown." *Oregonian.* 18 October 1996.

—. "Building the academic city." *Oregonian.* 23 February 1997.

—. "Multnomah County Library: A good read on history." *Oregonian.* 6 April 1997.

—. "Ice house comes in from cold thanks to pioneering partners." *Oregonian.* 12 April 1997.

—. "Is anyone building a sense of place?" *Oregonian.* 2 November 1997.

—. "Building 1997." *Oregonian.* 28 December 1997.

—. "Controversy at center court." *Oregonian.* 26 April 1998.

—. "Architect delivers some peace of mind." *Oregonian.* 3 May 1998.

—. "A Matter of Refinement." *Oregonian.* 5 July 1998.

—. "Eastern poetry meets Western rules." *Oregonian.* 3 January 1999.

—. "One community under God . . ." *Oregonian.* 30 April 1999.

—. "Peter Walker: On Portland landscape." *Oregonian.* 25 June 1999.

—. "Urban Renewal Meets infill." *Oregonian.* 27 June 1999.

—. "'Snoutless' Houses Make Better City Neighborhoods." *Oregonian.* 30 June 1999.

—. "River District rapids." *Oregonian.* 7 July 1999.

—. "Romantic's eulogy for Lovejoy Ramp." *Oregonian.* 19 August 1999

—. "High history, ho-hum architecture." *Oregonian.* 29 August 1999.

—. "City inspires project." *Oregonian.* 19 September 1999.

—. "The art of allegory." *Oregonian.* 4 October 1999.

—. "A powerhouse example of restoration." *Oregonian.* 10 October 1999.

—. "On the waterfront: More than a park." *Oregonian.* 17 October 1999.

—. "It makes a village: Adidas embraces a Portland neighborhood." *Oregonian.* 31 October 1999.

—. "Cinderella Complex." *Oregonian.* 14 November 1999.

—. "A landmark in art museum's expansion." *Oregonian.* 21 November 1999.

—. "The architecture of boom." *Oregonian.* 19 December 1999.

—. "Setting the Standard." *Oregonian.* 31 December 1999.

—. "Big changes for a little 'burg named Hollywood." *Oregonian.* 30 January 2000.

—. "Brewing a neighborhood." *Oregonian.* 27 February 2000.

—. "Re-sculpting the void." *Oregonian.* 3 March 2000.

—. "Hotel boom, aesthetic bust." *Oregonian.* 19 March 2000.

—. "A garden slowly awakens." *Oregonian.* 20 March 2000.

—. "Downtown and the university." *Oregonian.* 14 May 2000.

—. "Airport canopy works, but not as it should." *Oregonian.* 28 May 2000.

—. "High rise compromise." *Oregonian.* 8 October 2000.

Gringeri-Brown, Michelle. "The Craftmanship Spirit Lives On." *American Bungalow.* Number 19, Fall 1998.

"A Guide to Portland Architecture." Portland: The Portland, Oregon Chapter of The American Institute of Architects, 1968.

Haught, Nancy. "Shelter from the storm since 1965 . . ." *Oregonian.* 10 February 2000.

Hawkins, William John, III. *The Grand Era of Cast-Iron Architecture in Portland.* Portland, Oregon: Binford & Mort, 1976.

— with William F. Willingham. *Classic Houses of Portland, Oregon: 1850-1950.* Portland, Oregon: Timber Press, 1999.

Hill, Jim. "Study calls Oregon Convention Center a success." *Oregonian.* 13 April 1995.

—. "Developer seeks Weinhard site." *Oregonian.* 5 August 1999.

Historic American Buildings Survey/Historic American Engineering Record http://www.cr.nps.gov/habshaer/

"Historic Resource Inventory: Selected Properties." Portland, Oregon: Bureau of Planning, City of Portland, Oregon, May 1984.

Hogan, Dave. "New home for federal courthouse nears completion." *Oregonian.* 13 February 1997.

—. "New U.S. courthouse a $106.6 million buy." *Oregonian.* 12 November 1997.

Hogue, Kendra. "Landmark Listing." *Oregonian.* 3 September 2000.

Hortsch, Dan and Jeff Manning. "Adidas moving to Portland." *Oregonian.* 19 December 1998.

Huxtable, Ada Louise. *The Tall Building Artistically Reconsidered: The Search for a Skyscraper Style.* Berkeley, California: University of California Press, 1984.

Johnson, Barry, and Randy Gragg. "Portland Art Museum." *Oregonian.* 19 November 1995.

Kearney, Trevor. "Renovated Laurelhurst Theater is getting a thumbs up." *Oregonian.* 20 January 2000.

Keates, Nancy. "Portland's Pearl District pushes hip image." *Wall Street Journal.* 29 July 1998.

Kiyomura, Cathy. "Voices ask The O." *Oregonian.* 21 December 1995.

Koeper, Frederick and Marcus Whiffen. *American Architecture: 1607-1976.* Cambridge, Massachusetts: The M.I.T. Press, 1981.

Langdon, Philip. "How Portland Does It." *Atlantic.* November 1992.

Learn, Scott. "OSHA finds fault with renovated City Hall." *Oregonian.* 1 February 1999.

Leeson, Fred. "U.S. Bank will hold block sale." *Oregonian.* 12 May 1999.

—. "Seeking a faithful restoration." *Oregonian.* 21 February 2000.

MacColl, E. Kimbark. *The Shaping of a City: Power and Politics in Portland, Oregon, 1885 to 1915*. Portland, Oregon: The Georgian Press, 1976.

—. *The Growth of a City: Power and Politics in Portland, Oregon, 1915 to 1950*. Portland, Oregon: The Georgian Press, 1979.

—. *Merchants, Money, and Power: The Portland Establishment, 1843 to 1913*. Portland, Oregon: The Georgian Press, 1988.

Maddux, Percy. *City on the Willamette: The Story of Portland, Oregon*. Portland, Oregon: Binford & Mort, Publishers, 1952.

Marlitt, Richard. *Nineteenth Street*. Portland, Oregon: Oregon Historical Society Press, 1978.

—. *Matters of Proportion: The Portland Residential Architecture of Whidden & Lewis*. Portland, Oregon: Oregon Historical Society Press, 1989.

Maves, Norman Jr.. "Creator of Yule tradition . . . ." *Oregonian*. 29 September 1999.

Mayer, James. "Portland skyline keeps a low profile." *Oregonian*. 29 October 1995.

Mayes, Steve. "Portland is growing out but won't be growing up." *Oregonian*. 29 October 1995.

—. "Structures sprouting in downtown enhance." *Oregonian*. 8 May 1996.

—. "Fox Tower begins work on unsure footing." *Oregonian*. 23 August 1997.

—. "Tax break for venerable property may be history." *Oregonian*. 3 September 1999.

McMath, George A., and Thomas Vaughan. *A Century of Portland Architecture*. Portland, Oregon: Oregon Historical Society, 1967.

Meyers, Michelle. "Betting on the farm." *Oregonian*. 24 February 2000.

—. "Growing with a busy city." *Oregonian*. 2 November 2000.

Moe, Richard and Carter Wilkie. *Changing Places: Rebuilding Community in the Age of Sprawl*. New York: Henry Holt and Company, Inc., 1997.

Morris, Rebecca. "30 years of planning produce city for the '90s." *Oregonian*. 19 February 1990.

Nesbit, Sharon. "Vintage Edgefield: A History of Multnomah County Poor Farm." Portland, Oregon: McMenamins, 1995.

Nicholas, Jonathan. "Treasures—Your call." *Oregonian*. 16 July 1995.

—. "The best house in Oregon is bought by someone used to the sun." *Oregonian*. 21 November 1999.

Nokes, R. Gregory. "Still in the ring." *Oregonian*. 1 August 1999.

Norman, James B., Jr. *Portland's Architectural Heritage*. Portland, Oregon: Oregon Historical Society Press, 1991.

—, Pieter T. Dykman and Dwight A. Smith. *Historic Highway Bridges of Oregon*. Portland, Oregon: Oregon Historical Society Press, 1989.

Ochsner, Jeffrey Karl, editor. *Shaping Seattle Architecture: A Historical Guide to the Architects*. Seattle, Washington: University of Washington Press, 1994.

O'Donnell, Terence and Thomas Vaughan. *Portland: A Historical Sketch and Guide*. Portland, Oregon: Oregon Historical Society, 1976.

Oliver, Gordon. "Portland Tackles Hot Spots . . ." *Oregonian*. 1 January 1997.

—. "On one city Block, Portland's past and future meet." *Oregonian*. 23 August 1999.

—. "Landmark teeters toward its demise." *Oregonian*. 6 September 1999.

Pancrazio, Angela Cara. "The last vestiges of Portland's Little Italy." *Oregonian*. 23 August 1998.

Parente, Michele. "Rare Chinese gift travels rocky road: A sister city dilemma." *Oregonian*. 30 November 1996.

—. "City Hall opens, flaunting facelift." *Oregonian*. 30 March 1998.

Pement, Jack. *Oregon Historical Vignettes*. Portland, Oregon: Binford & Mort, 1974.

Polson, Mary Ellen. "Heights of Portland." *Old House Journal*. January/February 1999.

Potential Historic Preservation Districts. Portland, Oregon: Prepared and printed by the Portland Historical Landmarks Commission and the Portland Bureau of Planning, 1978.

Ritz, Richard E., FAIA. "Masonic Building no monstrosity." *Oregonian*. 16 November 1989.

—. *A History of the Reed College Campus and its Buildings.* Portland, Oregon: Reed College Office of Publications, 1990.

—. *An Architect Looks at Downtown Portland.* Portland, Oregon: Greenhills Press, 1991.

—. *Central Library: Portland's Crown Jewel.* Portland, Oregon: The Library Foundation, 2000.

Roos, Roy E. *The History and Development of Portland's Irvington Neighborhood.* Portland, Oregon, 1997.

Ross, Marion Dean. "Architecture in Oregon: 1845-1895." *Oregon Historical Quarterly.* March 1956.

—. *A Century of Architecture in Oregon: 1859-1959.* Eugene, Oregon: School of Architecture and Allied Arts, University of Oregon, 1959.

Row, D.K. "Conceptual restraints." *Oregonian.* 17 December 1999.

Schmertz, Mildred F., FAIA. *Zimmer Gunsul Frasca: Building Community.* Rockport, Massachusetts: Rockport Publishers, 1995.

Schoenberg, Wilfred P., S.J. *A History of the Catholic Church in the Pacific Northwest: 1743-1983.* Washington, D.C.: The Pastoral Press, 1987.

Schwartz, Matt. "Behind the Seersucker Curtain." *Willamette Week.* 14 July 1999.

Scott, Jackie. "Fixing up the Vista House for visitors . . ." *Oregonian.* 6 May 1999.

Silvis, Steffan. "Reaching for the Sky." *Willamette Week.* 10 November 1999.

Simmons, Bob. "Mission Possible." *Old Home and Historic Property Magazine.* 17 October 1999.

Smith, Herbert L. Jr. "Small Centers for Shops." *Architectural Record.* May 1985.

Snyder, Eugene E. *Skidmore's Portland: His Fountain and Its Sculptor.* Portland, Oregon: Binford & Mort, 1973.

—. *Portland Names and Neighborhoods: Their Historic Origins.* Portland, Oregon: Binford & Mort, 1979.

—. *Early Portland: Stumptown Triumphant.* Portland, Oregon: Binford & Mort, 1984.

—. *We Claimed This Land: Portland's Early Settlers.* Portland, Oregon: Binford & Mort, 1989.

—. *Portland Potpourri: Art, Fountains, and Old Friends.* Portland, Oregon: Binford & Mort, 1991.

"Tallest buildings challenge climbers." *Oregonian.* 29 August 1996.

Tankersley, Jim (with contributions by Janet Adamy.) "The tall tale of Portland's two towers." *Oregonian.* 25 July 1999.

Terry, John. "A flip of a coin makes Portland for Maine." *Oregonian.* 12 October 1996.

—. "Buildings stand test of time . . ." *Oregonian.* 28 February 1999.

—. "Smith brothers' imprint extensive and enduring." *Oregonian.* 16 April 2000.

Tess, John M. *Uphill Downhill Yamhill: The Evolution of the Yamhill Historic District in Portland, Oregon.* Portland, Oregon: National Trust for Historic Preservation, 1977.

Turnquist, Kristi. "Location, location, location!" *Oregonian.* 30 November 1999.

Ukman, Jason. "Turning old house into a home again." *Oregonian.* 25 October 1999.

Vaughan, Thomas, editor, Virginia Guest Ferriday, associate editor. *Space, Structure and Style: Building in Northwest America, Volumes One and Two.* Portland, Oregon: Oregon Historical Society, 1974.

Vitta, Maurizio, editor. *Zimmer Gunsul Frasca Partnership: Between Science and Arts.* Milan, Italy: l'Arca Edizioni, 1998.

Wiederhold, Kathleen M. *Exploring Oregon's Historic Courthouses.* Corvallis, Oregon: Oregon State University Press, 1998.

Wilkinson, Jim. "Broadway: A Bridge too Dangerous?" *Oregonian.* 10 February 1997.

Willamette Week. 25th Anniversary Issue: Portland 1974-1999. 10 November 1999.

Willamette Week. Best of Portland. 19 July 2000.

Wiseman, Carter. *Shaping a Nation: Twentieth-Century American Architecture and Its Makers.* New York: W.W. Norton & Company, 1998.

Wood, Sharon. *The Portland Bridge Book.* Portland, Oregon: The Oregon Historical Society Press, 1989.

Yim, Su-Jin. "High tech high-rise." *Oregonian.* 12 June 2000.

INDEX